DATE DUE

Restructured Resistance

Restructured Resistance

The Sibley Commission and the
Politics of Desegregation in Georgia

Jeff Roche

The University of Georgia Press | Athens and London

© 1998 by the University of Georgia Press
Athens, Georgia 30602
All rights reserved
Designed by Louise OFarrell
Set in 10.5/14 Minion by G & S Typesetters, Inc.
Printed and bound by Braun-Brumfield, Inc.
The paper in this book meets the guidelines for
permanence and durability of the Committee on
Production Guidelines for Book Longevity of the
Council on Library Resources.

Printed in the United States of America
02   01   00   99   98   C   5   4   3   2   1

Library of Congress Cataloging in Publication Data
Roche, Jeff.
Restructured resistance : the Sibley Commission and the
politics of desegregation in Georgia / Jeff Roche.
p.   cm.
Includes bibliographical references (p.   ) and index.
ISBN 0-8203-1979-1 (alk. paper)
1. Georgia. General Assembly. Committee on Schools.
2. School integration—Georgia—History.
3. Georgia—Politics and government—1951–
I. Title.
LC214.22.G46R63   1998
379.2′63′09758—dc21   98-2660

British Library Cataloging in Publication Data available

For Cathy

CONTENTS

PREFACE

There is no limit to what you can achieve
if you don't care who gets the credit.
—Robert W. Woodruff

This book has been a five-year labor of love. During that period I have run up quite a tab of academic debts. I would like to thank many of those who have helped me—hopefully as sort of a first payment. I would like to thank my mother, Sheila; my brother, Chris; and my stepfather, Doug, for believing in me for the many years when even I thought I would always be just a bartender. Without the guidance of my grandparents, Ina Earle and Christopher B. Martin, who taught me how to work, I would not be writing these words today.

The reference staff of Pullen Library at Georgia State University offers any researcher or student a tireless, positive attitude. The individual staff members are genuine in their efforts to help, and I thank them, not only for this book, but for all of their assistance in the four years I attended the university. I am also grateful to the staff of the library's Special Collections Department, especially the staff of the Georgia Government Documentation Project who have brought Georgia politics to life through their efforts in building an outstanding oral history collection.

The Robert W. Woodruff Library Special Collections Department at Emory University is a first-rate facility and holds a renowned collection of personal papers, but it is the staff under Linda Matthews that makes it such a truly enjoyable place to do research. The staff members are helpful, encouraging, interested, and extremely knowledgeable.

I could not have finished this manuscript without the help of the Inter-library Loan Office here at the University of New Mexico's Zimmerman Library. Every member of that staff deserves a hearty thank-you, especially Brian Freels-Stendel. Thank you.

Many different people have read at least portions of this manuscript, and each contributed to its final form with suggestions, comments, or the friendly red question mark. Any mistakes or misinterpretations, however, belong entirely to me. I would like to thank Ronald J. Zboray, who helped me understand the power of the public hearing and its role in the distribution of community knowledge, and Donald Ratajczak for pointing out the important economic changes taking place in the South after World War II and forcing me to understand Sibley's place within that evolution.

I especially want to thank my former boss, point guard, and friend Cliff Kuhn, for reading this manuscript in its entirety and offering immeasurable advice on how it could be improved, for the many hours he spent explaining Georgia politics, and for his continually challenging my assumptions until I learned to ask myself the tough questions that all of us would rather avoid.

I also owe an incredible debt to two University of New Mexico professors who helped me prepare the book for publication. Howard Rabinowitz took valuable time to read and comment on the entire manuscript. His suggestions and comments were immeasurable as he helped to clarify my thinking and place the Sibley Commission within a larger context of southern history. David Farber offered counsel and support in the frantic last few weeks as the book was going to press. His practical, no-nonsense advice was exactly what I needed at that juncture.

I owe my greatest academic debt to and reserve my largest thanks for my mentor John Matthews. Without him, this book would not have been possible. During my first quarter of graduate school, while flailing for a subject for a paper in a New South seminar, Dr. Matthews suggested the Sibley Papers might be mined for an appropriate topic; five years, one master's thesis, and one completed manuscript later, I am finally finished with that paper. Thank you, Dr. Matthews, for if this book is my child, then surely you must be its grandfather.

Lastly I would like to thank the person who made this book and everything good in my life possible—my wife, Cathy. Thank you, Cathy. This is for you.

INTRODUCTION

At ten o'clock in the morning of 3 March 1960, John Sibley rapped his gavel on the judge's rostrum of the Americus County Courthouse and brought the first hearing of the Georgia General Assembly Committee on Schools to order. Sibley, who in the course of his career had served as general counsel for Coca-Cola, president of Atlanta-based Trust Company Bank, and partner in the South's premier law firm of King and Spalding, had been appointed by Governor Ernest Vandiver to head the school committee. Sibley told the gathering that the state of Georgia confronted one of "the most important questions . . . in many generations": how would Georgia respond to the mandate of *Brown v. Board of Education*? Sibley explained that white Georgia's massive resistance movement to school integration had produced a crisis: Georgia was at risk of abandoning its public school system in a futile effort to preserve Jim Crow. At the "Sibley hearings" Georgians, forced by the *Brown* ruling and growing national pressure, prepared once again to meet or to make a New South.[1]

In the years following World War II, no other region in the United States experienced a greater metamorphosis than the South. Rapid change was fueled by the African American civil rights movement, which brought about a fundamental revolution in the South's social and political structure. But rapid urbanization also forced changes as southern cities became key engines of the post–World War II economic boom. The region's economic system moved beyond one-crop agriculture based on a plantation system of sharecropping and tenant farming and became a diverse, multifaceted segment of the national economy. Economic growth and civil rights collided in Atlanta and the result forever altered the political structure of the state. Georgia moved beyond one-party factionalism hallmarked by demagoguery and bitter race-baiting into the era of two-party politics with powerful national politicians of both races and both parties.[2]

Change did not come easily to most white southerners deeply committed to tradition and maintaining their unique culture. In the midst of a whirlwind of change, white southerners viewed school segregation as a critical symbol of southern distinctiveness. They clung to conservatism and resisted any challenge to the system of white supremacy, believing that change could undermine the entire structure of their society. In 1954, after the Supreme Court declared school segregation unconstitutional in *Brown v. Board of Education of Topeka,* southern political leaders embarked on a program to preserve Jim Crow in schools. Georgia and its state politicians, especially governors Herman Talmadge and Marvin Griffin, and "kingmaker" Roy Harris, led this massive resistance movement.[3]

This study seeks to examine how the desegregation of public schools in Georgia reflected the evolution of southern society, economics, and politics. The story begins in 1946, when Georgia stood at a crossroads. In one direction lay social, political, and economic progress. Straight ahead, however, the road looked hauntingly familiar. Georgia remained on its customary course. In the 1946 gubernatorial election, the people responded to potential reformation by electing a man who represented the past—Eugene Talmadge, a three-time former governor who based his platform on preserving the racial status quo.

The 1946 election marked the genesis of Georgia's defiant stance against change. White Georgians turned to Talmadge to save the white primary (which had been outlawed by the federal courts earlier that year), revealing their distress over changes in race relations. For many, the demands of southern African Americans for racial justice and an end to segregation represented the peril of progress. Georgia's political leaders, most of whom represented rural white farmers (black Georgians had been effectively disfranchised since the turn of the century), understood the fears of their constituents and worked toward preserving a static society. The efforts of politicians to calm the anxiety of rural whites culminated in the massive resistance movement of the period from 1954 to 1961. Movement leaders promised to preserve segregated schools, even at the cost of eliminating public education.

Five months after *Brown,* Georgia passed an amendment that prepared the state to convert public state-supported education to a "private" school system in the event a federal court ordered the schools integrated. The Georgia General Assembly continued to refine its private school strategy every annual session until 1961. The main thrust of Georgia's new school laws was a requirement that the governor cut off funding to any school that allowed black and white schoolchildren in the same classroom. Affected schools would then convert to private segregated institutions, and the parents would receive grants for tuition from the state. Subsequent federal court decisions, however, ruled that a state could not withhold funding from a single school or school district because of a court-ordered desegregation, and that if one school were closed due to integration, the state would have to abandon all support of the public schools.

Efforts to retreat from resistance were hindered by two separate but symbiotic factors: the popularity of massive resistance and the almost deafening silence from those among the white population who might challenge the sanctity of preserving segregation. For twelve years, Georgia politicians clamored to the stump in every crossroads hamlet, declaring their devotion to defiance and swearing their fealty to "the southern way of life." They promised their audiences that although Dixie was undergoing a second Reconstruction, with fervor, forbearance, and faith in resistance, southern tradition would prevail. White Georgia believed them. Public sanction of defiance and the doctrine of segregation left little room for dissent. Indeed, public discussion of segregation was forbidden in polite society. Further complicating attempts to desegregate Georgia's schools was the masterful achievement of resourceful resistance politicians who had bound their program to the ideology of segregation. Most cotton farmers and small town businessmen could not distinguish between segregation and resistance, because for years they had heard the two issues inexorably intertwined in political addresses, newspaper editorials, and feed store deliberations. However, it was this politicalization of segregation that eventually provided for the termination of massive resistance and the recognition of token change.

The private school plan created a schism between those dedicated to the preservation of education and those committed to absolute segregation. Events reached crisis proportions in 1959, when a federal court ordered the Atlanta school system to desegregate. However, the court allowed the Georgia General Assembly an opportunity to change its mandatory school closure laws before implementing its decision. The state was left with the possibility of abandoning public education and converting to the private school system engendered in 1954 or the option of accepting some degree of token desegregation.

The assembly responded, during its next session early in 1960, by creating the "Sibley Commission," whose primary, *stated* goal was to ascertain what the citizens of Georgia wanted to do in the face of the crisis. The panel held an open forum in each of Georgia's ten congressional districts. The commission heard from more than 1,600 witnesses, each stating a preference within a carefully constructed set of options: either to allow for a change in massive resistance law that would permit small amounts of desegregation and preserve public education or to maintain segregation through defiance and private schools. Sixty percent of witnesses preferred absolute segregation to public education when forced to choose between them. However, when the commission submitted its report in May, it recommended that the state abandon massive resistance and adopt a more practical position.

The Sibley Commission and its subsequent report were primarily the work of one man—John Sibley. The creation of the commission, although originally a political ploy to buy time for the governor and other state leaders before the desegregation of the public schools, became, in Sibley's hands, an instrument of change. The seventy-one-year-old chairman dominated the commission's members; he not only designed the hearing schedule but drafted all but one of the committee's official statements. Over the course of the hearings, Sibley manipulated witnesses and constrained them to respond only within a precisely prepared range of options. After the hearings, Sibley wrote and presented the final report advocating a new form of resistance— one that preserved public education and segregation. The Sibley report represented a realistic, corporate-style decision. Massive resistance was bad for business; threats to public schools slowed investment. Sibley and his associates were segregationists, but they were businessmen first. Regardless of his motives, when the school situation reached a point of critical mass, Sibley, representing the "powers that be in Atlanta," a designation he did not deny, stepped in and preserved public education.[4]

The commission hearings established Sibley and the committee as experts in the conflict between federal law and state segregation statutes in regard to the public schools. The committee's two options for witnesses at the hearings came to represent the only two alternatives for Georgia's response to the school crisis. The immense diversity of opinion in the state was funnelled into either a defense of resistance and private schools to protect segregation or the adoption of new techniques that would secure segregation for most of Georgia without threatening public education. Although some witnesses were certainly driven by loftier motives—African Americans and some progressive whites demanded an immediate end to segregation and racial injustice—most witnesses were concerned primarily with saving the public schools or preserving segregation. The commission's two options did not force them to choose between segregation and schools; it only asked them to state a preference for one form of resistance or another. The men of the committee studied every southern technique to preserve segregation and incorporated every applicable strategy into an alternative to massive resistance. In acquiring its position as the expert in the school crisis and offering a more pragmatic defense of Jim Crow as an alternative to massive resistance and school closures, the Sibley Commission seized the segregation issue away from resistance politicians.

The recommendation to abandon massive resistance, while representing a significant shift in Georgia's political and social position, was, most importantly, new, subtle, and within the limitations established by the *Brown* decision. In January 1961, when the school crisis unexpectedly changed venue and threatened the future of the University of Georgia (the alma mater of most members of the General Assembly), Governor Ernest Vandiver and the legislators adopted the recommendations of the Sibley Commission and ended Georgia's massive resistance. The Atlanta public schools peacefully desegregated nine months later.

This book describes how massive resistance ultimately failed in Georgia and why the Sibley Commission's restructured resistance succeeded. The earliest leader in the massive resistance movement, Georgia seemed curiously ill-prepared when the time came to test its defiant resolve. Certain causes for the collapse of Georgia's resistance are perhaps unique: the political domination of resistance at the expense of a grassroots defense of segregation, the premature appearance of defiant posturing, an open school movement that mobilized before a crisis, a rupture in a courthouse-boardroom alliance that had thrived for sixty years, and businessmen expropriating the segregation issue to preserve public education in the name of industrial expansion.

This story does not demonstrate the success of the civil rights movement in Georgia, although there were spectacular achievements. Nor is this a tale of racial moderation winning out over the excesses of racial politics. It is the story of how a business elite working in conjunction with political leaders crafted a new form of segregation. And this story can be found across the South.

The public nature of the Sibley Commission hearings also reveals how "typical" southerners reacted to the events that swirled around them. Whites and African Americans, women and men, sharecroppers and wealthy businessmen, sophisticated urbanites and rednecks, homemakers and political activists, presidents from the Chittlin Eaters Club, chambers of commerce, Lions Clubs, and NAACP chapters, the plaintiffs and defendant in the Atlanta desegregation case, ministers, sheriffs, mayors, and Klansmen, all participated in what a contemporary observer described as "a typical southern, particularly low-style Georgia occasion."[5] And although Georgia's exact situation was unique, the reactions of its citizens were not. The civil rights movement and white reaction were not monolithic behemoths slugging it out on some historical battlefield, but the result of thousands of different decisions, made by thousands of people, all over the South throughout this period. Events in Georgia were not decided only by heroes and villains working for good or nefarious ends, but by individuals whose responses were drawn by multitudes of reasons, some noble, some vulgar, many selfish. Whether a NAACP leader calling for an end to segregation, a businessman arguing for an end to massive resistance to preserve economic growth, a mother of school-aged children appealing for a continuation of education, or a Citizens' Council member parroting "states' rights," the witnesses before the Sibley Commission shared a southern reaction to the civil rights movement.

Georgia, in the years following the work of the Sibley Commission, shares a legacy with the rest of the South after the cessation of the region's white resistance to grant civil rights to black southerners. The death of the white primary and the birth of "one man, one vote" in southern politics led to the end of Black Belt domination and the emergence of urban political strength. The split between business interests and rural politicians helped usher in a new era of two-party politics as business changed its political philosophy after dismantling massive resistance and racist whites searched for new champions. And the creation of a new form of segregation based on geography in urban areas and intimidation in rural counties succeeded, not so much because it had been tried and tested in the South, but because it resembled the North's pattern of segregation. The nation had united under the banner of legal but not mandatory segregation.[6]

This book ends at the birth of restructured resistance. Georgia's schools remain deeply segregated, and many schools systems staved off any form of integration for several years after 1961. An analysis of the continuation of segregation remains for another time or perhaps another historian. This book is primarily the story of the Sibley Commission, and after the autumn of 1961, its job was finished. Until now its story had never been fully told. Other historians have tended to concentrate on the immediacy of the desegregation of the University of Georgia, or the rise of open school advocacy groups, or the failures of integration in Georgia's (and especially Atlanta's) public schools, but these studies have not paid adequate attention to the Sibley Commission as the vital link between all these events and issues.

The commission and its hearings exposed the changes taking place in Georgia's political and social structure—the strength and determination of African American cries for racial justice and the equally determined white defense of white supremacy, the growing economic power of Atlanta and corporate recognition that market forces would determine social policy, and the growing realization among all Georgians that change was inevitable. The commission and its hearings reveal a continuity in the slow evolution of both southern and national race relations. The Sibley Commission's recommendation that Georgia abandon massive resistance and focus on the continuation of public education created a deliberate new form of defiance—a restructured resistance—rooted in contemporary practicality and corporate pragmatism.

Restructured Resistance

CHAPTER 1

It Elects All the Governors

"Negro and white man
playing Seven-Up.
The Negro win the money
But he feared to pick it up."
—Roy Harris, reciting an old rhyme
to explain how to preserve segregation
in the wake of the *Brown* decision

In the spring and summer of 1947, one year after a very peculiar gubernatorial race, two men, James Mackay and Calvin Kytle, attempted to answer the question "Who runs Georgia?" They attended sessions of the General Assembly and interviewed politicians, businessmen, preachers, newspaper editors, teachers, and community leaders from all over the state. Their interviews included questions about corporate influence on political matters, the resurgence of the Ku Klux Klan, local interest in labor and unionization, how certain counties conducted voting procedures on election day, and who represented various political factions at a local level. At the end of their research, Mackay and Kytle concluded that the state's large corporations ran Georgia by using politicians and the political structure to dilute the power of the voters. They titled their report "We Pass . . . On Democracy: Who Runs Georgia." Roy Harris, perhaps the most politically powerful and well-connected man in the state and a chief beneficiary of the existing system, promised when interviewed for the report that "the Negro is going to motivate Georgia politics for years to come." This is the story of Harris's prediction and its ultimate conflict with Mackay's and Kytle's conclusions.[1]

The election that spurred Mackay and Kytle to study the machinations of state politics, the gubernatorial election of 1946, also provided the impetus for Georgia's massive resistance movement. Before that election, it seemed possible that the state could move toward a new era of progressivism. Ellis Arnall, a nationally recognized reform-minded governor, had, in his four years of office, attempted to bring the state into the American political and economic mainstream. The state's economic focus shifted away from its agrarian roots, and businessmen's attempts to lure industry to Georgia proved successful. Cities like Atlanta emerged as powerful national entities and threatened the dominance of rural-based politicians. The state's black population also challenged Georgia's strict social controls created to guarantee white supremacy.

Two seemingly unrelated events, however, detoured the state onto the road of resistance and racially motivated politics. First, in 1944 the United States Supreme Court ruled the white primary unconstitutional in the Texas case *Smith v. Allwright*.[2] Two years later, a federal court invalidated Georgia's white primary. Second, Ellis Arnall's attempts to succeed himself as governor led to a split between Arnall and his would-be successor and Speaker of the House Roy Harris. The governor's efforts angered Harris and drove him to not only defeat Arnall's bid at succession in the General Assembly but to support and run a gubernatorial campaign for the leader of the opposing faction, Eugene Talmadge.

Changes in Georgia's political and social climate allowed Eugene Talmadge to use effectively the abolition of the white primary as his central campaign issue in 1946. For many white Georgians, the primary issue reflected their fears of the transformations in society that they confronted in the immediate postwar period. Outward migration from rural areas, growing urbanization, an evolution in the class and racial structure, and a steady march toward progress scared many people. The state's one-party political system, described by one observer as "paternalistic at best, and autocratic at worse,"

even with two factions, could not offer enough alternatives in this time of social upheaval. Georgia's options became more restricted when the party's limited factionalism waned and reactionary social conservatives consolidated
their political power. Political leaders quickly retreated from progressivism
and appealed to the preservation of white supremacy to answer any challenge
facing the state.[3]

Georgia's anachronistic county unit system, a method of electing statewide officials by giving each of the state's 159 counties a certain number of
"electoral" votes, heavily favored rural areas with small populations and prevented drastic social change by forcing anyone running for statewide office to
compete for the allegiance of each county's ruling junta. The conservative
Black Belt region, the forty-four counties with a black population percentage
of forty-five or more that cut a wide swath down the middle of the state, controlled most of the state's county unit votes. Office seekers were compelled to
cater to these social traditionalists. During the 1950s, because of outward migration with no corresponding loss in political representation, the Black
Belt's power in the General Assembly was at its peak.[4]

Rural whites in Georgia feared any change in the elaborate dual structure
of Jim Crow. The nascent political power of black Atlantans, the perceived
racial liberalism of governor Ellis Arnall, and a growing national intolerance
of southern segregation led many white Georgians to cling desperately to the
racial status quo. Race relations in the state had remained largely static since
the turn of the century. Any movement toward progress or progressivism
took place within the vacuum of segregation that prevented any meaningful
exchange between white and African American leadership on a state level. As
these two cultures headed toward confrontation, the lack of communication
was exacerbated by a white retreat into demagoguery. Governor Ellis Arnall,
considered a racial moderate, described the setting. "In those days . . . the Negroes were regarded as chattel slaves. They lived in that section of town; they
worked for white folks, but if you shook hands with one you were doomed. I
remember when I started shaking hands and people said 'oooh.' If you had
one in your home you were an outcast. And anybody talking about Negroes
being people were crazy."[5]

The white primary and various other restrictions all but eliminated any
political power for Georgia's black population. The state and local communities enforced segregation in schools, colleges, parks, golf courses, movie

theaters, restaurants, hotels, taxis, buses, and even baseball parks. Atlanta Mayor Ivan Allen Jr. described a racial liberal as anyone "who felt vaguely uncomfortable over the mistreatment of people with black skin."

African Americans in Georgia and the South looked to Washington for help to alleviate the disparity in social and political conditions between blacks and whites, and the federal legislature could do little to help them. Democratic rule in the South had produced a powerful contingent of southern senators and congressmen who refused to change anything that could threaten southern social norms. The southern bloc in Congress would stop any piece of legislation that might imperil white supremacy.[6]

After World War II, other federal branches looked south and sought to change the black population's inferior status. The rhetoric of the war, the independence movements of African nations, northward migration of southern blacks, the increased bellicosity and political assertiveness of those who stayed in the South, cold war ideology, and the willingness of the Supreme Court to attempt to cure social ills all brought the southern institution of segregation under censure. In the years following the war, the Supreme Court heard several cases from black litigants challenging the constitutionality of state-supported institutions of white supremacy. The court sided with the plaintiffs in many of these cases.[7]

By attacking the ramparts of white supremacy in the South, the court provoked a defensive posture from southern politicians who made it an opponent and an issue to gain election. In Georgia after May 1954, when the Supreme Court ruled in *Brown v. Board of Education of Topeka* that segregation in the public schools was unconstitutional, the issue of race, heretofore the almost exclusive domain of Black Belt politicians, eclipsed all other concerns in state elections. Proponents of massive resistance reduced every campaign to one dedicated to preserving the institutions of white supremacy. The progressive "New Deal" faction of the Democratic Party buckled under the strain of racial politics, much as its Populist ancestor had the previous century.

"Massive resistance" spread through the South as the region's politicians rallied together in a crusade to save their institutions of racial control. Resistance took different forms in the various southern states. North Carolina, for example, took a pragmatic approach very early that exchanged small amounts of desegregation in the hopes that the state could avoid additional pressure for drastic change. Georgia and other states adopted private school plans that threatened the abolition of public education when faced with agitation for integration. Other southern states took measures somewhere between the Georgia and North Carolina approaches. All states, however, adopted new techniques and strategies to confront desegregation crises as they developed. Georgia took the early leadership in this resistance campaign in large part because its politicians, without factional competition, moved farther and farther to the right on the segregation issue. In 1946 race and the white primary served as an opportunity for Eugene Talmadge to salvage his career, but by 1956 the politics of race, segregation, and resistance were pure political survival.

As the policies of massive resistance gelled, a distinction between segregationists and resisters developed. For the purposes of this book, the term "segregationists" will refer to those dedicated to the preservation of the maximum amount of *legal* segregation. They were not willing to break laws, close schools, or threaten their communities with potential chaos. The term "resisters," on the other hand, will denote those who believed that a plan of maintaining complete and absolute separation of the races, no matter the costs, provided the only defense of segregation. State politicians among the latter group created Georgia's massive resistance movement in an attempt to retain unequivocal segregation in the schools. The resisters believed that the threat of a conversion to private schools and the withdrawal of the state from the realm of public education would prevent even token amounts of integration. The seemingly subtle differences between the segregationists and resisters grew as Georgia plunged deeper into the sublime waters of massive resistance.

1946

The 1946 governor's race provided a startling preview of massive resistance, because within this race existed all the elements of Georgia's defiant response to the civil rights movement. It was the first election since the disfranchisement of African Americans, following the Populist revolt of the 1890s, to feature large numbers of black voters on the rolls, an indication of their growing dissatisfaction. The primary candidates represented the two dominant spheres of political influence: Eugene Talmadge, the champion of the poor white farmers of middle Georgia, and James Carmichael of Marietta, fighting for the interests of the Piedmont region and the urban, commercial concerns of the state. Most important, race was the vital issue in the campaign. Carmichael, almost by default, inherited the mantle of the progressive, anti-Talmadge faction of the Democratic Party. Former governor E. D. Rivers, a New Dealer and uncrowned head of the progressive faction, provided a third choice in the primary.[8]

The progressive faction of the Democratic party can trace its modern roots to Eugene Talmadge's early nemesis, Richard B. Russell. In the 1936 governor's race E. D. Rivers, linking himself to both Russell and Franklin Roosevelt, defeated Charles Redwine, a Talmadge candidate, using a pro-"New Deal" platform. In 1942 Ellis Arnall took over the progressive leadership when he defeated Talmadge for governor. Talmadge, while governor in 1941, tried to stop certain professors from teaching "integration" and restructured the Board of Regents to do his bidding. The Southern Association of Colleges and Secondary Schools responded by refusing to accredit Georgia's colleges. State Attorney General Ellis Arnall, a Rivers ally, used the issue to defeat Talmadge in the 1942 gubernatorial election.[9] In late 1945, Arnall attempted to change the state constitution to permit his own succession. This act alienated Roy Harris, the powerful Speaker of the House and "heir" to the progressive mantle and governor's office, and E. D. Rivers, who had hoped to run for governor in 1946 with Arnall's backing.[10] Rivers ran anyway, and Harris became Eugene Talmadge's unofficial campaign manager.

The 1946 campaign strategies of the three candidates seemed very simple and straightforward. Rivers called attention to his record as governor and to his years as the leader of the anti-Talmadge forces. Carmichael made a plea for honest, efficient government, pledging to continue the progressive reforms of Arnall. Talmadge, at the urging of Roy Harris and his son and campaign manager Herman, adopted a dual platform of reform and white supremacy. But rarely in Georgia politics are campaigns simple and straightforward.

With Carmichael as their candidate, Arnall and the progressive faction hoped to capture the loyalty of the growing business and industrial interests in the state. Carmichael, the former head of the Bell Bomber plant in Marietta, had substantial ties to the Atlanta business community, and if he convinced this group to back the progressive faction, it could effectively destroy the Talmadge camp. These commercial interests had supported Talmadge, albeit discreetly, in the past because they preferred his frugal, conservative approach to state government. Eugene Talmadge, however, was not a young man, and his personal charisma was the main reason for the success of his faction of the party. With no logical heir to the Talmadge coalition in sight, Arnall and the progressives hoped to defeat Ol' Gene one last time, break the political power of Talmadgism, and take firm control of the state.[11]

Talmadge would be a very difficult candidate to defeat. During his twenty-five years in public life he built a formidable political machine, capturing the loyalty of two opposite ends of the economic spectrum. He played the politics of the stump, swearing his allegiance to the poor white farmer while approaching state government with an economic philosophy that won the fidelity (and campaign funds) of the state's business and industrial leadership.[12] One longtime state politician and former secretary of the state Senate explained another appeal of Talmadgism. "It is conviction, often as not. Take old man Darby [a member of the state Senate]. He's a banker and an old Southern gentleman, really. He just doesn't think Negroes should vote. And with him, that's enough. There are others, of course, who vote with Talmadge because they think they stand to get [the] most out of his administration, and there are others who out of a sense of loyalty—they are beholden to the Talmadge crowd for past favors." [13]

As a campaign strategist, Roy Harris offered the former governor an impressive knowledge of county unit campaigning and a bevy of county commissioners loyal to Harris who could deliver their counties' votes to Harris's candidate. Many state leaders considered Harris the most powerful or dangerous man in the state.[14] He had managed E. D. Rivers's first (and unsuccessful) campaign for governor in 1928; Harris then brought Rivers victory in 1936 and 1938 and worked as campaign manager for Ellis Arnall in 1942. His reasons for helping Talmadge were as much personal as political; he viewed the election as a political showdown between himself and Ellis Arnall. Besides being upset that Arnall did not back him for the governorship, Harris did not like the racial moderation exhibited by Arnall and feared the direction the progressive faction was taking. Harris was also temporarily out of a job. A reform movement in his home county of Richmond led to the defeat of Harris and his Cracker Party in early 1946. The Crackers, an Augusta political machine organized by wards and based on patronage, had run city politics for many years and the election loss to the newly formed Independent Party hurt Harris's chances for higher office. In a preview of the primary later that year, Harris, sensing defeat in the days before the city elections, turned to the race issue and claimed that his opponents would integrate the schools and streetcars.[15]

Harris believed deeply in white supremacy and in the 1946 campaign blended a progressive social platform with Talmadge's socially conservative philosophy. Harris and Herman Talmadge convinced Gene to add old-age pensions, teacher pay raises, massive road building, appropriations for hospital building, acceptance of labor unions, and some assistance to veterans to his platform. Both Talmadge and Harris knew what defeat could mean and developed a strategy to ensure victory that deserves a lofty place in the annals of Georgia's long and colorful political history. The plan had three basic parts. Talmadge stumped the state, making traditional racial appeals to Georgia's white farmers, using the white primary issue as the catalyst for his fiery oratory. The second part of the plan involved the third candidate, E. D. Rivers— as long as Rivers was in the race, he would split the anti-Talmadge vote. Eugene and Herman Talmadge also attempted to disfranchise or scare off as many black voters as possible in the months before the election.[16]

Carmichael had reason to believe his 1946 campaign would be successful. The year opened with a new twist in Georgia politics as voter registration was higher than it had been in many years. With the invalidation of the white primary, African Americans registered to vote in record numbers; some 135,000 registered in 1946, up from only 20,000 in 1940. In Georgia's three largest cities, Augusta, Savannah, and Atlanta, African Americans organized unprecedented voter registration drives. Aside from the increase in black voters, other factors helped to double the voting rolls in 1946, including the elimination of the poll tax, the lowering of the voting age to eighteen, and the return of soldiers from the war. Since most of these new voters could scarcely be counted Talmadge supporters, this increase should have been very beneficial to Carmichael.[17]

Eugene Talmadge offset the power of these new voters with a basic racial appeal. The most important plank in his gubernatorial platform was the restoration of the white primary and the maintenance of white supremacy.[18] Talmadge viewed the invalidation of the primary as the federal government's first step in destroying southern institutions of racial control and warned listeners to avoid the smoke screen of his opponents and peer deeply into their rhetoric to "see a raging holocaust burning away at the very foundations of our southern traditions and segregation laws." Talmadge claimed that the destruction of the white primary was the work of communists and that "northern radicals, local quislings, and controlled newspapers seeking to mix the races" ran the Carmichael campaign. The Ku Klux Klan attempted to link Carmichael to black voters by offering them ten dollars to attend his political rallies. Talmadge told audiences that Carmichael sought an end to segregation. He claimed that the end of the white primary would lead to the election of black senators and governors and that any white politician who wanted to get elected would have to succumb to the political wishes of the black population. In the week before the election, Talmadge promised a Columbus audience that he alone could restore the white primary.[19] "They say that it's the law, and Nigras will vote in the primary—this year, next Wednesday—and it stops right there! What do I say? I say it's the law this year, and some of the Nigras will vote, the fewer the better, but I add to it this: if I'm your governor, they won't vote in our white primary the next four years."[20]

Author Lillian Smith described Talmadge's effect on his audiences during a campaign stop in Rabun County. "Race prejudice was almost non-existent till a month or so before the primary. The people, by and large, I think have an amazing degree of tolerance for the Negro. That's why a man like Talmadge is so dangerous. He came up here for a campaign talk and whipped up race feeling where it had hardly existed before. I know, because my friends in the Negro community . . . told me. Talmadge fired the imagination of all our poor whites. He told them about mixing the blood and how uppity the black people were getting. That caused the poor whites to search out the Negroes in hopes of some excitement. White boys started sitting in the Negro balcony at the theater here. They would sit there and insult the Negro boys and girls, tease them, do all manner of little things, hoping something would happen."[21]

Eugene Talmadge not only railed against black voter registration but did all he could do to stop it. Talmadge used a little-known codicil in the Code of Georgia that allowed any citizen of the state to challenge the voting qualifications of another based on citizenship, residency, character, literacy, or interpretation of the United States Constitution. Those challenged were responsible for proving their qualifications and obtaining reinstatement. Talmadge mailed out thousands of challenge forms to his supporters throughout Georgia. In April of 1946 the *Statesman,* Talmadge's newspaper, published a standardized challenge form, on which a person needed only to fill out a name and a reason for the imputation of ineligibility. He concentrated his efforts in counties that were traditionally loyal to him and where increases in black registration were noticeably evident. Most county officials did little to help those confronted regain their eligible status. The disqualification of black voters in traditional Talmadge counties allowed him to concentrate his efforts in the areas where the race between him and Carmichael was much closer. This disfranchising strategy seemed to have had the desired effect, as black voters were challenged all over Georgia, with many not having the opportunity to respond before the primary. Talmadge supporters continued their disfranchising efforts through the primary election. On election eve the Ku Klux Klan burned crosses in counties with numerous registered black voters. In Soperton a black church was burned in the days before the election.[22] On the day of the primary, Savannah political boss Johnny Bouhan brought voting in black sections of the city to a virtual standstill. Many African American voters stood in line from 5 A.M. until the polls closed without an opportunity to cast their ballot. The successful efforts of Talmadge and his followers prevented enough newly registered voters from going to the polls that the former governor won many crucial counties where the margin of Talmadge's victory was less than the number of black voters disfranchised. Of the African Americans who received an opportunity to vote, 98 percent cast their ballots for Carmichael.[23]

E. D. Rivers's campaign also helped the Talmadge camp achieve its margin of victory. By running for governor, Rivers helped to defeat Carmichael by dividing the vote of those opposed to Talmadge. This division proved to be extremely effective, for Rivers won ten counties that probably would have gone to Carmichael and allowed Talmadge to win with a plurality in several more counties. The evidence is strong that if Rivers had not been in the race, Carmichael would have won. These two factors, Talmadge's attempts at disfranchisement and the subterfuge of a third candidate to siphon votes from Carmichael, enabled Talmadge to win the 1946 primary and in effect the governor's race. He needed both factors to win, however, because his appeals to white supremacy were not enough. The election results suggest that in 1946 it was possible for a moderate or progressive candidate to win an election for governor.[24] Most Georgians, however, especially politicians, believed Talmadge won because of his racial appeals. Years later, James Mackay, longtime DeKalb County representative and coauthor of "We Pass . . . On Democracy: Who Runs Georgia," remarked, "He [Carmichael] buckled under the strain of being called a nigger lover . . . you can't temporize on the humanity of other people. The Talmadge boys have been the best race baiters, and don't try to get into their field because they'll stomp on you."[25]

In the November general election Talmadge ran unopposed, but before his inauguration he died, and his death threw the state into turmoil. The constitution of 1945 did not specify who would fill the office in the event that the governor-elect could not assume his duties. Three different men staked their claim on the governor's office, none of whom had run in the primary or general election. Ellis Arnall announced that, as governor, he would remain in office until the matter was resolved. M. E. Thompson, the newly elected and first-ever lieutenant governor (the 1945 state Constitution created the position), asserted that the people elected him to the post knowing that it entailed possible succession to the governorship. The leaders of the Talmadge camp, however, pointed to a constitutional statute that stated when no one in the general election received a majority of the votes, then the Georgia General Assembly should choose the governor from among the top two write-in candidates in the general election. Roy Harris and others argued that the clause meant that the assembly should also decide the election whenever a winner was unavailable to take office.

Harris and another Talmadge stalwart, James Peters, fearing Eugene's poor health, spent the time between the primary and the general election organizing a discreet write-in campaign for Herman Talmadge. Indeed, it was widely rumored that shortly after his father's death, Herman promised M. E. Thompson that he would support his claim to the governor's office. However, before he announced his intention to support Thompson, Harris and Peters alerted the Atlanta press that the younger Talmadge planned to ask the General Assembly to elect him to fill his father's vacant chair.[26] Despite protests from Arnall and Thompson, the General Assembly, meeting in January of 1947, counted the write-in votes to select the candidates for the next governor. A problem for the Talmadge supporters arose when at first count it seemed that Herman was not among the top two write-in candidates. Carmichael had 669 votes and Talmadge Bowers, a Republican although he vehemently denied this party affiliation when addressing the General Assembly, had 619 votes. Both exceeded the number of write-in votes received by Herman in the general election. In the eleventh hour the Talmadges' home county of Telfair reported finding an additional fifty-eight "misplaced" write-in votes that placed Herman ahead of Bowers in the vote count. The Atlanta newspapers investigating the story later revealed that among those voters whose ballots had been found were several dead men who voted in alphabetical order. With Herman Talmadge now among the top two finishers in the write-in campaign, the General Assembly elected Herman governor at 1:50 A.M. on 15 January 1947.[27]

A storm of protest erupted all over the state, and Talmadge, rather than alleviate the public's fears of a coup d'état, locked governor Ellis Arnall out of his office and refused to respond to Thompson's claim to the governorship. During one evening of fervent demonstration, students from Georgia Tech and the University of Georgia hanged Herman in effigy and called him "King Herman the First." Another student held aloft a placard that read, "How Many Representatives were drunk when the Crown Prince was Crowned?"[28] Talmadge quickly settled into the role of governor, naming department heads and taking steps to carry out the platform his father used in the primary campaign. He sent bills to the Georgia Assembly calling for a sales tax and the restoration of the white primary.

M. E. Thompson, meanwhile, had been sworn in as lieutenant governor and sued in the Georgia Supreme Court to have himself proclaimed the rightful governor. The court agreed with Thompson and on 22 March 1947 ordered Herman to vacate the governor's office. The court ruled Thompson would serve as acting governor until the next general election in 1948. This ruling marked the end of a very strange episode in Georgia history but also signified the beginnings of Herman's leadership of the Talmadge faction and a new political paradigm. As newspaper editor Carey Williams put it, "things were changing after Talmadge won and died. I think the changes started right there after he died."[29] Those changes included a return to racial politics that predated other southern states by almost ten years. It also signified the beginning of the end for the progressive faction in the state.

Herman Talmadge

The controversy and strife that surrounded the 1946 gubernatorial struggle
left both the participants and the entire state drained. The Georgia Supreme
Court's naming of Thompson as acting governor until the next general election split the four year governor's term in half and severely reduced his effectiveness while in office. Thompson took over as governor after the General
Assembly had all but adjourned its 1947 session. William T. Dean, the presiding officer in the Senate and a supporter of Thompson, had used his control over appointments and knowledge of parliamentary procedure to block
many Talmadge programs until the State Supreme Court ruled on Thompson's claim to the governor's office.[30] When Thompson took over, the only
important unresolved issue was the white primary legislation, intended for
Herman Talmadge's signature. Thompson, although an ardent supporter of
the white primary, vetoed the bill, expressing both his ire toward Talmadge's
illegal usurpation of the governor's office and his belief that the bill as written
would be struck down in the federal courts. The 1948 session of the legislature
was equally ineffective as the members of the General Assembly failed to enact any substantive legislation until after the election between Talmadge and
Thompson later that year.[31]

The white primary proved to be the most emotionally charged and important issue in the 1948 governor's race. A pastor in Telfair County emphasized the magnitude of the race when he called upon the people to defeat Talmadge's "fascism" by practicing "moral militance" to "save democracy in
Georgia."[32] Herman promised to restore the white primary and made it the
key plank in his platform. Thompson swore fealty to the idea of a white primary, but did not offer a concrete plan to revive it. Many white voters grew
wary of Thompson, especially as African Americans continued to register in
large numbers. The Ku Klux Klan did all it could to check this increasing registration. Not only did the group step up the purging campaign of 1946, but
it placed small coffins on the doorsteps of Swainsboro's black leaders and
mailed threatening letters to other potential black voters.[33] Mackay and
Kytle noticed a key link between the importance of the white primary to voters and the black population percentages in their area. In the northern part
of the state, where the black population was limited, and in urban areas, the

white primary was not as important as in middle or south Georgia, where it was so effective "that the people [would] hardly listen to anything else." The division between north and south Georgia over political remedies to preserve white supremacy widened during the next several years.[34]

Although the 1948 governor's race signified an important political change, as the Talmadge faction successfully turned its mantle of leadership over to Herman Talmadge, the reemergence of racial politics allowed for a degree of continuity. Herman, Roy Harris, and campaign manager Ernest Vandiver exploited Herman's ouster from the governor's chair and cemented support for Herman's candidacy among the "wool hat boys." The allegations lodged by the Atlanta newspapers that Herman's write-in campaign was a fraud did not seem to hinder Talmadge's 1948 campaign. On the contrary, most Georgians believed that finding a mysterious last-minute box of votes was a typical and appropriate tactic in Georgia politics. Georgia's factionalism, based on political personalities, made it difficult to transfer political power, but in 1948 Herman Talmadge gathered his father's political forces around him. He adopted a similar campaign strategy to his late father's and claimed that Thompson was the candidate of Rivers and Arnall. Besides lambasting Thompson for vetoing the white primary bill, Talmadge claimed his opponent was full of liberal ideas and was the candidate of the Communist and Progressive parties. This strategy was necessary because the two men's platforms were very similar; both believed in the white primary and pledged to modernize Georgia's roads and highway department, to increase welfare benefits, and to revitalize the state's health care program. However, the 1948 election, like the race in 1946, revolved around white supremacy. Talmadge made race his central campaign theme, claiming, "My platform has one plank which overshadows all the rest . . . my unalterable opposition to all forms of the 'civil rights program.'" Talmadge asserted that he would fight the legislation to set up a Fair Employment Practices Commission and would prevent the white women and children in Georgia from working "under a Negro foreman or . . . beside a Negro." Thompson fought back as best he could but spent much of his time answering Herman's charges. He ran on a platform of progressive, honest government and responded to Talmadge's claim that he had been "denied" the fruits of victory in 1946 by stating "that they had been denied the *spoils* of victory. . . ." Talmadge won the election with 52 percent of the popular vote and 76 percent of the county unit vote.[35]

Talmadge, winning the election in 1948, encountered some of the same limitations that had hindered Thompson. He was in office only two years before facing a campaign for reelection. This prevented the governor from attempting any real change until he had a clear mandate. Given the close vote in the 1948 race, Talmadge proceeded very carefully and conservatively during his first term as governor. The 1950 election was a repeat of the 1948 contest with one very important new feature—Talmadge used the threat of school integration as a campaign tactic.[36] Genuinely committed to the sanctity of white supremacy, he believed that segregation was the only thing that prevented miscegenation. During the 1950 campaign, a full four years before the *Brown* decision, Talmadge, responding to two recent Supreme Court decisions that broke down segregation in graduate schools and a NAACP lawsuit filed in Irwin County that charged the local school system with operating unequal schools, promised, "As long as I am Governor, Negroes will not be admitted to white schools. . . . The good women of Georgia will never stand for the mixing of the races in our schools."[37]

Talmadge needed the segregation issue to stave off a charging Thompson, who had used the two years between elections to solidify his support. He willingly accepted the reins of the anti-Talmadge faction and made use of Herman's support for a sales tax a major issue in the campaign. This tactic appears to have been effective, since the 1950 race was even closer than the previous election. In Georgia, however, elections are not always as they seem. Thompson remembers that "on the night of the election, about eleven, I was ahead in the county unit vote and in popular vote. At that time the unit vote was the controlling factor. Then the returns just quit coming in. I had telephone calls from Meriwether, Terrell, and other counties telling me that I had carried those counties. The next morning they reported that Herman had carried those counties and there were about five hundred more votes for the race for governor than there were in any other [statewide] race at that time." Thompson accused Roy Harris of stealing fifty counties from him in the race, and Roy Harris replied that "it wasn't more than thirty five."[38]

The public career of Herman Talmadge represents the conflicting forces at work throughout the South during the massive resistance movement. He was ardently dedicated to two ideologies destined for confrontation; he sincerely believed in the value of absolute segregation and feared for white Georgia if the practice were abolished, and he also held a deep belief in the modernization and expansion of Georgia's economy. Like his father, who used both ends of the economic spectrum to gain a political advantage, Herman also aligned the two forces behind his political machinations. But in many ways Herman was the reverse side of the same coin. Eugene gathered business support by default simply by his naturally conservative political beliefs that served Georgia's business and industrial interests; his main concern was winning the loyalty of poor white farmers. Herman's first loyalty was to business and industry and the creation of a thriving economic climate, and he received the support of his father's "wool hat boys" because of his legacy and commitment to social traditionalism. This is not to say that both men did not nurture the support of both groups. That they were able to convince each of these coalitions that they were best suited to attend to its needs demonstrates each man's political skills.

The passage of a 3 percent sales tax provides perhaps the best illustration of Herman Talmadge's dual loyalties. Determined to keep the schools segregated, Talmadge needed to raise large amounts of money to equalize the disparities between white and black schools without raising licensing fees or property and corporate taxes. He decided that a sales tax offered the best and quickest method of increasing the state's coffers.[39] Georgia's economy was booming and he did not want to do anything that might threaten growth. Although voters rejected an earlier referendum that allowed a sales tax, Talmadge, after his victory in 1950, believed he had a mandate to ensure segregation and secured the tax in the General Assembly in 1951. He then equalized pay for black and white teachers and state allotments to all schools. In 1952 he created the state School Building Authority to raise two hundred million dollars worth of new funding and eliminate the disparity between white and black school facilities. In 1953 the General Assembly created a Commission on Education to ensure the equability of school facilities. By the time Talmadge left office, 53 percent of the state's budget went to education. This regressive new sales tax, which Talmadge promised would guarantee segregation, hurt the state's poor, including the farmers Talmadge claimed to represent. While turning to the "wool hat boys," who made his election possible, to pay for the equalization of schools, Talmadge slashed taxes and licensing fees for business. He also eliminated the state property tax and expanded the role of the state's Port Authority to secure trade and attract business to Georgia. Talmadge toured the country, quick to remind any corporate decision maker that Georgia offered a contented and cheap labor force. This effort endeared him to the business elite of the state without costing any rural votes. Herman quickly made many powerful friends in Atlanta and drew support from the *Atlanta Journal* and the city's largest law firm, King and Spalding.[40]

The sales tax and the equalization of school facilities were only the first steps taken by Talmadge in his fight against civil rights. Talmadge newspapers published pictures of interracial meetings and printed the relief rolls. In 1952 he proposed an amendment to make the county unit system applicable to all general elections (previously it was only used in primary elections) and used the Georgia Democratic Party's presidential campaign money to publish racist literature designed to win support for this amendment.[41] Had this effort been successful, Talmadge could have manipulated the county unit system to pass resistance legislation and avoid the numerical political strength of Georgia's urban areas. The county unit amendment failed largely due to an organized effort by the League of Women Voters and a new association, Citizens Against the County Unit, which publicized the danger of extending the unit system. They accused Talmadge of trying to build a statewide political machine that would use the county unit system to circumvent the will of the populace and the General Assembly if necessary.[42]

In 1953, Talmadge needed all the political power he could muster because he planned to create what he believed to be the ultimate defense of segregated education—the conversion to a statewide private school system. Late in the summer of 1950, Roy Harris, responding to the Supreme Court cases that outlawed segregation in graduate or law schools, wrote an editorial in his *Augusta Courier* that suggested that white taxpayers in southern states use their tax dollars to create a white school system free from state control. Other southern states considered Harris's idea, and South Carolina passed an amendment allowing for a private school system in 1952. During the fall of 1953, Herman Talmadge and his advisors (many of whom were constitutional lawyers with specific instructions from Talmadge to find ways to avoid any integration until the governor was safely out of office) prepared a private school plan for Georgia. The idea lacked specific details but basically provided that in the event a federal court forced a school or system to desegregate, the state would eliminate funding to that school and provide the parents of its students with tuition reimbursement. The School Building Authority would lease the school grounds and supplies to an independent individual to run as a "private" segregated school. After passing the Georgia General Assembly by the required two-thirds majority in the 1954 session, the amendment was slated for the November general election ballot.[43]

The idea of creating a private school system divided the state. To ensure the amendment's passage, Herman and his lieutenants used the Georgia Education Commission to generate positive public reception for the amendment. To that end the commission spent thirteen thousand dollars mailing nine thousand pamphlets, cards, and letters urging its passage. Talmadge, Attorney General Eugene Cook, and Lieutenant Governor Marvin Griffin, all members of the commission, stumped the state campaigning for the amendment. As Herman Talmadge described it, "We were doing everything we possibly could to take care to prevent the integration of the races in the public schools in the event of a nonfavorable decision from the federal courts." Opposition arose from the state's newspapers, the League of Women Voters, B'nai B'rith, the AFL-CIO, the Georgia Federation of Labor, Protestant church groups, school officials, and organizations who argued against the potential damage the proposition could mean to public education. Even Roy Harris protested the amendment; he did not believe that the measure would stand up in court, and he argued instead for the physical intimidation of black Georgians to ensure segregation. Other critics of the plan derided it for a lack of detail or any concrete measures to convert the schools. Despite the opposition, the private school amendment, coming before the voters six months after the Supreme Court decision in *Brown v. Board of Education,* passed by a vote of 210,488 to 181,148.[44]

Brown v. Board of Education of Topeka

In May of 1954 the Supreme Court ruled in *Brown v. Board of Education of Topeka* that the southern practice of school segregation was unconstitutional. The court claimed that separate schools violated the equal protection clause of the Fourteenth Amendment.[45] This decision unleashed a torrential reaction. As Charles Weltner, later a congressman from Atlanta, described it,

> Old sores were in an instant rubbed raw, and old wounds were ripped open. Public reaction to the decision was cataclysmic. Not a single responsible public voice was heard in its support. Every officeholder felt compelled to point out its mani-

fold evils. The speeches rolled. The state legislature was in a frenzy of reaction. Citizens organized. Resolutions were passed. Memorials were framed. In Congress, of course, the Southern Manifesto went the rounds. Lawyers argued the content of the decision, its legitimacy, impact, and style. The Attorney General of Georgia promptly denounced it as "illegal." The impeachers tried to impeach. Interposition was exhumed from the Sedition Act days. The Ku Klux Klan stirred from its slumber. The White Citizens Councils sprang into bloom. In Georgia, the legislature created something called the Georgia Education Commission, designed to preach segregation at taxpayers' expense. Rallies were held. The populace was aroused.[46]

Southern leaders expressed their determination to circumvent the decision of *Brown v. Board of Education*. Though some states had already taken measures to avoid integrating their schools and swore never to abide by the court's ruling, the decision still created a frenzied opposition throughout the South. One historian recently offered three reasons as to why, if the South knew the decision was coming (and surely it did, judging by the decisions rendered by the Supreme Court and the laws passed by southern legislatures in the years prior to 1954), the reaction against *Brown* was so intense. He suggested, first, that the ruling represented a federal encroachment upon the traditional social structure; second, that it was a *sudden* fundamental change and not a gradual one; and third, that it involved the schools and the South's fears of miscegenation.[47]

Initially, not all southern states reacted to the court's decision with defiance. The upper South and border states offered a tempered response. In Arkansas, Governor Jim Cherry said the state would obey the law, "it always has." Orval Faubus, running for governor, eliminated a stance of resistance from his platform when the public and press reacted negatively to it. Other campaigns in the South featured victories of moderates, calling for acceptance of the ruling, over fire-eating segregationists.[48]

In other parts of the South, state leaders appointed committees to examine the court's ruling and to present the best method of resolving the differences between state law and tradition and the decision. Private citizens also formed study groups that offered suggestions to the public. Governor Thomas Stanley of Virginia appointed one of the most important official committees. Stanley received the news of the *Brown* decision calmly, taking no immediate action except to call a meeting with the state's black leaders on 24 May 1954. They urged him to make Virginia an example of smooth integration. Later that summer Stanley appointed a thirty-two-man commission, led by state senator Garland Gray, to study the school question and make recommendations to the General Assembly. The Gray Commission recommended a plan of pupil placement, tuition grants, and local option (offering each community a choice of private or public integrated schools) when faced with integration. Before the legislature acted on any of these options, however, Virginia's ruling faction led by Senator Harry Byrd committed the state to following a course of massive resistance.[49]

President Eisenhower dreaded the Deep South's reaction to the *Brown* decision. This region had never been deeply committed to education, and the president especially feared that Georgia would abandon public schools. He worried about the long-lasting and devastating effect this lack of schools would have on the poor children of both races. Eisenhower, however, refused to comment publicly on the decision and left the matter to the courts. This silence, he privately hoped, would give the South time to adjust to the ruling and prepare its public school systems for the change. Everything depended on the court's decision in its implementation hearing set for May 1955.[50]

The Supreme Court in the hearing known as *Brown* II invited all state governments that practiced segregation to present briefs and oral arguments. This invitation, the court hoped, would force the states at least tacitly to accept the ruling of the previous year. Five states, Georgia, Louisiana, Mississippi, Alabama, and Tennessee, refused the invitation; South Carolina, an original defendant in the *Brown* case, could not refuse to present a brief in the implementation hearing. Most of the briefs filed by the southern attorneys asked for a long, gradual period in which to carry out the court's decision. Virginia warned the court that if it tried to act too quickly it would force southern states to resist the ruling. What the court decided in May 1955 was something of a compromise; it ordered the southern states to desegregate their public schools "with all deliberate speed." It left the task of interpreting their decision to the lower courts.[51]

On Capitol Hill, however, three important and influential national politicians, Richard B. Russell of Georgia, James O. Eastland of Mississippi, and Harry F. Byrd of Virginia, voiced their opposition to the philosophy behind the original *Brown* ruling. Entering the Senate in 1957, Herman Talmadge also fought the decision, but as a freshman senator, his voice did not carry the same weight as the three elder statesmen. Eastland battled the Supreme Court on the floor of the Senate, claiming that it based its decision on the recommendations of communist agitators. This argument, forged in the heat of the Cold War, enabled the segregationists to base their position on a nationally conservative ideology rather than white supremacy and southern interests. Talmadge published a pamphlet, *You and Segregation,* pursuing this line of debate further, stating that communists were using the court to destroy the Bill of Rights. He claimed the first item on the communists' agenda was the destruction of the Tenth Amendment, which guaranteed states' rights. This amendment was important, he continued, because as long as states had the power to resist the federal government, communism would not grow unchecked.[52]

Georgia Senator Richard B. Russell took a more traditional paternalistic approach and claimed that separate schools had provided more and better opportunities for black southerners. He accused reformers of being "more interested in destroying segregation than . . . advancing the education of the Negro race." Russell was in constant contact with the state leaders in Georgia, and, at his suggestion, the state refused to file a brief in *Brown* II. Russell claimed that if the southern states were not represented, the court would see the futility of its decision. Harry Byrd and Richard B. Russell prepared the southern leaders' written response to the *Brown* decision, the Declaration of Constitutional Principles or the "Southern Manifesto." This document, written in 1957 and signed by almost every southern senator and congressman, claimed the court had overstepped its authority and amended the Constitution without the express consent of the people.[53]

State officials and some community leaders in the Deep South responded to the *Brown* decision with contempt. Fifteen of the seventeen southern governors met in Richmond on 10 June 1954 to discuss their reactions and possible remedies to the court's decision. By October, four states prepared to resist the court order. Louisiana drafted an amendment for that fall's general election to allow the state to preserve segregation as a matter of "health and morals." Alabama proposed an amendment to its state constitution allowing for the abolition of public education. As already noted, Georgia had passed an amendment creating the option of private segregated schools, which Mississippi now emulated. Governor Hugh White, after the initial *Brown* decision, attempted to forge an alliance with the state's black leaders. In exchange for voluntary segregation and a promise not to attempt public school integration, Mississippi would attempt to eradicate the disparity between white and black schools. When the black leadership failed to approve this plan, Governor White adjourned the meeting and proposed an amendment to the state constitution calling for the abolition of the public schools. He said of this new plan and the possibility of the elimination of public education, "We have lived through Civil war, under the bayonet of the unsympathetic conqueror, through economic slavery for white and black alike, and through all manner of troubles; but our spirit, which is our own and which no power on earth can take from us, has remained unbroken." A grassroots movement to preserve segregation sprang up in Mississippi that called for each county to create a "Citizens' Council" of local businessmen that would use every means short of violence to preserve the social norms. By February 1956 most southern states had adopted some measures to defy the Supreme Court decision.[54]

Georgia's political leaders reacted swiftly to the court's decision in *Brown v. Board of Education*. Herman Talmadge returned from a hunting trip and promised that Georgia "will not comply with the decision. Even if federal troops were sent down . . . they wouldn't be able to enforce it." After his initial press statement on the decision, the governor's office received more than one thousand telegrams, and all but five supported Talmadge. Herman continued to vilify and challenge the court over the next few months, claiming that Georgia would not abide by the ruling and would resist "even if it is the sole state in the nation to do so." Talmadge urged Georgians to stand firm because the final arbiter would be the people: "As long as the people resist on the local level in a determined manner there is little that the federal government can do to enforce its desegregation decision." Georgia Attorney General Eugene Cook hosted a group of his fellow state attorneys to discuss possible legal defenses. Cook also published a pamphlet, "The Georgia Constitution and Mixed Public Schools," in which he claimed that in the matter of schools states had the final authority, and the Georgia constitution required school segregation. He said that if the Supreme Court struck down separate schools, "free common schools fall with it."[55]

Resistance was not the only immediate political ramification of the court's decision. In declaring segregation illegal, the court altered the course of southern politics. Race, again, eclipsed class for poor to middle-class white farmers. Nowhere was this more evident than in Georgia. *Brown* enabled Black Belt politicians to wield their power in the state house against the town and up-country politicians. At its peak during the 1950s, rural political power, accentuated by the county unit system, allowed Georgia's less populated areas to dominate state politics at the expense of urban centers. Since Tom Watson attempted to unite the farmers of the state against the city and business interests, Georgia politicians had used antagonism against the state's cities as a political tool. The rise of resistance in response to the growing clamor for civil rights emanating from Atlanta, Savannah, and Augusta exacerbated this situation. The call by African Americans to the federal government to step between Georgia and her own citizens and the corresponding decisions of the Supreme Court compelled some politicians less preoccupied with race to toe the Black Belt line because of a devotion to the principle of states' rights. Regardless of their motives, resistant politicians continued to promise white Georgians that defiance alone could prevent any change in the social sphere.[56]

Perhaps reflecting the confidence in the promises of political leaders, rural-based newspapers expressed a cautious optimism that the *Brown* decision would have little impact on the state. Many editors assured their readers that if the courts invalidated legal segregation, blacks and whites in Georgia would work out a voluntary system for separate schools. They promised that segregation would continue under a system that satisfied "the thinking aspects of both races." Roy Harris, in his political mouthpiece the *Augusta Courier,* applauded the statement of a group of African Americans in Glascock County (on the occasion of the opening of a brand new brick school building) that urged the continuation of segregated schools. Harris and other segregationist editors believed that continuing the equalization of school facilities would prevent agitation for integration.[57]

After the court's *Brown* II ruling, the state's urban newspapers (many believed that the cities would be the first to desegregate) expressed relief. The *Atlanta Constitution* felt the decision would end the politics of resistance, insisting that the verdict was "no call to arms for demagogues and race baiters . . . [and] must be a bitter blow to those who were ready to ride to glory on a hate platform. It will be received with relief by the reasonable majority of both races." The city's afternoon paper, the *Atlanta Journal,* called for the South to take "local responsibility" and hoped that with enough time and local action, "the South can achieve a solution both lawful in the eyes of the courts and satisfying to the people of the South." In Augusta, the *Chronicle* praised the decision for allowing the South enough time to prepare for the changes integration would bring and called it "a distinct triumph for the southern viewpoint" because with a broad interpretation of the decision "segregation in the classroom could continue for years, or for decades, or even forever." [58]

After the initial shock of the *Brown* decree and the implementation decision waned, Georgians retreated to a stance of watchful silence. Most did not believe that anything would actually change. African Americans, for a variety of reasons including fear of reprisal, moved very cautiously toward ending school segregation in Georgia. Whites, convinced that their political leaders could change or fight the decision, "behaved as if nothing important had happened or was going to happen." The state's politicians used the decision to win or to stay in office, promising their constituents that Georgia would never integrate its schools. And from the time the *Brown* decision was announced until the standoff in Little Rock, Arkansas, in the autumn of 1957, Georgia's political leaders dedicated themselves to the politics of massive resistance. [59]

The Philosophy and Politics of Massive Resistance

The 1954 governor's race offered a wide field of candidates as both factions of the Democratic Party were in disarray. The *Brown* decision and Georgia's commitment to massive resistance disrupted the traditional choice in the governor's race between the progressives and the social conservatives. The more moderate faction could not withstand the pressure of the race issue and was hindered by M. E. Thompson's two consecutive defeats at the hands of Herman Talmadge. Georgia's economy was strong and growing, and Talmadge had used money from the sales tax and various fund-raising ventures to improve the state's hospitals, roads, and schools. These improvements and his defiance toward the federal government made Talmadge a very popular governor, but in 1954 he refused to name his successor. Three of the nine announced candidates in the campaign were closely tied to the Talmadge camp. Because of the Supreme Court's edict, the Talmadge faction was strong enough to divide its own votes and still elect a governor. What had cost James

Carmichael the election in 1946 now could not help the progressive forces. The threat of a major disruption in Georgia's social structure gave Talmadge and his minions almost total control over state politics.[60] Corresponding with the increased popularity of those associated with Talmadge was the rising influence of the Black Belt in the state's county unit voting patterns. In 1954, 30 percent of the county unit vote belonged to counties that had a black population of 30 percent or more.[61] Massive resistance held a basic appeal to the whites of this area; since the 1920s their economic way of life had gone through fundamental changes. Many poor African Americans lived in the plantation counties, and large landowners relied on segregation and a static society to provide inexpensive labor and a clear definition of employee and employer relations. Any change in that relationship, including civil rights, scared the rural white elite.[62]

The front-runners in the field for the Democratic nomination for governor included Lieutenant Governor Marvin Griffin; Speaker of the House Fred Hand; Agricultural Commissioner (a traditional step to the governor's chair) Tom Linder; a popular anti-Talmadge state representative from Brunswick, Charles Gowan; and M. E. Thompson. As eventual winner Griffin recalled later, "a fellow out running against that field, in the vernacular of we Wiregrass Georgians, had to steer his stumps to get by them in 1954." Although Talmadge would not support any of the candidates publicly, he later claimed Griffin was his personal choice.[63]

In a widely publicized and discussed campaign event, each candidate appeared before the Georgia Education Commission and testified how he or she would preserve segregation in the state.[64] Not all of the candidates supported the private school amendment. Charles Gowan recommended a local option plan to give each community a voice. Hand gave an equivocal answer about the need to preserve public education and southern tradition. Thompson, on the other hand, argued for a constitutional amendment nullifying the Supreme Court decision. Other candidates' suggestions included such original ideas as abolishing the Supreme Court, an amendment to the United States Constitution to provide states with the final authority over their schools, and relocating every black citizen out of Georgia and providing them with employment. Perhaps the strangest idea of all, proposed by Tom Linder, recommended that the state conduct a poll of every citizen, asking whether the respondents preferred segregated schools. According to Linder, anyone who answered negatively could be declared insane, sent to Milledgeville, and locked up in the state's mental hospital. On the campaign trail Linder later amended this idea and suggested that the state open integrated schools and then commit anyone who attended the integrated school to the state hospital. As Roy Harris pointed out years later, "They can say what they please about the nigra issue and all this [as] racist but it elects all the governors."[65]

Marvin Griffin won the election handily by associating himself with the recent achievements of the Talmadge administration, promising to preserve segregation "come hell or high water," and committing himself to states' rights, low taxes, and the continuation of the county unit system. He received 234,690 popular votes and 302 county unit votes. As Charles Weltner described it, "Georgia politics remained Georgia politics, except more so. The issue in the gubernatorial race of 1954 was segregation and the County Unit System. The question was who was most for them—for never a syllable was uttered against either. Marvin Griffin was elected by an overwhelming county unit vote, although two-thirds of the people of Georgia voted against him."[66]

A few months after the Griffin inauguration, when the Supreme Court ruled in *Brown* II and ordered the southern states to desegregate their schools "with all deliberate speed," many in the South breathed a collective sigh of relief. Georgia's leaders, however, although pleased the court did not call for immediate desegregation, continued their preparations to resist the original decision. The newly elected lieutenant governor, Ernest Vandiver, thought "the Supreme Court in some small measure attempted to correct an obnoxious decision." House Speaker Marvin Moate promised "to use all means possible to put it off in Georgia." Denmark Groover, a longtime state politician, believed that the verdict was "less vicious than it could have been but that decision is not presently binding on the state of Georgia." Georgia's new Governor Marvin Griffin added, "No matter how much the Supreme Court seeks to sugarcoat its bitter pill of tyranny, the people of Georgia and the South will not swallow it." Georgia prepared to defy the decision. Herman Talmadge claimed "a line is drawn. The time has come when all must get on one side or the other."[67]

Talmadge's call did not go unheeded. Even before the *Brown* decision, southern states exhibited signs of a modern regional solidarity against perceived federal encroachment. When segregation in southern graduate schools was threatened, fourteen southern governors met in 1947 in an attempt to establish a regional black graduate school. Southern black leadership, however, showed little interest in the project and it was abandoned. The short-lived 1948 "Dixiecrat" split from the Democratic Party, responding to Harry S. Truman's platform, suggested a degree of southern unity. And after the Supreme Court graduate school decisions in the *Sweatt* and *McLaurin* cases in 1950, racial politics led to the defeat of two prominent moderate southern politicians, Claude Pepper in Florida and Frank Graham in North Carolina.[68]

South Carolina joined Georgia in the early leadership of massive resistance, forced into that role as a defendant in the original *Brown* lawsuit. James F. Byrnes and Strom Thurmond led the racial political resurgence in the Palmetto state that passed the first private school amendment in November 1952. That amendment was the creation of Marion Gressette, who chaired a committee to study the possibility of forced integration. Gressette concluded that the state could not be forced to integrate private schools. However, the amendment narrowly passed and the vote divided along the traditional South Carolina fall line that separated the state's Black Belt region from the upcountry.[69]

After the two *Brown* decisions, resistance in the South slowly gelled into a recognizable form. From 1954 to 1964 the former states of the Confederacy passed more than 450 laws to avoid the court's decision. Many created the possibility of a private school system; others planned to abandon state control over individual school districts, thereby forcing African Americans interested in desegregating schools into filing separate lawsuits in each individual district; and still others designed a system of placing pupils into separate schools using criteria other than race (gerrymandered school districts for example) and made school transfers practically impossible.[70]

The massive resistance movement, however, represented much more than political actions to preserve segregation in education. Southern leaders resurrected the saints, heroes, and emblems of the Confederacy and applied their powerful symbolism in their fight. By wrapping their effort to preserve segregation in the stars and bars of states' rights philosophy, these men, raised on stories of Reconstruction and the glory of the Confederacy, sought to recapture the spirit of Southern Unity. To justify their fight, they used the writings of John C. Calhoun, who had given racism an "aura of high morality."

They picked apart the words of Thomas Jefferson and James Madison looking for sentiments of strict constitutional constructionism, favoring state
sovereignty. They venerated Jefferson Davis, Robert E. Lee, and Stonewall
Jackson for their fierce determination in fighting for the southern way of life.
Southern leaders convinced themselves and their constituents that they were
fighting for a just and noble cause and that the South was a victim of northern aggression. Herman Talmadge once said that he expected an upcoming
session of Congress to be the "meanest, most vicious since Andrew Johnson [because] they are determined to reconstruct the South for the second time."[71]

John C. Calhoun's idea of interposition and James Madison's and Thomas
Jefferson's concept of nullification were two ideas southern leaders used to
combat the court's decision. Briefly stated, interposition is the notion that
since the Constitution was a compact between individual states, each state
could claim sovereignty over the national government unless the Constitution specifically granted certain authority to the federal government. Since
the document contains no mention of public schools, southern leaders
claimed the court's decision had no bearing within their state. Echoing this
interpretation, South Carolina state Senator Marion Gressette explained that
"this being true, the state cannot be forced to appropriate money for schools
contrary to the public interest." Roy Harris, meeting with a group of southern political leaders in Virginia in early 1956 recommended that all southern
states adopt a resolution of interposition. Four governors were strongly in
favor of the idea; Thomas Stanley of Virginia, Marvin Griffin of Georgia,
George Timmerman of South Carolina, and James P. Coleman of Mississippi
agreed to adopt interposition. Griffin wished to take his opposition one step
further and opt for nullification, claiming that the Supreme Court decision
was null and void in his state. As legal stratagems, however, nullification and
interposition were chimerical at best; southerners had used these arguments
in the years before the Civil War and failed. Even so, most southern states
adopted some measure of interposition as a symbolic gesture.[72]

Southerners did not rely only upon historical justifications for rational-
ization of their actions. They also used a new, very powerful tool available to
politicians seeking absolution for an agenda of the extreme right. The cold
war left America in mortal fear of communism; southern politicians, accus-
tomed to accusing their political opponents of being less "southern," simply

twisted this argument against the Supreme Court and any racially progressive politician and charged them with being less "American." In his pamphlet *You and Segregation,* Herman Talmadge came just short of denouncing the Supreme Court as a communist agency. In Georgia, Eugene Cook campaigned to link the NAACP with the Communist Party. The Georgia Education Commission received an increase in funding and evolved from a political sounding board to an active undercover agency. It collected surveillance equipment worthy of any proper covert organization, using wiretap devices, pocket microphones, and telescopic cameras secretly to investigate the NAACP and the families of students requesting school transfers.[73]

The underlying philosophy of massive resistance was not a fierce dedication to states' rights nor a reliving of the glory of the South's history, nor was it an inexplicable fear of communism. It was a practical preservation of white supremacy. To many in the white population, a dual system of citizenship, in which African Americans received inferior treatment, made perfect sense. The idea of white supremacy was the stronghold of their personal and political beliefs. As *New York Times* reporter Anthony Lewis suggested, massive resistance had a "searing emotional impact. It has been made to appeal to the most susceptible tribal impulses: patriotism, racial purity, religious dogma, group solidarity, status and personal pride." The fear of many white southerners in allowing blacks the same freedoms as whites was social intermingling between the races.[74] The threat of miscegenation permeated the thoughts of these men and drove them to create a resistance movement, doomed to failure, but one which they hoped would give them time to understand the changes taking place in the South.

Defiance of the federal government began to permeate all levels of southern society; the politics of the era rubbed off on the populace. As *Atlanta Constitution* editor Ralph McGill observed, "This average Southerner with a deep sense of injustice is not a 'bad' man. He wants to be liked. He wants it understood he loves his country—and he does, as he has proved in war and peace. But at present he feels that his country does not love him. And he is sad, angry, resentful, and defiant." Perhaps the most obvious representation of that defiance was the phenomenal growth of the "Citizens' Councils." Organized in Mississippi in 1954, the councils were usually made up of businessmen, and, unlike the Ku Klux Klan, worked in the open, using economic pressure rather than violence. "The white population in this county controls the money," explained one member, "and this is an advantage that the council will use in a fight to legally maintain segregation of the races. . . . We intend to make it difficult, if not impossible for any Negro who advocates desegregation to find and hold a job, get credit or renew a mortgage." The councils grew quickly throughout the South. Most chapters of a council had four committees: Political and Elections provided a yardstick for political candidates and discouraged black registration; Information and Education collected and distributed segregation information; Membership and Finance recruited members and collected a five-dollar membership fee; a Legal Advisory committee provided legal counsel for members. The councils grew in popularity all over the country and published articles in *Harper's Magazine, U.S. News and World Report,* and *Atlantic Monthly.* By 1958 they were producing and airing federally subsidized television programs justifying to audiences the practice of segregation. The Citizens' Councils were pragmatic, grassroots organizations dedicated to preserving segregation in every community. They never caught on in Georgia; Georgia's version of the council, the States' Rights Council of Georgia, became another arm in the state Democratic Party under the control of Roy Harris.[75]

The States' Rights Council of Georgia (SRC) started with great fanfare; among the earliest members were Herman Talmadge, Marvin Griffin, and Harris. The group originally planned to open chapters in all one hundred and fifty-nine Georgia counties, but the SRC did not attract a large following. Nor did the Atlanta-based resurgent Ku Klux Klan. The reason for the failure of both the SRC and the Klan to generate a substantial enrollment during the peak of resistance lay in the success of Georgia's politicians in gathering support for the programs of political resistance. Men like Harris and Griffin, rather than using their prestige to recruit members into the SRC, believed it would better serve as a political tool for their faction of the Democratic Party. Harris described the SRC as the "the old Talmadge ringleaders . . . the folks we depended on, and that was the organization." This is not to say that the white people of Georgia were apathetic about segregation, because as the Sibley Commission hearings show, they were very dedicated to its preservation. What it does say is that the politicians who had been using the race issue for eleven years to get elected and to stay in office had effectively convinced the populace that Georgia would never integrate its schools. And the people believed them.[76]

Perhaps this belief in the policies of resistance stemmed from the flurry of legislation passed by the Georgia General Assembly. Beginning in January 1955, the General Assembly passed laws to thwart the *Brown* directive. In preparation for an adverse ruling in the implementation hearing later that spring, the assembly enacted legislation that would withhold funds from any school expected to integrate and passed resolutions urging constitutional amendments to deny federal authority over state schools and give states full control over education. One year later the assembly prepared the state for a conversion to a private school system. Legislation passed that year included provisions for fire inspections of private schools, the leasing of school property to private individuals, tuition grants to parents, and the extension of retirement benefits to private school teachers. The assembly further made it a crime to trespass on closed school property and allowed for the suspension of retirement benefits to school officers failing to enforce school segregation. Entering a new phase in its challenge to federal authority, the assembly in 1956, with only one dissenting vote from Atlanta's Hamilton Lokey, passed House Resolution 185, which called for the state to adopt interposition. The following year the assembly strengthened the governor's emergency powers and enabled him to suspend mandatory attendance laws, gave the Georgia Education Commission power to hold public hearings, and passed a resolution asking for the impeachment of six Supreme Court justices for "high crimes and misdemeanors."[77]

Laws designed to prepare the state for conversion to a private school system were part of a subtle strategy based on the belief that most black Georgians preferred segregation and sought primarily equality in facilities and expenditures. Private schools, the legislators reasoned, could be used as a threat and a last resort. The ambiguity of the court's order in the *Brown* case meant that each community could continue segregation until a court order forced a white school to admit black pupils. As long as no one sued in federal court, life would continue as before. Federal Judge Elbert Tuttle described the strategy of many southern legislators including Georgia. "Politicians would fight for a delay of another year; and they wouldn't comply with the law unless they themselves were compelled by a court order. And that meant that there had to be a litigant in every school district in the South. If the issue involved was desegregating the courthouse or the drinking fountains or waiting rooms in the trains [they would fight] . . . because time was worth fighting for in the

minds of these officials." Georgia legislators coupled their private school legislation with large increases in school spending in an effort to eradicate the
disparity between the white and black schools, hoping that the black population would accept voluntary segregation in exchange for improved school facilities. Between 1949 and 1955, Georgia spent $274 million on public schools,
more than any other southern state in the same period with the exceptions of
Texas and North Carolina, more than five times that of Mississippi, and eight
times that of Alabama. Indeed, by the time Herman Talmadge left office,
spending on black students had increased almost eightfold in fifteen years.
The black community saw this increase in spending as a joke; the new schools
dubbed "Supreme Court schools" were empty from the beginning as white
people moved out of the inner city faster than the schools were built. (In Atlanta's transitional neighborhoods, often both black and white schools were
built to ensure that the white school stayed white.) This exodus occasionally
created sublime conditions. School officials, allowing black pupils to use a
formerly white school building, boarded up the front entrance and forced the
new student body to use the back door. In case the wave of school improvements was not enough, there was the danger of converting to private schools.
Certainly Roy Harris understood this danger. When the Georgia Education
Commission made its first recommendations to the General Assembly to
adopt a private school plan, Harris voted against it, claiming that the risk of
closing schools with no recourse would be more effective. Eugene Cook and
Herman Talmadge thought the intimidation of a switch to private education
would be enough to discourage any would-be integration advocates. The
threat was used all over the South; as one state senator from Alabama put it,
"there are more ways than one to kill a snake. . . . We will have segregation in
the public schools . . . or there will be no public schools." [78]

   Georgia's leaders based both the private school plan and the equalization
of school facilities on an interpretation of the Supreme Court decision by a
federal judge in South Carolina. Judge John J. Parker, ruling on a local desegregation case, claimed that "what [the Supreme Court] has decided, and
all that it has decided, is that a state may not deny to any person on account
of race the right to attend any school that it maintains. . . . Nothing in the
Constitution or in the decision of the Supreme Court takes away from the
people freedom to choose the schools they attend. The Constitution in other
words does not require integration. It merely forbids discrimination. It does

African American Population in Georgia, 1960

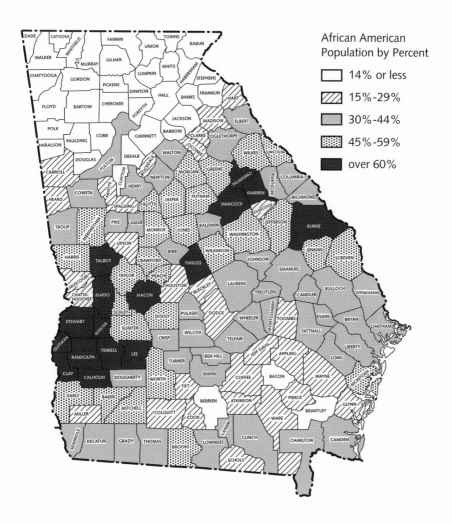

African American
Population by Percent

- [ ] 14% or less
- [/] 15%-29%
- [▒] 30%-44%
- [▓] 45%-59%
- [■] over 60%

Compare the figures from this map with individual counties' testimony. Most of the counties with large African American populations sent white delegations to appear before the Sibley Commission to testify for segregation at all costs. The counties with a small African American population supported other options.

not forbid such segregation that occurs as the result of voluntary action. It merely forbids the use of governmental power to enforce segregation." Georgia's political leaders simply convinced themselves that they could prevent integration with legislation.[79]

Resistance in Georgia was first and foremost a political function; the state's leaders stood firmly in their vigil against any change in Georgia's social structure. Attorney General Eugene Cook did all he could to ensure that the state practiced segregation "twenty-four hours a day, seven days a week, and three hundred sixty-five days a year."[80] In 1956 the General Assembly voted to incorporate the Confederate battle flag as part of the official state flag as a symbol of defiance. The State Board of Education banned books that did not teach the southern viewpoint, including a children's songbook that had replaced the word "darkies" in a Stephen Foster tune.[81]

At times the constant vigil over segregation took on embarrassing proportions. Georgia's leaders, promoting the state as a vacation spot, invited a group of Canadian miners, the rescued victims of a cave-in, to the state for a free holiday. The publicity turned sour; one black miner was forced into segregated lodging during his stay. Perhaps the most disconcerting event of the period was the controversy surrounding the 1956 Sugar Bowl football game. Georgia Tech, in the heyday of its football glory, was invited to play the University of Pittsburgh squad. A vice president of the States' Rights Council wired Tech coach Bobby Dodd expressing his protest that Tech would be involved in an integrated contest (the Pitt team had a black player). Although both Tech and the University of Georgia had played integrated sports teams in the past, Marvin Griffin asked the Board of Regents to forbid any Georgia school from participating in a nonsegregated athletic event; he felt the state must make a stand and not play the game. For many students and other Georgians this interpretation of the state's commitment to segregation was simply too strict, and a fierce protest swirled around the Capitol. Some twenty-five hundred students from Tech and the University of Georgia converged upon Capitol Avenue, burned Griffin in effigy, overturned trash cans, pulled out fire hoses, and demanded that Griffin "grow up." Another demonstration at the governor's mansion lasted until the early hours of the morning, and among the demonstrators was the governor's son, Sam Griffin. The Board of Regents quietly calmed the controversy when it ruled that, since Tech played the game out of the state, it was permissible.[82]

Ironically, Roy Harris, by creating a stifling political atmosphere with no place for moderation, actually helped to bring the downfall of Georgia's massive resistance. Harris's strategy of transforming segregation into a political, rather than a social issue, left it exposed to the changing winds of political fortune. Georgia's politicians paid proper homage to white supremacy while privately admitting the issue was "phony." (Disingenuous or not, until 1961, no politician outside Atlanta could afford to campaign as a racial moderate or vote against the torrent of massive resistance legislation that flooded the floor of the General Assembly.) Bill Shipp, a political reporter for the *Atlanta Constitution* who started work in the 1950s, later explained how difficult it was for an outsider to understand the complexities of race politics or "how thoroughly ingrained race was in the political structure of the state and how race was used as a subterfuge and a dodge so that politicians would not have to promise what they should have been talking about. . . . Instead, they talked about preserving our way of life."[83] Former Speaker of the House George T. Smith believed that in times of "social uprising," however, politicians are primarily motivated by political survival and were "genuinely . . . afraid of the massive change . . . . Uncertainty is a foundation most about fear."[84]

By 1958, Georgia's plan to resist integration was firmly in place. Roy Harris, proud of his achievement, boasted that "as a result [of our efforts] sentiment became so unified in Georgia that there was no real effort made over five years to integrate the schools in Georgia. So far as I am concerned, I propose never to surrender. I may be hung. I may be shot. But regardless of what happens there will be no surrender on my part. . . . If one little nigra is entitled to go to Henry Grady High School in Atlanta, then all nigras are entitled to go to some high school with whites."[85] However, when Harris took his resistance revival on the road in an attempt to convince the white people of Arkansas that they, like Georgia, could defy the federal court order, it led to a series of events that destroyed the legal underpinnings of massive resistance.

Little Rock

President Eisenhower's lukewarm commitment to enforcement of the *Brown* decision allowed the defiant attitude of the South to fester. He believed that federal intervention would be ineffective and would trample on powers that properly belonged to the states. He privately hoped the matter of implementation would be postponed until he was out of office. However, his wish remained unfulfilled because a formerly progressive politician, sensing the mileage that could come from a strong stand against the government, challenged the court's decision and forced Eisenhower into action.[86]

The most celebrated fight between the federal government and the southern resisters took place in Little Rock, Arkansas, in the autumn of 1957. Federal courts had ordered the city to desegregate its public schools, and the first students to integrate Central High School were set to start classes in September. A few days before school began, Marvin Griffin and Roy Harris, at the invitation of an Arkansas Citizens' Council, came to Little Rock. Governor Orval Faubus, although hesitant, invited them to stay with him at the governor's mansion. Addressing large crowds, Griffin and Harris protested the upcoming integration of Little Rock schools and agitated the gathering. They claimed that Georgia, through a program of massive resistance, had avoided all integration and would continue to do so. The crowd took to heart what the men had to say, and when school began a few days later an angry throng gathered outside Central High School to protest. Those present to hear Georgia's segregationist emissaries were not the only ones who heeded their message; Faubus, witnessing the crowd outside the school, feared violence and called out the Arkansas National Guard to control the people gathered to protest. The next day he ordered the guard to prevent the students from entering the school. By directly defying the federal government, Faubus became a new hero in the fight for segregation. The South, with the passage of time having slowly eroded the living memory of the Confederacy, grappled for a new identity to set itself apart from the rest of the nation and had settled on segregation. Faubus became the first new hero in the fight; like Davis, Lee, and Jackson, he defied the federal government in a direct confrontation and changed the course of massive resistance.[87]

President Eisenhower, though sympathizing with the South's position, and even agreeing with the idea of states' rights, would not allow direct defiance of a court order. He federalized the Arkansas National Guard and changed its mission to protecting the students entering school. To angry southerners, once again "federal" troops occupied the South to enforce the decrees of a hostile national government. But defeat could not lessen Faubus's position as the leader of the resistance movement; indeed in southern mythology there were few heroes who emerged from battle with the federal government victorious. After Little Rock, Reconstruction comparisons were natural and became an integral part of southern oratory. Herman Talmadge, keenly aware of both the historical and modern fight for southern tradition, compared the use of troops in Little Rock not with federal occupation but with the Soviet invasion of Hungary.[88]

The Little Rock standoff proved to be the turning point in the massive resistance movement. The federal courts responded to the crisis with a flurry of decisions designed to break resistance permanently. However, these decisions did not stop the mountain of defiant legislation passed in the South after Faubus's stand. The noted historian of the period, Numan Bartley, contends that massive resistance reached its peak in the year following the Little Rock crisis as southern states passed more and more massive resistance legislation.[89]

Some Georgians, however, experienced Little Rock differently. The state's next governor, Ernest Vandiver, who was elected in 1958, appalled at the Arkansas governor's actions, claimed "Faubus is not a sincere segregationist, and what he's going to do over there in Arkansas is going to speed up integration here and elsewhere in the South five or ten years. They're cheering him, when actually he's cutting our throats." Vandiver was no resister caught up in the symbolism of defiance; he wanted to protect segregation and was as practical and pragmatic about it as he possibly could be on such an emotional subject. Another factor affected Georgia's massive resistance stand after Little Rock, when the negative publicity and resulting economic slowdown in Arkansas's business development awoke a sleeping giant. State business and industrial leaders, fearing for the economic future of Georgia, began actively to involve themselves in protecting public education and ending massive resistance. Most people, however, refused to believe integration could happen in Georgia, and the political rhetoric of the defiance movement only strengthened this belief. Ralph McGill, in 1958, described Georgia's state of mind: "There are even now literally thousands of good Southern people who believe the court's action to be illegal and not applicable to them, because a governor, a senator, a congressman, an editor or some other person of position has so said or written."[90]

CHAPTER 2

Uneasy Bedfellows

Georgia's experience with massive resistance established a white supremacist hegemony that left seemingly little opposition. The political races of the 1950s and the rhetoric of the General Assembly and governor gave the appearance of a solid citizenry, wholly dedicated to the tenets of segregation and political resistance. This impression, however, simply was not true. A small but vocal minority struggled to be heard above the deafening roar of silence on the segregation question.

A Genteel Tyranny

The leaders of the massive resistance movement largely succeeded in silencing most southern opposition. Most newspaper editors or ministers would call only for moderation, unable to make a stronger stand for fear of retribution. The *Atlanta Constitution*'s Ralph McGill lashed out at the "mob" of public opinion that "terrorized or silenced any who might dare oppose it." A high-ranking church official claimed, "the atmosphere in Georgia now is one which denies freedom of speech on the segregation question. Freedom of speech is not denied by law; it is now being denied by fear. . . . Free discussion is curbed by fear of reprisals—social and economic reprisals." Almost one year after the Supreme Court's ruling in *Brown v. Board of Education of Topeka*, the Southern Regional Council released a statement condemning southern politicians for their "concerted attempt to stamp out independent thought and stifle all dissent with respect to school segregation. . . . There are thousands of southerners, white and Negro, for whom the demagogues do not speak, and whose voices have been little heard above the din of controversy. Ultimately these southern voices will repudiate fraudulent leadership on the school issue." The statement criticized the resisters for their efforts to dodge the Court ruling. "Such an attitude promotes paralysis of public thought, and thereby forfeits a valuable opportunity for advance discussion and planning to insure smooth transition to integrated schools." The report singled out the actions of Georgia, Louisiana, South Carolina, and Mississippi for "busily creating dangerous illusions and enacting defiant measures. Some political leaders in these states are assuring the people that the schools will remain segregated indefinitely, if not forever, even though public education may be abolished in the process. These threats and the legal stratagems devised to carry them out are better adapted to hoodwink the people than to preserve segregation." In Georgia, Charles Weltner protested the fact that "no one was telling the truth to the people. . . . There was total silence on the matter throughout Georgia. The leadership at the state level was mute." One southern newsman agreed. "To know that period of the South is to know that it was frozen in silence. People were not discussing the issue. Neighbor and neighbor were afraid of each other. Conformity was established by precedent. And for a man who might doubt the wisdom of segregation to sit down with his neighbor and say, 'Hey, I'm not sure we're right' could have ruined that man in most Southern states."[1]

Fear and ignorance were not the only forces working to the advantage of those committed to segregation through resistance. The decline of the progressive faction in the Georgia Democratic Party contributed to the public's political apathy. Those opposed to the defiant stance of Georgia's resistance movement lacked a method or an avenue to vent their frustration. They needed an issue or event to prove there were issues Georgians cared about more than segregation.[2]

The destruction of political moderation occurred throughout the South. Historian Michael Klarman identifies an ironic twist to massive resistance politics in his "backlash thesis." He contends that as the post-*Brown* South retreated into demagoguery, politicians used the racial fears of poor and middle-class whites to destroy moderation. The southern fire-eater's reaction to *Brown* brought attention to the region and molded northern opinion against the southern leaders. Eventually, Klarman asserts, this concern gelled during the civil rights protests of the mid-1960s and helped civil rights leaders in their fight to break down the barriers of southern white supremacy.[3] In Georgia, however, another element quickened the pace toward desegregation—the state's business leaders, fearing an adverse economic climate if massive resistance threatened public education, abandoned the state's political leaders and sought a quick resolution to a potential school crisis.

Business desertion of its conservative political allies marked the end of a coalition that had prospered since the last part of the nineteenth century. The Populist movement's efforts to alleviate the pitiful conditions of southern farmers in the 1890s forged a courthouse-boardroom alliance between Georgia's rural politicians and its businessmen. These two forces, socially, politically, and economically conservative, saw the inherent danger that Populist ideology meant to their control over the South. The boll weevil infestation of the 1920s reinforced this coalition, when Georgia turned to industry to help revive the local economies of small and medium-sized towns. The state's leaders amended the constitution, creating tax exemptions for new businesses. State politicians and businessmen recruited new commercial interests to Georgia, promoting cultural tradition and an intense aversion to organized labor. Smaller towns and cities often provided new industry with land grants and other allowances. In Atlanta a national advertising campaign, "Forward Atlanta," promoted the city's favorable business environment. In rural Georgia, these small-town industrialists quickly formed an alliance with the local planter class. The state's county unit system made a small-town industrial center even more politically powerful than could have been possible in a larger city. Throughout Georgia, the rural coalition of small-town business owners and the planter class united with the Atlanta business community and supported conservative political factions because they shared an interest in limited taxation, frugal government, and a captive labor force.[4]

Calvin Kytle and James Mackay explained the system. "Our romantic cultural tradition, our violent paroxysms of race prejudice, and the continued absence of a strong labor movement tended to obscure what was happening to us, to make it easier for industrialists and financiers to perpetuate a kind of genteel tyranny." The large plantation or mill owners who provided county leadership fought to preserve segregation, because it established a rigid social structure that kept wages low. To this end, they formed county political machines or "courthouse rings" that controlled politics at a local level and delivered their county's unit votes to the particular faction or candidate that promised to protect the status quo. These men were also motivated by personal vanity. "It's a thing of pride with them," one observer commented. "They just want to be in a position where the people will ask them how to vote, where politicians will seek them out, and where they can have the privilege of calling on the governor and being assured an audience."[5]

Although courthouse rings controlled politics at a local level, Georgia's large corporations dominated the state's political affairs. The county unit system made this domination possible. By forcing candidates to run political races in each of Georgia's 159 counties, the system provided little protection against corporate influence over state affairs because of the large amount of money required to run a statewide campaign and corporations' willingness to "play politics" and provide the money needed. Although Georgia law prohibited corporations from directly contributing to campaigns, individuals within certain companies gave thousands of dollars to candidates. Often, these financial representatives gave money to both candidates in a particular race. Kytle and Mackay concluded that businessmen could not "risk their interests to the vagaries of politics [because] they must be above factionalism; they must dominate all factions. If the faction they've supported the most doesn't happen to win, they must be able to switch promptly and without too much additional expense to the faction that does." The most dominant corporate influences were the public utilities, railroads, pipelines, trucking companies, liquor dealers, soft drink companies, banks, independent contractors, and textile mills. These companies not only used the county unit system to control elections but maintained a strong lobbying presence at the capitol when the General Assembly was in session. In spite of corporate abuse of the county unit system, rural politicians continued to defend it, convincing their constituents that without the guaranteed rural representation that county unit voting provided, "city machines" would rule the state.[6]

Eugene Talmadge best personifies the unification of Georgia's socially conservative rural politicians, struggling to maintain a racial status quo, and the economically conservative visionaries striving to build an industrial

Georgia. Talmadge was a throwback to the old Redeemer-style governors of the post-Reconstruction South; his fiscal policies centered on limited government, low taxes, and support of business. However, as federal government involvement in the affairs of state citizens grew, Talmadge's main concern evolved into the preservation of white supremacy as a means of social control.[7] He formatted his governmental programs to keep the large numbers of landless poor, both black and white, powerless and able to provide cheap labor for agriculture and industry. To this end he fought vigorously against any labor union uprising. In September of 1934, during a textile workers general strike that erupted throughout the South, Talmadge declared martial law in Georgia's communities where strikes were held and locked up striking workers in the stockade at Fort McPherson. His aversion to labor unions and his commitment to maintaining the established social structure benefitted the small-town textile mill owner or manufacturer. An example of Talmadge's enigmatic duality is provided by the issue of the "three dollar tag." While governor, Talmadge fought for a change in the method the state taxed automobiles. He argued that it was not fair for Georgia's poor farmers to buy a "ten dollar tag" for a "three dollar car." As governor, Talmadge secured the passage of an ad valorem tax and flat three dollar fee for each tag. Although farmers, whom Talmadge claimed to represent, benefitted from the change in the fee structure, corporations with large fleets of trucks or automobiles benefitted more. As one man put it, "while saving the little men pennies, [Talmadge] saved the big men thousands."[8]

The two separate forces that characterized the Georgia economy during the first half of the twentieth century, a rapidly growing industrial sector and a plantation agricultural system struggling to overcome its own anachronistic structure, both benefitted from segregation, disfranchisement, and many landless poor. But the economy of the state evolved during this time as the agricultural base gave way to a corporate, industrial foundation that became less and less colonial and more rooted in the red clay of Georgia. The plantation system, designed to keep money and power in the hands of local wealthy landowners, transformed due to an outward migration of workers that coincided with technological developments and enabled these men to replace workers with cheaper, more productive machines. During the Great Depression, Eugene Talmadge's intense hatred of New Deal policies and refusal to accept wage supports originally benefitted the plantation owners. But during

Georgia's brief flirtation with the New Deal under the E. D. Rivers administration, large farmers received capital through farm price supports and were able to replace even more workers with farm machinery than would have otherwise been possible. Georgia's absentee industrial and transportation ownership, which also profited from Talmadge's aversion to the New Deal, continued to capitalize on restricted credit with high interest rates and discriminatory freight rates. However, rising labor and transportation costs in the Northeast and Midwest prompted many business owners to move their production facilities to Georgia, thus making the state less of an economic colony.[9]

After the Second World War, the courthouse-boardroom alliance also transformed as the business leaders increased their power because of a flourishing economy and active involvement of certain governors dedicated to industrial recruiting. When Herman Talmadge proved to be more concerned with economic growth than many of his predecessors, he gained the unabashed support of the business elite in Atlanta. The chief partner of the city's most prestigious law firm, Hughes Spalding, whose son edited the *Atlanta Journal,* liked Talmadge for his pro-business outlook. Robert Woodruff, the head of Coca-Cola, supported Talmadge throughout the politician's long career. The Atlanta business community wanted to preserve the environment that fostered so much of the city's success and called upon the state's political leaders to continue to fight for the status quo.[10]

A new generation of firebrand governors, dedicated to both the maintenance of white supremacy and a growing economy, emerged during Georgia's massive resistance campaign. Herman Talmadge vigorously sought to extend an atmosphere conducive to attracting and building banking, agriculture, industry, and transportation firms in Georgia, but he will be best remembered for his leadership in defying the Supreme Court. Business leaders applauded his efforts to alleviate the disparities between white and black schools and used the new schools as a lure for potential industrial relocation. Marvin Griffin, who once suggested locking up integrationists so far in the back of Georgia's jails they could not be reached with a "black jack sapling," also fostered a pro-business atmosphere. Between 1955 and 1959, more than one thousand manufacturing plants opened or expanded in the state, due in no small part to Griffin's many forays outside Georgia to recruit business. However, the two basic thrusts of Talmadge's and Griffin's philosophy were destined for confrontation, and when forced to choose between them, they chose the political option and pursued massive resistance.[11]

As beneficial as segregation was to promoting a healthy economic climate for industrialists, the fight to preserve it began to have the opposite effect. Racial moderates urged business leaders to get involved and use their influence to promote open discussion of the South's problems before the "secessionist policies" of the resisters went too far. Business leaders operating on a national or international scale faced a serious dilemma: appealing to two groups with opposite feelings on the segregation question. As historian Numan Bartley noted, they walked "a tight rope between presenting a national image free of bigotry and a home profile that demonstrated sufficient concern for segregation." Robert Woodruff of Coca-Cola discreetly promoted civil rights causes, hired black employees in offices far from the South, and limited Coca-Cola's public displays of racial moderation to events covered only by the black press. Woodruff and other members of the Atlanta business community saw that racism was wrong, but more importantly, that any negative feelings massive resistance created were bad for business. As Georgia's defiance escalated, business leaders looked for a way to resolve the situation amicably. In 1956, the executive vice president of the Georgia Chamber of Commerce, Walter T. Cates, denied that Georgia's racial problems slowed industrial growth, but warned that increased tension brought on by more negative publicity could change that.[12]

Early Opposition to Resistance

Even before the Supreme Court's decision in the *Brown* case, the NAACP experienced a cascade of victories in its fight to overcome racial inequality. The organization targeted state-supported segregation and won many cases in the federal courts. These decisions, besides ending discrimination in some local communities, brought the plight of black southerners to national attention.[13] Georgia's NAACP in 1950 filed cases against the Irwin County and Atlanta school boards, claiming the facilities for black schools were not equivalent to the white schools in the districts. Two years later, the NAACP sued the Atlanta School Board, stating that separate education for the races denied black students equal protection under the law. These cases, pending the decision in *Brown v. Board of Education,* were dismissed when they did not come to trial by 1956. Fear of reprisals against the black community due to zealous white defiance that appeared after the Supreme Court's 1954 decision and an apprehension of the possible reaction of lower federal courts discouraged the NAACP from directly challenging Georgia's school segregation laws for four years.[14]

During the early 1950s, the African American leadership in Georgia used a combination of compromise and growing political power to attain its objectives. In Atlanta and other large cities in the state, the black leadership worked with city officials in a spirit of mediation to achieve mild but gradual progress in racial equality. The Atlanta Negro Voters League, formed by John Wesley Dobbs and Austin T. Walden in 1949 in response to the growing power of Talmadgism, provided a bloc vote for Atlanta African Americans that was used to elect moderate candidates. Black voter registration continued to climb—from 145,000 in 1952 to 163,000 four years later. In 1953, the League used its influence to elect the first black member of the Atlanta School Board, Atlanta University president Rufus E. Clement. Atlanta's black community also pressured city leadership to desegregate the police force in 1949, city buses in 1953, and golf courses in 1958.[15]

In 1958, armed with federal court rulings that grew out of the Little Rock controversy, the city's NAACP leadership also moved to desegregate Atlanta's public schools. Twenty-eight parents, specially chosen by the organization, sued the Atlanta School Board. The plaintiffs, led by Vivian Calhoun, sought not individual student admission to white schools but an end to segregation in the Atlanta School District. The man on the bench, 62-year-old Frank A. Hooper from Americus, Georgia, had served in the General Assembly during the 1920s and was a state superior court judge from 1943 to 1949, when he was named to the United States District Court in Atlanta. The case made its way slowly through the court system, and on 5 June 1959, Hooper decided for the plaintiffs. Eleven days later he ordered the Atlanta School Board to submit a plan for desegregating its schools. Under Georgia law, if the city implemented its desegregation plan, the state would close the Atlanta schools. Hooper, sympathetic to the conflict between his ruling and Georgia's massive resistance laws, gave the school board until December to present its plan. In his ruling he called for the state to overturn mandatory school closing laws.[16]

Even the most ardent segregationists . . . now recognize that racially segregated public schools are not permitted by the law. . . . This court can not at this time make any other ruling except a ruling to the effect that the operation of racially segregated schools in Atlanta violates the Fourteenth Amendment. . . . To make any other ruling would only add to the confusion which already exists in the minds of so many of our good citizens, and the build up in the breasts of our citizens hopes of escape which would soon be torn to shreds by rulings of our appellate courts on review.[17]

While the African American community worked to eliminate mandatory segregation, protests against Georgia's plan of protecting Jim Crow emerged. One of the first challenges to Georgia's headlong rush into massive resistance came when Herman Talmadge attempted to implement a sales tax during his first administration. He sent a referendum to the citizens of the state wrapped in the guise that the three percent tax was needed to stave off integration. The people turned down the proposal by a three to one margin. The *Cobb County Times* accused Talmadge of using the race issue as a "tool to establish a statewide political machine."[18] Many Georgians also objected to the private school amendment, which narrowly passed 210,488 to 181,148 in November 1954. The majority of people in urban counties voted against it, and it passed by the slimmest of margins in the Piedmont area of the state. Georgia's newspapers opposed the measure by a four-to-one margin. Leaders in the fight against the private school amendment expressed incredulity over the apathy the state demonstrated toward public education.[19]

The private school plan and the methods used to pass the amendment even brought out detractors in political circles. An Associated Press poll revealed that half of the assembly members queried had reservations about the feasibility of the proposal. Even the governor-elect, arch-segregationist Marvin Griffin, showed some second thoughts about the viability of the plan. And Lieutenant Governor Ernest Vandiver expressed discomfort with the "gestapo tactics" used by the Georgia Education Commission to pass the amendment and warned them not to substitute "intrigue" for "sincerity, sound thinking and legal procedure."[20]

Other southern states that implemented private school plans heard similar protests. In South Carolina, the state's upcountry region bitterly opposed the private school amendment. The upcountry, with a far lower percentage of black schoolchildren in its school systems, did not feel the same pressure to convert the schools. When Mississippi proposed an amendment to abolish public education, a group calling itself the Friends of Segregated Schools fought the measure, accusing resistance leaders of using the threat to with-hold public school funding as something other than a "last resort."[21]

Responding to the private school plan and other resistance legislation in Georgia, a dedicated group of representatives in the General Assembly banded together; determined to fight the rural bloc of politicians forcing the state into defiance of the Supreme Court. The "Sinister Seven" earned their moniker because "time after time when one of the 'defiance bills' would come up for a vote, all the lights would be green [indicating a yes vote], ex-cept for the seven red votes of the Sinister Seven." The seven included state representatives Hamilton Lokey, James Mackay, Bill Gunther, Bill Williams, Fred Bentley, Bernard Nightingale, and Muggsy Smith. State senators Everett Millican and John Greer also fought massive resistance in the General As-sembly. These legislators could not believe the lengths their fellow congress-men were willing to go to preserve segregation. Hamilton Lokey categorized the resistance laws as having been "designed to frighten Negroes into re-maining in the status quo. These laws involved such things as threats to close schools, economic sanctions etc. . . . Laws designed to make it difficult, costly, and time consuming for negroes to qualify for entrance into white schools. . . . [and those that] primarily shouted 'Nigger, Nigger' for the pur-pose of reelection by the authors." In reply to the legislation that threatened public education, Lokey and James Mackay drew up a declaration that in-sisted Georgia must have open schools. Only eight House members in the Georgia General Assembly (the Sinister Seven and Hugh McWhorter) signed the document. The "Public School Declaration" demanded the support of public schools, the right of petition and of assembly, and discussion of the school problem. It also called for defiance to legislation that might destroy public schools, give the power to close schools to one man (the governor), or allow schools to switch to private operators, and forsake public education.[22]

A Living Institution

These men were among the earliest visible leaders of an open school move-ment. James Mackay coined their motto, "I will not vote to destroy a living institution to preserve a dying one." When the *Calhoun* decision drew near, and clearly the judge could only rule in favor of the plaintiffs, the Sinis-ter Seven and state senator Everett Millican spoke on behalf of education throughout the state. From the beginning, the men only discussed the value of open schools rather than the merits or liabilities of segregation. The introduction of the private school plan and the threat to public education created a division between segregation and resistance. This fracturing of the two issues allowed proponents of open schools to argue for another form of resistance that did not involve sacrificing education. This attempt to separate the school question from segregation became an axiom of open school movements throughout the South. In their speeches, the open school advocates pointed out to audiences the conflict between federal court rulings and Georgia law, hoping to show their listeners the implications of continued resistance. Emory University professor John Griffin hosted a series of lectures on segregation in 1957. He invited prominent southern newspaper editors to discuss the issue. The participants included Sylvan Meyer of the *Gainesville Times,* Ralph McGill, Harry Ashmore of the *Arkansas Gazette,* and Reed Sarratt of the *Winston-Salem Observer,* who proposed moderation in the segregation question, and James J. Kilpatrick of the *Richmond News-Leader,* James Hall of the *Montgomery Advertiser,* and Thomas Waring of the *Charleston News and Courier,* who argued for southern defiance. Two years later Griffin hosted another series of lectures, called "Crisis in the Schools," which featured discussion on the benefits of public schools with limited integration and proposals for private schools to maintain absolute segregation. James Mackay was among those who spoke for the former. Outgoing governor Marvin Griffin and constitutional attorney Robert Battle Hall (who would later serve on the Sibley Commission) argued for serious consideration of the private school plan that they had helped to construct. Lokey also continued his fight for open schools and, in a speech given in the spring of 1959, claimed that many communities in Georgia would not face any threat to their public schools if resistance were abandoned because of the scarcity of black children in their districts or because no one would sue to integrate the schools. But these men confronted an often hostile public; after an open schools speech in Atlanta, some segregationists convinced of the validity of resistance called Muggsy Smith a "scalawag, communist, mongrelizer, [and a] Bolshevik."[23]

Early in 1956, Roy Harris described Atlanta as the "Achilles heel" in the fight to preserve segregation in Georgia. He pointed to the city's black colleges and their influence, Atlanta's "leftists and left-wing groups," and the susceptibility of the Atlanta newspapers' dedication to segregation and de-nounced the political power of the city's black population. Atlanta presented problems to Georgia's fire-eaters for other reasons, most notably the city's connections and influence outside Georgia and the South. As the major southern transportation center, Atlanta came under northern influence more than most other southern cities and yearned for national and interna-tional acceptance. But for all the city's national prominence, state politics kept it weak within the borders of Georgia. When Hamilton Lokey first en-tered the Georgia Assembly as a representative from Atlanta, Speaker Fred Hand appointed him chairman of the "lookout committee." When Lokey asked what his duties involved, Hand told him, "Why sir, do you see that chair over there? You take that chair and put it by the window, and you sit in that chair and look out for the next two years."[24]

The African American leadership of Atlanta and the white business estab-lishment desired a positive, growing economic climate. These two groups, along with the administrations of Mayor William Hartsfield, moved slowly forward in the arena of civil rights with a minimum of conflict during the 1950s. The city's black business, church, and college leadership had confi-dence in Hartsfield and believed that the city's race relations progressed at a reasonable speed. Whenever the city chiefs seemed to drag their feet, the black establishment could usually pressure them into picking up the pace. These two groups worked together well because neither wanted to threaten Atlanta's unique climate as a haven for racial moderation and economic growth; these two ideals depended upon one another for survival. It was this symbiosis that frightened Roy Harris and the other resisters.[25]

Atlanta thrived throughout the first part of the twentieth century in large part due to its dedication to and dependence upon a growing business envi-ronment. Perhaps no other southern city was more devoted to the principles of the New South than Atlanta. Mayor Hartsfield relied upon the support of the city's major business concerns: Rich's Department Store; Citizen's and Southern, Trust Company, and First Atlanta banks; the Ivan Allen [office supply] Company; and Coca-Cola. In return for this support, business lead-ers insisted on charting the course of the city. Whenever a significant decision concerning Atlanta needed to be made, Hartsfield requested the counsel of the city's commercial establishment. As former political reporter Celestine Sibley (no relation to John A. Sibley) described it, "In Atlanta it was always the Chamber of Commerce, the silk stocking crowd, who were effectively in charge."[26]

William B. Hartsfield's pragmatism and practicality enabled the city to escape the turbulence of the 1940s and 1950s civil rights movements. Hartsfield put Atlanta's growth ahead of maintaining anachronistic traditions. He met the African American community's pleas for justice head on, working with black leaders to resolve differences, and did not, like so many other southern leaders, simply wait for problems to go away. Very early after the *Brown* decision, Hartsfield went to Governor Marvin Griffin and asked that the state allow Atlanta to hold a referendum on whether to close its schools in case of forced integration. In response to Griffin's inflexibility on the segregation issue, Hartsfield said, "I don't give a damn what Griffin or anyone else said. I refuse to let Georgia go through another period of ignorance." Once when asked to speak to a group dedicated to the preservation of separate schools, Hartsfield's approach to the podium was met with cat-calls and boos. He lashed out,

> You asked me to come here. I didn't want to come. Now are you going to listen to me or act like a bunch of bums? I am mayor of a great city. What would you want me to do as Mayor of your town? Do you want me to put on a sheet and burn down a few houses? .... Do you want me to kill a few? All right, while you've been running around mouthing "Nigger Lover" at everybody in sight, we've been building a great city. And we're going to go on building. Nothing is going to stop us. You hear me?

The mayor's enlightened racial attitude guided Atlanta during its fight against the state's leaders and their determination to close the city's schools rather than allow integration. Hartsfield's racial attitudes were, in addition to being enlightened, practical politics. Atlanta, after 1944 and especially after 1946, had a very large black voting population, and Hartsfield appealed to a unique coalition of black and affluent white voters to maintain power. This alliance allowed Hartsfield to win elections even when the majority of white Atlantans voted against him. There were many white people in Atlanta who did not share Hartsfield's or the Atlanta business community's racial pragmatism.[27]

With the city's political leadership firmly behind the open school movement, Atlanta seemingly presented a united front when facing off against the resisters in the state legislature. As *Calhoun v. Latimer* moved closer to a decision in 1959, Atlanta's leaders and open school advocates continued to build the impression that the issue at stake was open schools and avoided any argument about segregation. One Atlanta group largely responsible for open school advocacy was Help Our Public Education (HOPE), Inc., an organization of mostly white homemakers who rallied together to protect public education in Atlanta. HOPE experienced a large measure of success, and many city leaders and influential organizations supported the group's efforts, including the Atlanta Board of Aldermen, the city's PTAs, the League of Women Voters, and the Atlanta Chamber of Commerce. As the showdown between federal and state school laws approached, Atlanta presented a serious economic and political threat to massive resistance.[28]

Churches and Schools

The Supreme Court's decision in May of 1954 caused great consternation among white southern churches. The leaders of most national church organizations praised the decision after it was announced. But local ministers were torn between the intense feelings the decision brought out in their congregations and official national policy. This period was perhaps the most difficult time for religious leaders in the South since the arguments over slavery split many churches into southern and northern divisions. The national leadership called for members to obey the law and act in a Christian manner. The Southern Baptist Convention claimed the decision was "in harmony with the constitutional guarantee of equal freedom to all citizens and with the Christian principles of equal justice and love for all men."[29]

In Georgia, the arguments over cooperation with the *Brown* decision caused division not only between local churches and their national administrations but also between state organizations and city associations. The official newspaper of Georgia Baptists, the *Christian Index,* edited by John J. Hurt, advocated cooperation with the Court's decision. Hurt urged his readers to approach the problem carefully and "prayerfully." His paper condemned racial demagogues and organizations dedicated to the preservation of segregation.[30]

Although Hurt, as editor of the official organ of the Georgia Baptists, urged cooperation, its membership sharply divided over the issue. The *Brown* decision dominated the Georgia Baptists' conventions every year until the desegregation of the Atlanta schools in 1961. In 1956, the group deferred a statement calling for acceptance of the decision as the law of the land and in accordance with Christian principles. The next year the convention rejected a public policy that would have supported massive resistance and an approval of segregation. At the following convention, the Baptists slowly approached the open school movement and drafted a statement asking members to get involved with the public school question. In the autumn of 1960, with the threat to public schools looming over Georgia, a segregationist sect in the convention drafted a statement supporting segregation as a stabilizing societal force and beseeching members to resist integration. When this statement was brought before the convention, it was defeated by a large margin.[31] This defeat reflected a trend seen in many circles throughout the South—as the possibility of losing public education came closer to reality, segregationist stances softened and open schools were embraced.

Individual cities in Georgia also reflected division over the issue. When the Augusta Evangelical Ministers Association urged cooperation with the Court, it was ridiculed by other ministers who lambasted the moderate stance. The ministers dedicated to resistance unleashed such an outcry that the Evangelical Ministers Association's plea for acceptance of *Brown* appeared to be the work of a very small minority of Augusta clergy. In Columbus in 1959 a minister was fired and labeled an integrationist for calling for "creative contact between the races."[32]

In Atlanta a group of eighty-seven ministers signed a statement in 1957 calling for open schools, in spite of Georgia law. The following year, 387 ministers signed a similar declaration that stressed free speech, adherence to the Supreme Court decision, open communication between the races, and the preservation of public education. The document met with intense reaction from resisters in the state. A new group, the Evangelical Council, formed in response and released their own statement that claimed integration was "satanic, unconstitutional, and one of the main objectives of the Communist Party," and the Georgia States' Rights Council derided the ministers who signed the 1957 declaration, calling them "enemies of Christ."[33]

A survey of the church leaders who signed the Atlanta declaration revealed that many of them also urged their church members to support the open school movement. Many ministers, as the possibility of desegregation came closer to reality, used the pulpit to prepare their congregations for the immense changes that would come with integrated schools. The survey of church leaders shows that 63 percent of those responding to the poll spoke to their congregations about desegregation, while most of the remainder held positions in the church that would not offer opportunities to speak (administrators, teachers, and the like). The men who preached did so very carefully, making the subject of desegregation part of a broader theme. The three most popular topics incorporating the subject were: an explication of Christian doctrine and the reasons some people were afraid to adopt these principles when it might affect social surroundings; an attempt to persuade listeners to have faith in God's love and mankind's shared burden of sin; and the exhortation of the congregation to follow Jesus Christ's example of recognizing both sides of an issue and helping brethren regardless of color. By concentrating on these principles during the school crisis, ministers hoped to guide their flocks and appeal to a sense of Christian responsibility and the creed of helping their fellow man. Many church officials privately urged their members to get involved in the open school movement while the official position of the church was neutral. Church support was very important to the open school movement; for many people their minister was the only voice of authority speaking in behalf of public education.[34]

The Atlanta Press

There can be little question that the moderate views of the Atlanta press helped the open school cause. The city's two daily newspapers, the *Atlanta Journal* and the *Atlanta Constitution,* with the latter's powerful editor Ralph McGill, gave the public a lucid alternative to the impassioned racial fears of the massive resistance politicians and their newspapers.[35] Television, a relatively new source of information in the late 1950s, offered another moderate voice, accompanied by the power of the moving picture. These views in many ways reflected their audience, targeting editorials toward a perceived public moderation. This approach had a symbiotic effect. As most mass communications experts agree, what the media stress as significant is directly correlated with how much importance the public gives an issue. An editorial emphasizing the importance of maintaining a healthy, racially clearheaded focus both influenced and reflected the attitudes of the reader or the viewer. During the public school crisis, the editorial staffs of the city's newspapers and television stations underscored both the magnitude of the problem and the importance of maintaining Atlanta's reputation as a modern moderate city. The citizenry, in turn, treated the problem with proper respect and worked to alleviate the situation quickly.[36]

Ralph McGill, an outspoken opponent of segregation, repeatedly warned the South during the 1950s that it could expect a Supreme Court ruling that would find school segregation unconstitutional. McGill argued that school segregation made no financial sense and in 1953 claimed that it held no quarter in the modern world. Speaking in Daytona, Florida, early in 1954, McGill averred "universal education and universal segregation are uneasy bedfellows. . . . When public education was a matter of one room schools, two such schools in each neighborhood were no great drag on the public purse." But Ralph McGill knew his duty was "to seek in every way to ameliorate the problem [the conflict between southern devotion to segregation and federal law], knowing it cannot be solved."[37] As Georgia rushed into resistance that jeopardized the public schools, McGill spoke and wrote on the need to preserve education at every opportunity. Early in 1959, McGill, invited to speak in Augusta, stressed the importance of keeping the schools open.

> One thing must be plain to us. We must all defend public education as the necessary foundation for our form of government. To speak the phrase, "close the schools," means a previous process of closing the mind has been completed. The mind must be shut before doors to schools may even be thought of as closed. There are already minds and schools closed in the South. There will be more. . . . I mean no irreverence when I say that while public education may be crucified on a cross of willful decision to end it, it will rise again out of the wreckage. But a whole generation of children will suffer grievous and lasting discrimination. The South has put more sweat and tears into education than any other area. Yet, today the political power pattern plans to close them in four or five states. For all the South's struggle and progress, her needs and lacks in education have remained unmet. She is not alone, but to be willing to destroy the advances made is almost too fantastic to believed at a time when the need for more and better education has been violently thrust upon us.[38]

Other southern newsmen followed McGill's beacon of editorial prudence. James S. Pope felt it was an editor's responsibility to offer a moderate viewpoint to offset both the "demagogue" bent on reelection and the "intellectual and doctrinal integrationist" who did not understand the complexities of integration. The newspapers of Atlanta worked hard to create an atmosphere of moderation, and to a large degree they were successful. Perhaps the Atlanta press simply reflected the feelings of the city. As David Altheide and Robert Snow suggest, editors choose who and what they attack and rarely "single out" someone or something that would evoke a strong negative response from the majority of their audience. (The opposite, however, also holds true. Many other newspapers in Georgia and the rest of the South supported resistance.) Bill Shipp believed that the Atlanta media was responsible for creating an aversion to violence and a slow evolution in the opinion of citizens that massive resistance was "socially unacceptable." [39]

Television provided the open school advocates with a forceful new weapon in their struggle against massive resistance. Vivid, shocking images that people received in their own homes brought the violence of defiance closer than any other source of news. The school crisis at Little Rock and the intense fury of the desegregation of New Orleans' public schools exerted a powerful impact on public opinion. Network coverage of the integration of southern schools helped prepare Georgia for the inevitable. Television images offered a sense of objectivity that newspaper stories and editorials could not. Resisters could rail about the left-wing sympathies of a Ralph McGill and make listeners understand the editor's bias, but they could do little to assuage the revulsion people felt watching children being spit upon.

Locally, Atlanta television station WSB-TV was at the forefront of the open school crusade. Former WSB news director Ray Moore reflected on television's role in the school crisis and the civil rights movement:

> We were an escape valve. We were part of a bloodless revolution. Discrimination and suppression such as was practiced here could have easily erupted into much more violence than it did, had it not been particularly for the T.V. news media . . . it gave the Black a voice. It gave him a reason to cry out and it gave him a forum on which to state his grievances and to be heard by silent whites who sat in their living rooms and either got mad as hell or else, "You know, maybe there's something to that. Maybe we have been unfair. Maybe something ought to be done about that." [40]

In the station's second-ever news documentary, Moore portrayed the efforts of the open school advocates and the struggles Georgia would face if the state lost its public schools. The station's editorials advocated uninterrupted public education and chronicled the efforts of HOPE. In many ways television and newspaper support created the illusion that HOPE was a massive grass-roots organization far more powerful than it really was.[41]

The Atlanta media's coverage, especially that of Ralph McGill and WSB-TV, promoted HOPE's cause and enabled it to reach many more people than would have otherwise been possible. McGill had been looking for someone to enlist community support for open schools for many years and rallied behind the HOPE movement, offering it not only news coverage but open succor and patronage. Dale Clark and Ray Moore's documentary on HOPE in 1959 gave the organization unprecedented exposure. Their presentation on the school crisis looked at the efforts of both the private school promoters and the open school advocates. At the end of the half-hour program, Moore offered an editorial on the importance of preserving public education. In his statement, Moore reminded his audience that WSB was their "friend" and in that role it was the station's responsibility to tell its viewers of the dangers of private schools, their responsibility under the law, and the value of public education. As he remembered, it was not a "very bold and brave editorial, but in the tenor of those times, under those circumstances, we were the first business in Atlanta to stick our heads above the parapets and get shot at."[42]

HOPE

HOPE deserves praise and commendation for its members' tireless efforts to preserve the public schools and avoid a social catastrophe. This enigmatic group of homemakers worked extremely hard to ensure that their children received the best education Georgia could provide. Their outstanding successes include gathering support from throughout the state, garnering publicity for their efforts in persuading the assembly to overturn resistance legislation, working to attract the help of business leaders, and most importantly, recognizing the importance in separating the segregation question from the school issue.[43]

When *Calhoun v. Latimer* went to trial in 1958, Atlanta confronted the seriousness of the conflict between federal court rulings and Georgia law. The very real possibility of losing public schools loomed over the city. Many thought the Georgia General Assembly would suspend public education just to spite the city and the Court. The assembly would then contend that it was really the Supreme Court that had closed the schools. This spurred Muriel Lokey (the wife of state congressman Hamilton Lokey) to invite some of the League of Women Voters leadership to her home to form a new organization dedicated to finding some way out of the public school imbroglio. The early leadership included Mrs. Lokey, Fran Breeden, and Maxine Friedman. Helen Bullard, a campaign manager, speech writer, and assistant to William Harts-field, gave the association its name and offered her unique political savvy and experience. Another battle-scarred veteran of fighting the rural-dominated General Assembly, Frances Pauley, former president of the League of Women Voters, joined HOPE at the onset. With a firm eye on its objective, HOPE moved forward in its attempt to preserve public education—the first organization of its kind to appear in the South before a court-ordered desegregation.[44]

Among the major accomplishments of HOPE, the most important was the separation of the question of segregation from the struggle for open schools. The resistance leaders had forged schools and segregation into one issue. HOPE's daunting task was to convince the populace that segregation and schools were two distinct matters. This effort forced HOPE into some very difficult decisions. It concluded very early, for example, that the organization could not be interracial as that would only provide fodder for anyone accusing the alliance of promoting integration and not just open schools.[45] Some of HOPE's early leaders were associated with various progressive organizations and causes seen as "liberal," and the group fought that stigma. One woman provided HOPE with southern credentials that no one could dispute—Nan Pendergrast was from an old and prominent Atlanta family (it was rumored that her grandmother had been born during the Battle of Atlanta), and she served as a primary spokesperson for the enterprise.

Pendergrast represented most of HOPE's membership. Unlike its leaders, most of the group's members were apolitical and joined the organization only to preserve education. The leaders knew this, and from the very beginning fought only for the perpetuation of public schooling. While upsetting some more progressive members of the group who felt that HOPE should take a stronger stand, Pendergrast, Lokey, and others realized that the only way HOPE could be successful was to avoid a discussion of segregation and focus solely on schools. Consequently, HOPE did not contest segregationist strategies like pupil placement or local option that other southern states used to maintain separate schools because these plans did not threaten public education. To push for anything stronger could have alienated many of its potential supporters and give its enemies weapons to use against the organization.[46]

HOPE faced serious opposition, not only in trying to change the laws of Georgia but from other Atlanta organizations dedicated to preserving segregated schools using existing state laws. Two such groups, MASE (Metropolitan Association for Segregated Education) and GUTS (Georgians Unwilling To Surrender), provided spirited adversaries. GUTS leader, restauranteur, founder of Atlanta's White Citizens' Council, and occasional mayoral candidate, Lester Maddox, claimed that his organization was not anti-black, but only against forced integration. Maddox used his restaurant's newspaper advertisements to promote MASE and GUTS. When HOPE began its bumper sticker campaign with the slogan "We Want Public Education," MASE countered with its own stickers that read, "Me Too, But Segregated." By 1960, MASE claimed to have more than five thousand members and early that year asked the plaintiffs in the *Calhoun* case to withdraw their lawsuit in the interests of both races.[47]

Bumper stickers were a visible but small part of HOPE's much larger publicity campaign, a campaign with three goals in mind: first, to win support in the legislature by showing how important the school issue was to Georgia's citizens, thereby enabling moderate legislators to come out in favor of schools without the immense public backlash the politicians feared; second, to enlist the support of businessmen, showing them how important public schools were to the economy; and third, to recruit large public support for their fight. In their effort to receive the acceptance of Georgia's private citizens, HOPE sponsored speeches by politicians and community leaders sympathetic to its cause; held rallies; sent mass mailings, news letters, and press releases; and encouraged local chapters in Georgia communities. The members petitioned the General Assembly, packed the gallery when the legislature was in session, and held private audiences with many of the state's influential politicians. To win the support of the business community, the group experimented with economic threats, direct appeals, and pamphlets showing what massive resistance cost the cities of New Orleans and Little Rock.

Public statewide support of HOPE's efforts was critical to the organization, for if it was seen as only an Atlanta enterprise, the chances for its success dimmed. The group sponsored speakers all over the state and attempted to form chapters in every city. HOPE leaders would go into a small town and begin to telephone women they thought would be interested in the school effort. Many times the recipients of these phone calls thought they were the only ones concerned; HOPE brought them together. At one such effort in Rome, the local chapter of the Citizens' Council showed up in force. The council had engaged in an economic pressure campaign against HOPE members, harassing them and occasionally attempting to have them fired from their jobs. When the council members arrived at HOPE's meeting site, a church on the edge of town, the local HOPE organizer invited them in and welcomed their participation. There the council members saw not fiery integrationists but concerned parents and teachers. The housewives and mothers who made up most of HOPE's membership were one of the group's biggest assets. No one could claim these women were wild-eyed "race mixers"; they were simply concerned with the future of Georgia's schools.[48]

One of the most important events in HOPE's attempts to gather public support was a rally held in March 1959 in Atlanta's Tower Theater. The "Fill the Tower with HOPE" rally was a huge success, drawing more than fifteen hundred people. Mrs. Gordon Wilson, who had headed the Little Rock open school movement, gave the keynote speech. Ralph McGill, William Hartsfield, Sylvan Meyer (a moderate newspaper editor from Gainesville), and the evening's hostess Fran Breeden joined her on the program. The elderly Mrs. Wilson described the distress that the lack of public schools created for her city. The event, widely covered by the state and national press, gave HOPE great recognition. By the time of the Sibley Commission hearings, its mailing list exceeded thirty thousand.[49]

HOPE still faced serious opposition both from resistance politicians and local segregationist groups. The week following the Tower Theater rally, Roy Harris and another segregationist, Peter Zack Geer, rented the theater and hosted their own rally in support of resistance. The two men drove the crowd into a frenzy and at one point gave the audience Ralph McGill's and Hamilton Lokey's home telephone numbers. Harris instructed the gathering to call the men at three o'clock in the morning and tell them exactly how they felt about integration. Lokey, upon receiving his first wake-up call, promptly hung up the phone and rang Harris in his hotel room. Lokey told Harris that each time he received an early morning phone call, he would immediately call Harris to tell him about it. MASE also sent out flyers that reprinted news clippings about violence in northern integrated schools and treatises on the subject of miscegenation. Early in 1959, HOPE sent GUTS leader Lester Maddox a letter asking for a contribution; Maddox sent the group a Confederate ten-dollar bill and a note that read, "Here is my contribution—I didn't think you would have the gall."[50]

HOPE's finest hour came in the early days of 1960. After Judge Frank A. Hooper's *Calhoun* ruling, everyone waited to see what action the Georgia General Assembly would take. HOPE sprang into action. The leaders constructed a plan that would bombard the legislators with evidence of the public's support of open schools. The women put HOPE literature on every legislator's desk two and three times a week during the assembly's session. If that were not enough, they packed the gallery of both the House and Senate every day the assembly met. The women wore HOPE arm bands, white gloves, and pillbox hats. They were assigned partners and a specific day of the week to attend the sessions. Instructed not to speak to the press, the women turned over any questions to Frances Pauley, Fran Breeden, Judy Neiman, or Betty Harris, one of whom was always in attendance. One day during the assembly session, HOPE dropped a "four story high" open schools petition with ten thousand signatures from the gallery to the floor below. Just before the end of the session, representatives from HOPE and other organizations concerned about the public schools paid visits to senators Herman Talmadge and Richard B. Russell at their homes. They asked the solons to back open schools and to do what they could to limit the "inflammatory speeches" made by Georgia's politicians. The climax of the campaign came when Talmadge and Russell made their annual appearance before the assembly. They met not the usual cheers and applause from the upper gallery, but a cold silence. The two men looked up and saw the women of HOPE sitting calmly with their hands in their laps and their hats on their heads. When the men stepped to the podium and began to address the crowd, the group's members held aloft eight-inch by ten-inch signs that in block letters read, "WE WANT PUBLIC SCHOOLS."[51]

Although HOPE's actions during the 1960 session of the General Assembly garnered the group a great deal of publicity, HOPE's most successful public campaign involved the luring of business into the fold of open school advocacy. After the success of the Montgomery bus boycott in 1956, the South became a hotbed of boycotts and other economic sanctions. The HOPE leadership, aware of the success of these endeavors, launched its own program of economic pressure. In 1960 the group printed up small stickers that read, "If the schools shut down, this account may also close"; these reminders were to be stuck to members' checks when they were shopping or paying bills. A much more effective technique was simply to explain to businessmen the costs of continued resistance.[52]

The campaign to recruit business support for HOPE's cause began in earnest early in 1959. In January of that year, Hamilton Lokey used his influence over the Atlanta Bar Association and sent out a circular to its members asking his fellow counselors to join him and call for changes in Georgia's laws to allow for uninterrupted public education. The following month HOPE sent out a questionnaire to every Atlanta business employing more that twenty-five people, asking the respondents their opinion on the school crisis. At one point Nan Pendergrast went to Harrison Jones, the president of the Coca-Cola Company, and asked him for his company's support. Jones responded by telling Pendergrast that "integration was coming; it had to come. But it wasn't coming quite yet, and those of them who got out in front were going to have rotten tomatoes and eggs thrown at them." Jones told her that business would help but would "follow at a respectful distance."[53]

There is ample evidence to believe that HOPE was very successful in gathering business support for its cause, at least the support of some big businesses, who, while encouraging the group's efforts, preferred to be discreet. Muriel Lokey believed that HOPE was being observed and helped all along the way by corporate Atlanta.

> I would say, that someone of influence high up in the business community of Atlanta—. See, I think the business community knew what was going to happen. They were, in my opinion, extremely slow in coming out because it wasn't safe, but they were monitoring us. And we were being monitored to make sure we weren't communists, or something like that. . . . But, anyway, they really wanted a pipeline, I think, into what we were doing because I have learned later from reading little things. I have forgotten where I read this [that Robert Woodruff was very interested in open schools and] . . . worked behind the scenes. Whoever they are, I think someone was monitoring us and sent some employees through this big company with a regional office here simply to work with us and to report back what was said.[54]

The business community sent money surreptitiously. Volunteers appeared whom no one had seen before, worked by themselves, and did not attempt to get close to anyone else in the group. Three volunteers that helped with fund-

raising and security caught the eye of Frances Pauley. When HOPE held its
rally at the Tower Theater, one of these volunteers "arranged" for two hundred plainclothes security officers to work at the event. Later, the same volunteer helped Pauley confiscate an audiotape made by the Georgia Education
Commission with plans to doctor the tape and misrepresent what was being
said at HOPE meetings. Asked years later by the HOPE leader why the three
volunteers were so interested in assisting the organization, the young man replied, "our company [International Business Machines] told us to, and told
us they would back us and HOPE financially, and that we had to keep an accurate record of everything that happened." [55]

The Economics of Education

Georgia's business community helped HOPE and promoted open schools
not because of any enlightened sense of racial justice, but for reasons of
sound, economic pragmatism. Existing business and industry benefitted and
prospered through the first half of the twentieth century due to the politics
of rurality: segregation, the county unit system, disfranchisement, and demagoguery, which provided a healthy political atmosphere for growth because
business was able to control government, limit corporate taxation, and maintain a powerless, inexpensive labor force. But the state's corporate establishment outgrew the brand of simple political machinations the Black Belt
politicos provided. In five years, from 1954 until 1959, an average of 150 new
plants a year valued at more than $414 million opened in Georgia. During
those same years, 352 existing plants expanded their operations at an average
value of almost one million dollars per expansion. By 1960, virtually every
Fortune 500 company had an Atlanta office. [56]

This astonishing growth of industry (and the craving for even more expansion) coupled with an equally impressive rise in urban population in the
postwar years, something Georgia financiers had been desperately seeking
since Reconstruction, forced them to review and change many long-held political, economic, and social beliefs. In an attempt to lure more industry into
the state, Georgia Power (the state's largest electric company), along with the
Georgia Municipal Association and Georgia Tech's Engineering Experiment
Station, created a "Certified City Program" to ensure that cities seeking industrial development provided certain criteria that businesses sought in a

plant location. The amenities that a "Certified City" included were recreational facilities, good schools, adequate fire protection, and overall physical appearance. Business leaders deemed this type of assurance necessary because of intense competition from other southern states, all of which offered the basic attractions of little or no taxes, an aversion to organized labor, and low wages. Atlanta business leaders also worried that a perceived lack of political power under the county unit system might scare away investment. Recently arrived businessmen believed the system could harm industry by placing their company and employees under the political thumb of a rurally dominated General Assembly. Another factor in the changing attitudes of business leaders was the growing purchasing power of African Americans. Robert Woodruff's longtime advisor, Ralph Hayes, reminded him that the number of black consumers in the United States was equal to the entire Canadian population, and that the stagnation of Georgia's political and social structure limited the potential of this little explored consumer market.[57]

The largest concern for business leaders, however, came from the negative publicity generated by massive resistance. The northern press demonstrated significant concern for black civil rights causes and portrayed white southerners as "racist, savage, ignorant, and violent." As resistance continued, northern interest in civil rights causes intensified. In the year following the *Brown* decision, people in the North were just not that interested; only 6 percent felt that segregation was a number-one concern, compared with 33 percent in the South. This number, of course, went up every time a southern demagogue did something to bring attention to the plight of black southerners.[58]

The policies of massive resistance not only aroused northern ire, but created concern for the stability of southern schools. The precarious position of public education forced any business or industry considering opening an office or plant in the South to weigh its options carefully before choosing a location. In an article published in the 8 July 1960 edition of *Harvard Business Review,* Helen Hill Miller warned southern business recruiters that the men who made up the growing professional managerial class were unlikely to want to look for employment in an area with an unsettled public school question. She professed that business leaders could not ignore this problem nor could they afford to disregard the purchasing power that a large plant might bring an area. In 1958, Atlanta's Ivan Allen called for a change in business strategy. "It's an axiom of business and capital investment that it doesn't fear

good business or bad business but the things that business and the investment of capital dislikes is uncertainty, chaos and confusion. The present situation is just that. . . . It's time for some constructive leadership and not a
negative policy." Facing a potential school crisis in Atlanta, the president of
Citizen's and Southern bank, Mills B. Lane, predicted that the state would lose
one new or existing plant every day the schools were closed. Dr. Louis Rader,
manager of a General Electric plant in Waynesboro, explained the position of
many business leaders: "A strong system of public education is very important among those factors that attract new industry into a state and keep
industry already here from moving away." Support for such an argument
was readily available. Businessmen needed only to look toward the massive
failure in industrial recruitment that followed the debacle in Little Rock,
Arkansas.[59]

Little Rock, until the fall of 1957, had experienced steady growth and industrial expansion. From 1950 until the crisis at Central High School, the city
averaged five new plant openings a year valued at $8,335,000 and creating
twenty-five hundred new jobs. During the same period forty-five existing
plants expanded and those expansions were worth $9,558,000. In 1958 and
1959 no new plants opened in Little Rock and only two plants expanded,
worth a mere $593,000. The head of the Little Rock Industrial Development
Corporation, Everett Tucker, spoke throughout the South, warning anyone
who would listen about the pitfalls of resistance. He told audiences that it was
"sort of an insidious thing. The principal damage comes about when you
don't even know that it's happening to you. You just don't hear from XYZ
Company that it's on the prowl for a new plant location." He would end his
speech with "an allusion, it reminds me of having to see a bad movie the second time. If we can in any way prevent your buying tickets to this second
showing, we feel our meager efforts have been amply repaid . . . keep control
of your schools with the local school boards where it belongs; try to keep the
politicians from diverting the issue to their own selfish ends; and, finally keep
your public schools open. You will never regret it. I realize that all of these
things are easier said than done. We didn't do any of them in Little Rock."[60]

In her article, Ms. Miller advised business leaders that they "may find it de-
sirable to participate in state and local efforts to ensure the availability of continuous, modern public school systems." Following this advice meant that
southern businessmen would have to sacrifice absolute segregation for eco-

nomic growth, a sacrifice many were willing to make. It was vital to the business interests of Atlanta that they gain a firm grasp on the school situation—they could ill afford to leave it in the hands of rural legislators who campaigned against the city as often as they campaigned for segregation. Indeed, closing the Atlanta schools could reap big political rewards for rural office seekers.[61]

Industrialists throughout the South faced many of these same concerns and joined their brethren in Georgia in opposing resistance. Many commentators concluded that these men were motivated by a spirit of moderation. This moderation, however, was driven by practical cost accounting. Business leaders, rarely in the forefront of any social issue, moved slowly to protect the public schools and usually only when confronted with an immediate crisis. Their interests, primarily driven by a desire to increase industrial development, often conflicted with their community's desire to maintain the status quo. Southern businessmen sympathized with segregationists and were often willing to use all means short of closing schools to preserve Jim Crow.[62]

The southern business elite slowly grasped the link between an atmosphere of perceived racial moderation and economic prosperity. In North Carolina, businessmen controlled state politics and made an early conscious effort to refrain from outward defiance to the *Brown* decision; the state's economic development continued unabated. Tennessee business leaders did likewise and announced that the Volunteer State would not resist the Supreme Court ruling; they experienced similar positive economic results. Industrialists in other states, however, were not as successful in restraining politicians bent on defiance. In 1956, the head of the Baton Rouge Chamber of Commerce urged state officials not to defy the Court, warning them of the economic dangers of resistance. Political leaders ignored his pleas. In New Orleans the lack of concerned business leadership helped the hard-core segregationists gain control of that city's school crisis with disastrous results. After the city's schools were desegregated, most white parents took their children out of public schools. Angry mobs of whites gathered near the desegregated schools, taunting and spitting upon the small children on their way to class (New Orleans chose to begin integration with elementary school students). Television images from New Orleans were broadcast nationwide, and the city's reputation plummeted. Virginia experienced a severe economic downturn due to that state's massive resistance policies until business leaders finally convinced the governor of that state to abandon defiance. Business involvement at the moment of a school crisis in cities like Dallas or Charlotte helped desegregation efforts go smoothly. In the cities like Little Rock or New Orleans, where business was paralyzed by fear, or apathy, or both, it usually went poorly, and business suffered—along with countless children, black and white.[63]

In Georgia, as *Calhoun v. Latimer* approached implementation, state business leaders looked to the rest of the South and quickly saw the advantages of gaining firm control over the school situation. They joined forces with the increasingly vocal open school advocates to ensure the continuation of public education. There were, however, many obstacles to overcome: the curtain of silence that surrounded segregation in rural Georgia (most calls for open schools emanated from the urban areas), the severe weakening of the Democratic Party's progressive faction that limited possible political action, and the resister's masterful weaving of segregation and schools into one issue. The corporate executives of Atlanta's largest companies, Coca-Cola, Trust Company Bank, Ivan Allen Company, and the law firm of King and Spalding put subtle pressure on their new governor, Ernest Vandiver, to end massive resistance and accept token desegregation. Vandiver responded by forming the Sibley Commission, whose public hearings allowed John Sibley, a member of the Atlanta business elite, to interpret and explain the school crisis. The commission hearings also provided open school advocates and resisters with a sanctioned forum in which to air their views.

CHAPTER 3

The Whole Ballgame Changed

In the 1958 gubernatorial election, Georgia first turned from rabid segregationist rhetoric and elected a man considered by many to be the racial moderate in the race. By any standards other than the political yardstick used to
measure southern politicians in the 1950s, Ernest Vandiver's campaign would
be considered a savage and race-baiting defense of segregation. But in 1958,
racial politics had moved so far to the right that Vandiver was perceived as the
"moderate" candidate, an epithet he did not desire nor deserve. His administration was the first to confront the reality of school desegregation and the
inherent conflict between federal law and massive resistance. Ernest Vandiver
inherited the responsibility of preserving public education and segregation,
and as was usually the case, political and business considerations were deeply
involved. Frank Hooper, the judge in *Calhoun v. Latimer,* understood Vandiver's position and gave the governor time and opportunity to rewrite resistance legislation. Toward that end Vandiver created a public commission to
study the problem, canvass the state, survey the opinion of the people, and
offer alternatives to integration or the closing of public schools. The Sibley
Commission performed this task admirably and in the process made the
prospect of abandoning massive resistance possible and palatable, and in the
end even preferable.

No, Not One

The 1958 gubernatorial election presented another alternative to the severe weakening of the Democratic Party's factionalism. In 1954, a host of candidates tried to exploit the demise of the progressives; in 1958, one man, Ernest Vandiver, claimed sole possession of the Talmadge faction. His loyalty to the "wool hat boys" could not be questioned; his father had been a county organizer for Eugene Talmadge, and in 1936 Ernest Vandiver gave his first political speech in support of Talmadge's senatorial campaign. Vandiver assisted Talmadge again in 1946, and in return the governor-elect named him an executive aide, a position Herman honored during his short 1947 term as governor. Vandiver and Herman Talmadge were close friends; Herman served as one of Vandiver's groomsmen and Vandiver managed Herman's 1948 gubernatorial campaign. After that election, Talmadge appointed him director of the state's selective service and adjutant general, positions he held until elected lieutenant governor in 1954. During his four years in that office, Vandiver offered a passionate, yet practical voice for segregation. He opposed the bombastic posturing and meaningless symbolism of massive resistance and countered that the South could achieve its goals without violence, using imaginative legislation to stay ahead of court decisions. In April 1957, speaking to a group of Georgia county commissioners, he suggested that the state attempt to foster "an atmosphere of mutual respect and a real determination among all of our people to solve our problems without federal dictation or outside interference." He assured them that integration would never occur if citizens acted with "absolute firmness and unyielding determination." Vandiver, throughout his career, showed a contempt for pure race-baiting politics. He appealed to people's sensibilities and rationalities on very emotional subjects and very rarely lowered his political style. He is representative of the politicians who followed him into office who wanted to elevate Georgia politics from the "yahooism" that had been the political norm. He understood that there were no real resistance options available to the South that would completely prevent desegregation and that it was better to pull back from direct defiance and preserve the maximum amount of segregation.[1]

The 1958 governor's race once again exploited the chaotic nature of ineffective one-party politics. Herman Talmadge, the only stabilizing force in the faction that now bore his name, was elected to the United States Senate in

1956—effectually removing him from the daily affairs of state politics. Herman avoided becoming involved in the election, and the two most powerful members of his faction fought for the job. Marvin Griffin, unable to succeed himself, searched for a candidate to oppose Ernest Vandiver, his lieutenant governor (and political arch rival). Vandiver had campaigned against Griffin during his years as lieutenant governor, repeatedly questioning Griffin's political methods and integrity. The final showdown was during the 1958 General Assembly session when Griffin proposed a one hundred million dollar rural road authority, the purpose of which was to raise the money necessary to provide paved roads for Georgia's farmers. Griffin's underlying motive was to use the money to give his candidate for governor, Roger Lawson, a huge supply of campaign road promises that could be used to influence individual county commissioners' control over their county's unit votes. Vandiver and other members of the General Assembly recognized this motive and fought against the measure, eventually defeating it and Lawson's short-lived gubernatorial campaign. After the rural roads fight, Vandiver secured the backing of several of the state's influential politicians, including Lawson. Griffin, however, won the final legislative skirmish between the two men when he created the Stone Mountain Memorial Commission, over Vandiver's objection. The commission, sanctioned to purchase Stone Mountain (a huge granite monolith about thirty miles east of Atlanta) and finish a carving of southern Civil War heroes on the north face, was having trouble in the General Assembly, in large part due to Vandiver's opposition. Griffin warned Vandiver that the Stone Mountain issue could be used against him in the governor's race and he should "give a little thought down there, that I'd hate like hell to run this summer against Jeff Davis, Robert E. Lee and Stonewall Jackson. The weather's too hot." [2]

Perhaps many other potential gubernatorial candidates believed that the political weather was too hot as well. Surely the politically wise understood that Georgia's next governor would face a situation that would force him to choose between abandoning either segregation or education. After 1955, federal court decisions continued to broaden and strengthen the *Brown* decision, and after federal intervention in Little Rock, the courts went on the offensive, attacking the ramparts of resistance legislation. When the *Calhoun* case went to trial early in the 1958 election year, the inevitability of confrontation became increasingly obvious.

Vandiver's lone opponent in the Democratic Primary, Bill Bodenhamer of Ty Ty, Georgia, a Baptist preacher and executive secretary of the States' Rights Council of Georgia, campaigned exclusively on the segregation issue. He stumped the state in bright red armbands, using his pulpit-honed speaking skills to accuse Vandiver of being weak on segregation, hosting an alleged integrated campaign barbecue, and receiving an endorsement from the NAACP. Bodenhamer was well financed by revenue commissioner (and Griffin crony) T. V. Williams, who used his position to secure campaign funds from liquor interests. Every week Bodenhamer ran campaign speeches on one hundred different radio stations. He chastised Vandiver for his relationship with Bob Jordan, whose brother ran an interracial farm, Koinoina, near Americus, accusing Vandiver of promoting integration by association. Ralph McGill described Bodenhamer's tactics as a "campaign of political abuse that shocked all but the most extreme."[3]

The main thrust of the Vandiver campaign was a call for clean, honest government. He railed about the corruption of the Griffin administration and pledged to revitalize state government, a common theme among the political generation that came of age after World War II. Vandiver also pledged his fealty to segregation and the county unit system. But Bodenhamer's message was a strong one, and without sophisticated polling techniques, Vandiver had no real clue as to how the race might turn out. After a speech before the Clairmont Civitan Club in DeKalb County, in which Vandiver stated that his position was the responsible stand on segregation and "not the extremist position" of either side, his campaign was forced to make a tougher stand in favor of segregation. The next day the *Atlanta Constitution* ran a headline claiming Vandiver took the "middle of the road" on segregation. Vandiver refuted the headline saying it was misleading and "there could be no 'middle road' on this issue."[4]

That night Vandiver met with some of his advisors, including Peter Zack Geer, William O. "B" Brooks, Bob Russell, and Jim Gillis, to prepare a new campaign speech.[5] Brooks and Geer convinced Vandiver that he needed to adopt a strong segregationist stance to counter both Bodenhamer's accusations and the newspaper's headline. Vandiver's new speech embraced defiance and segregationist bombast and averred that the federal government lacked the necessary force to integrate Georgia's schools. But the men felt they needed a simple phrase to capture the essence of Vandiver's stance that everyone could remember and repeat. That night they coined Vandiver's new motto, "No, not one."[6]

His new stump speech now closed with,

> We will not bow our heads in submission to naked force.
> We have no thought of surrender.
> We will not knuckle under.
> We will not capitulate.
> I make this solemn pledge. . . .
> When I am your governor, neither my three children, nor any child of yours,
> will ever attend a racially mixed school in the state of Georgia.
> No, not one.[7]

Vandiver's successful "No, not one" campaign contributed to a landslide victory. He captured more than 90 percent of both the county unit and popular votes. After November's general election, Herman Talmadge summoned the governor-elect to his home in Lovejoy. When Vandiver walked into his old friend's living room, Talmadge introduced him to Walter Cochrane and several other prominent members of Georgia's black community. The men spent the afternoon discussing the possibility of desegregating the schools under a Vandiver administration.[8]

Shortly after this meeting, Vandiver set to work on the best way to preserve the schools with the maximum amount of segregation. He assigned a team of attorneys including Griffin Bell, Charles Bloch of Macon, and Holcombe Perry from Albany, to investigate the conflicts between Georgia's massive resistance legislation and recent federal court rulings. They suggested that the state adapt its private school plan and allow the governor to close a single school or district rather than a city- or county-wide school system. In the week before Vandiver took office, Judge Boyd Sloan ruled in *Hunt v. Arnold* that Georgia State College (a business school in downtown Atlanta) could not deny admission to four African American women based solely on their race. Sloan did not, however, order their immediate admission. On his inauguration day, Vandiver ordered Georgia State to halt registration indefinitely and then turned to the General Assembly to pass a law that forbade college admission to anyone over the age of twenty-one (all four plaintiffs exceeded the new age limit). Vandiver then presented an "arsenal of legislation" to the 1959 General Assembly to streamline the private school plan. The solons allowed for state income tax credits to pay private school tuition, enabled the governor to close a single school, including a university, assured pay to teachers in the event of a school's closing, and called for correspondence courses to replace class work during a possible interim between a public school's closing and the opening of a private school. They also passed a provision forbidding the creation or use of an ad valorem tax to fund integrated education, in the event Atlanta tried that measure to save its schools. The legislation passed during Vandiver's first days in office, described by the Speaker of the House as "the best first week since I've been here," typified the course of massive resistance during Vandiver's administration. He publicly maintained a recalcitrant position toward the *Brown* decision while he privately sought a method to forestall or prevent direct defiance.[9] Of major concern to resistance leaders including Vandiver was the constitutionality of the heart of Georgia's resistance program—the private school plan. The program had never been tested in court. In 1956 Charles Bloch prepared to bring the plan before the state Supreme Court in order to gain a ruling on its legality. He dropped his case, however, when he feared it might be moved to a federal court. Federal intervention was a common practice, especially in the Fifth Circuit Court of Appeals, which removed many civil rights cases out of the hands of local and state courts.[10]

The Phantom of State Control

Although many consider the stand of Governor Orval Faubus at Central High School the apex of modern southern defiance, the same can be said about the legality of massive resistance legislation. Arkansas had no resistance legislation in place in 1957, because the state had no plans to resist the *Brown* ruling. When the governor defied the federal government, he quickly turned to the General Assembly to enact laws to circumvent the desegregation of the Little Rock schools, based on the defiance measures of other states (including Georgia). This action forced the federal courts to immediately rule on resistance legislation and begat three very important court rulings that destroyed the underpinnings of legal insurrection and had a focused impact on Georgia's resistance program. In September of 1958, the Supreme Court in *Cooper v. Aaron* denied a motion by the Little Rock School Board to delay integration because of the possibility of violence or disruption in the schools. Furthermore, the court gave power to the lower federal courts, in their battle against massive resistance, by ruling that no state could attempt to nullify the court's decision in *Brown v. Board of Education* directly or indirectly by "evasive schemes for segregation whether attempted ingeniously or ingenuously." The same day the Eighth Circuit Court of Appeals ruled, in *Aaron v. Cooper*, that the state could not operate private schools for the sole purpose of maintaining segregation. Another outcome of the Little Rock case made a governor subject to a federal court injunction and liable to criminal charges if he attempted to oppose the rulings of a federal court.[11]

The next year, the scene turned to Virginia. When Governor Lindsay Almond closed some Norfolk schools in an effort to avoid integration, parents of the affected children sued the governor to reinstate funding and reopen the schools. The Fourth Circuit Court of Appeals ruled in *James v. Almond* that Virginia could not close a single school or district solely to prevent integration. The court claimed that by closing only desegregated schools, Virginia had created a "different class" of citizens denied equal protection and access to state services as required under the Fourteenth Amendment. It ordered the state to reinstate funding to the affected schools or suspend *all* public education. In response, Almond appointed a special study committee to examine the conflicts between Virginia's massive resistance policies and the federal court decisions. The Perrow Commission recommended changing state law to incorporate local option, pupil placement, and a freedom of choice measure.[12] Local option turned control over school districts or systems to local school boards and allowed each community to decide whether to close its public schools when confronted with desegregation. Pupil placement established permanent school districts, based on the existing segregated school systems, along with an elaborate set of circumstances under which a student could transfer schools. Although the plan differed from state to state, the more popular criteria for deciding whether to permit a student transfer included: availability of classroom space or transportation (white school buses did not go through black neighborhoods), the psychological state or intelligence level of the student requesting a transfer, and the potential for economic or physical reprisals against the student or school. Because these criteria were not based on a student's race, the Supreme Court, in *Shuttlesworth v. Birmingham*, upheld the legality of this plan in 1958. Freedom of choice permitted children whose schools had been integrated to transfer to another segregated school or receive tuition grants from the state to pay for private segregated education. In April, Almond called the General Assembly into a special emergency session to overturn mandatory school closing laws and adopt the recommendations of the Perrow Commission. Virginia's retreat from resistance created a confusing scene in the statehouse. The General Assembly narrowly passed the new measures and "a number of legislators wept in the corridors of the Capitol because of the prospect of integration." [13]

Virginia's new method of preserving segregation closely resembled that of North Carolina. The business leaders and politicians of the Tarheel State adopted a pragmatic approach to preserving segregation early after the *Brown* decision. In 1955, the Pearsall Committee, a study group composed of white and black citizens, whose stated goal was to find a way to preserve the public school system, submitted its plan to the legislature. The group recommended that the state transfer authority over schools to local school boards and that it avoid any type of private school plan. The assembly accepted the recommendations and created pupil placement measures to limit school transfers. The next year the General Assembly buttressed the plan with freedom of choice laws and tuition grants. The Pearsall recommendations allowed the state to strictly limit the potential impact of desegregation. In contrast to much of the South, which engaged in furious resistance and wrathful defiance to the federal government, North Carolina *appeared* to be an oasis of moderation.[14]

In Georgia, people deliberated the state's next course of action following judge Hooper's decision in *Calhoun v. Latimer*. Representative Iris Blitch of Homerville told reporters that Atlanta should "get busy" and organize private education. Mayor Hartsfield asked the General Assembly to adopt a local option plan, so that Atlanta could vote whether or not to close its schools. He told the legislature "it would be a grave mistake" to hold the city "hostage" and warned that if absolute resistance continued, it would lead to the "eventual closing of every public school in Georgia, including [Georgia] Tech and the University of Georgia." Publicly, Vandiver stated he would obey *state* laws, but he hoped the "federal courts would not force the closing of a single school." [15]

In November 1959, the Atlanta School Board presented Hooper with its plan to desegregate the Atlanta schools. Its main thrust was a strict pupil placement plan with eighteen separate criteria to be considered in any school transfer request including: availability of transportation, student potential, classroom space, scholastic aptitude, curriculum, and the possible impact on the community in the form of violence, unrest, or economic retaliation. In addition to the transfer requirements, applications to change schools were only made available beginning May first and had to be completed and turned in by May fifteenth. Only twelfth graders could apply the first year, eleventh and twelfth graders the following year, continuing with an additional grade per year for twelve years. The strategy was to limit the amount of integration while still obeying the letter of Hooper's decision. Starting with the later grades, the school board reasoned, would reduce the number of student transfer requests (they believed that most seniors would not want to changes schools for their last year of high school) and initially limit the impact of desegregation to children whose racial attitudes were already established. Hooper approved the plan but put off its implementation until the General Assembly met in January 1960. He wanted to give the legislature an opportunity to change its mandatory school closing laws.[16]

Shortly after the *Calhoun* decision, Vandiver held a private meeting with other state political leaders and discussed the state's options in the wake of the ruling. Those in attendance included Roy Harris, Charles Bloch, Griffin Bell, Holcombe Perry, Georgia Assembly Speaker George L. Smith, representatives Frank Twitty and Carl Sanders, and constitutional attorney Freeman Leverett. This ad hoc committee of lawyers dedicated itself to the study of the school question. The men discussed the Alabama pupil placement law and the North Carolina local option plan. After the meeting, Vandiver advisor "B" Brooks requested advice from Richmond, Virginia, attorney William H. Burson on the best method of changing state law to save the maximum extent of both public education and segregation. Burson replied that Georgia should adopt a pupil placement plan with strict criteria for any school transfer and offer tax credits to parents who did not wish to send their child to an integrated school. He claimed that this would result in 99.9 percent segregation and then warned, "It would take courage and statesmanship of the highest order to advocate such a course, but I am firmly convinced that history will reserve its kindest treatment for the man who preserves public education with maximum local control rather than the man who destroys public education in the name of the phantom of state control. . . . There is nothing to be gained by marching ourselves into a corner nose first except to get our asses kicked."[17]

Vandiver's Quandary

As 1960 approached, Ernest Vandiver found himself in a precarious position. The decision in *Calhoun v. Latimer* had been reached, Atlanta's desegregation plan was approved, and Judge Hooper was offering the state an eleventh hour chance to change its laws before events reached crisis proportions. Vandiver felt he had two basic options, each holding an elemental appeal. He could disobey the court, deny Atlanta its school funds, and effectively close its school system. This move would make him wildly popular in the Black Belt region of the state and even something of a regional hero.[18] The positive aspects of this response would, however, be short-lived, not only because of the threat of federal charges against the governor but also because the parents of the affected children would surely force the issue back into court (the women of HOPE had all but promised this) and Judge Hooper, using *James v. Almond* as a precedent, would have no choice but to order Vandiver to reinstate the school funds or close every school in the state. This outcome would of course severely damage the state's educational system and destroy Vandiver politically. His other option was to make a case for the preservation of education and allow Atlanta to desegregate its schools. This action would bring Vandiver to national stature and make him a hero in Atlanta but a pariah in the rest of Georgia. This option also threatened him with criminal charges from the state, because Georgia law required the governor to suspend funding to any "mixed" school.

Vandiver's ambition further limited his options. The governor sought national stature and was a political ally of John F. Kennedy. The presidential election of 1960 offered Vandiver an opportunity to deliver Georgia's electoral votes to the Massachusetts senator and perhaps win a place in a Kennedy administration. Working within the confines of segregationist and resistance politics, however, forced Vandiver to be very careful not to disrupt his fragile hold as leader of the Democratic Party. Roy Harris still yielded an inordinate amount of power for a man outside elected office and could challenge Vandiver if given a clear issue. The governor's most pressing task was to find a way to convince the General Assembly to change mandatory school closing laws and allow Atlanta to desegregate without an embarrassing incident. Most of the state legislators, however, like Vandiver, had been elected on strong segregationist platforms and were unwilling to risk their political futures on what could turn out to be a very unpopular program. Griffin Bell described Vandiver's predicament after winning with the slogan "no, not one." "Well by the time he got elected the Supreme Court had decided the second Little Rock case . . . in which they said violence was no excuse. The whole ballgame changed." [19]

In the midst of Vandiver's difficulty came a threat to the Talmadge faction's control of the Democratic Party. Ellis Arnall came out of retirement and announced that the public schools must remain open and if Vandiver closed them he would use the issue to run for governor in 1962. Roy Harris responded by asking James Peters, the head of the Georgia Board of Education, to make a firmer stand for continued resistance. He claimed that segregation was a "political issue and not [a] legal issue." He wanted Peters to help mobilize the state's educational system for an all-out assault on desegregation. Peters, in turn, wrote to Harris and asked him to back away from massive resistance, warning him that "given twelve months to register 600,000 Negros and to convince the mothers and fathers the only way to re-open [the schools] is with him [Arnall] as governor, Ellis would be difficult indeed to defeat and Herman could very easily go down with him. Thus we would lose control over the government and entrench Ellis Arnall and the integrationists in the control of the government for decades to come." Peters believed that the public was turning away from resistance and that the next election would reflect this trend. He told Harris that unless something were done to avoid closing schools, "we are headed towards defeat and the loss of our power and influence in the government of this state." [20] The exchange between Harris and Peters accurately reflects the political nature of massive resistance in Georgia. As the confrontation between state and federal law loomed ever larger, Vandiver and other political leaders actively sought a means to limit the potential impact of a school crisis on the state's political structure.

The governor also had the state's economic future to consider. Like his predecessors, Talmadge and Griffin, he strove to improve Georgia's economic conditions. To this end, he actively recruited new business and industry and took pride in his administration's efforts to provide a favorable business environment. Vandiver spoke in person to corporate leaders considering opening southern offices or plants. He continued Georgia's tradition of providing conservative, frugal state government. He revamped the state's administration and streamlined governmental agencies, making Georgia even more inviting to commercial interests. In his first year as governor, 177 new plants opened in the state with an estimated worth of almost $40 million and 115 existing plants expanded their facilities at a value of $79.6 million dollars. Vandiver clearly understood that continued business development depended upon a prompt, amicable, and forthright resolution to the school dilemma.[21]

In any attempt to change Georgia's resistance, Vandiver faced another serious threat—the almost impenetrable wall of silence that surrounded segregation. The majority of white Georgians preferred to close the public schools rather than submit to even token integration. The political and philosophical ruminations of massive resistance penetrated deeply into the hearts and minds of white Georgia. Even in the cities, segregation was preferred to any unknown form of integration. A poll taken in Augusta, during Vandiver's election year, revealed that more than half the citizens favored segregation even at the expense of public schooling. In Atlanta, a city that enjoyed a reputation as a haven for racial moderation, most people did not question the sanctity of the separation of the races, and only in a few quarters—some churches and colleges—was its validity ever questioned. Although Atlanta's political, religious, education, business, and media leadership sought to foster a racially moderate atmosphere, reflecting the mood of the city's population, this attempt was made within the vacuum of a segregated society and was not meant as an alternative to the existing order. Although Atlanta had its racial liberals, they were a very small minority.[22]

Adding to Vandiver's predicament were those Georgians who believed that a conversion to private schools might prove beneficial, enabling the state to save enormous amounts of money and control schools' curriculum to eliminate liberal ideas. According to Charles Weltner, "The idea of desegregated schools was difficult to approach. . . . There was no open discussion of the vital issue that Georgians had to face sooner or later. If something did not happen to prevent it, the entire education system . . . would be scuttled, without so much as one voice raised in protest." [23]

Ernest Vandiver stood almost alone in the waning months of 1959. Herman Talmadge retreated from his vocal support of the private school plan when he realized that it was unworkable and that if Georgia converted to private schools, he could lose the support of the state's business community. The equivocal nature of the private school plan forced many in the state to reevaluate its utility as a form of defiance. The continued debate over private schools recast the argument and enabled open school advocates to protest resistance and avoid attacking segregation. Even some members of the General Assembly hinted that they might support open school legislation, but the only members who would introduce any open school bills were the delegations from Atlanta's DeKalb and Fulton counties, and no rural representative could afford to be linked with urban interests. Vandiver needed a way to forestall the implementation of the *Calhoun* ruling and give the state an opportunity to realize fully the implications of further resistance. Direct defiance of the court's order was not an attractive option for Vandiver; he had a deep reverence for the law and had difficulty imagining the adoption of an openly antagonistic stance against the federal government. As he put it, "Well, you either had a choice of seceding from the Union and we had tried that before, not being successful, or you had to obey the laws of the Supreme Court. [You] either followed the law or you didn't follow the law." But Vandiver was also a very practical man. The idea of a firm stand against the federal government still held a powerful appeal to any southern politician. In 1959, many in the South mentioned the name Orval Faubus in the same sentence with John Calhoun, Jefferson Davis, and Robert E. Lee.[24]

Vandiver's political beliefs included an ideal that the people, given the facts of an issue and an opportunity to express their opinions, would guide their political leaders onto the correct path. He would demonstrate this philosophy during the September 1960 primary election. He had a referendum placed on the ballot that would allow the people to choose whether the state would have unpledged electors in the November presidential election. Many southern political leaders argued that if the South rewarded a favorite-son candidate with Dixie's electoral votes, both Richard M. Nixon and John F. Kennedy would fail to receive the required number of votes to win the election. The race would then be decided by the United States House of Representatives where southern strategists believed that they could more easily control the outcome. Vandiver, although a Kennedy supporter, went along with this idea because he needed to maintain control of Georgia's Democratic Party and appease Roy Harris and others who expressed reservations about Kennedy's civil rights agenda. The September referendum allowed the governor to pass his predicament onto the voters.[25]

Late in 1959, Vandiver's chief of staff, Griffin Bell, came up with a plan that incorporated the idea of letting the populace decide the state's most controversial issue. Bell, a member of Vandiver's elite team of attorneys that included Buck Murphy, Charles Bloch, and Holcombe Perry, had been instructed by the governor to try to find a way out of the school imbroglio. Bell and the others traveled the South, talking to their fellow counselors and studying various local option plans, pupil placement programs, and other segregation strategies. He became convinced that the other southern states knew little more than Georgia and that Georgians simply needed to understand the facts and to be given an opportunity to vent their frustration. Bell claimed the genesis of the Sibley Commission came to him one night while he was sitting in his den. Although there had been school study groups in the South since the original *Brown* ruling, the Sibley Commission was the first to hold *statewide* hearings that allowed both blacks and whites to testify.[26]

Bell presented Vandiver with an idea that a study committee of prominent citizens should tour the state, present Georgians with their options in clear and concise language, and allow the people to determine the fate of public education. Once Georgia had spoken, Vandiver could approach the coming school crisis with a foreknowledge of how people might react to either continued defiance or compliance with the court's ruling. The governor wholeheartedly endorsed the plan and began to search for a chairman for the study committee.[27]

Afraid the panel would not be as effective if linked to the governor's office, Vandiver arranged for it to appear to have originated in the General Assembly. It is more likely that Vandiver worried that the idea of a commission might elicit a negative response. No one know how the public might react to a committee that could be perceived as questioning the validity of segregation.[28] Former Speaker of the House George T. Smith later claimed it was he who had the original idea for the commission as an effort to delay any implementation of the *Calhoun* ruling. The leaders in the assembly, even the most ardent resisters, went along with the idea of public hearings because they expected that the people, given an opportunity to express their feelings, would give them a mandate to continue resistance, even to the point of closing the public schools. But if the state were divided on the issue, as the presence of HOPE and other open school groups indicated, then statewide public hearings would give local politicians a way to measure the convictions of their own constituents.[29]

Ernest Vandiver, however, had much bigger plans for the delegation. He wanted it to clearly explain the choices that confronted Georgia, so that every citizen would understand exactly what continued resistance would mean to public education. He wanted the state actively to discuss and debate the issue. "Seeing the handwriting on the wall," he later recalled, "a group of my advisers and I met and discussed what we might do, on one hand, to delay the decision and, on the other hand, to give the people of Georgia a chance to study their alternatives. Under the laws of this era, they had two choices—either integrated public schools or no schools." Vandiver also hoped the public testimony would spark such an intense public debate that Georgians would demand a popular vote on the issue and relieve him completely from the responsibility of deciding the school question.[30]

The leaders in the assembly and Governor Vandiver chose George Busbee, a representative from Dougherty County, to present the bill that would create the General Assembly Committee on Schools during the 1960 session. The bill proposed that the committee hold public hearings in all ten of Georgia's congressional districts, allow witnesses to express their opinions on the school situation, and after the hearings, report its findings and recommendations to the General Assembly. The men who chose Busbee to introduce the measure felt that he could not be accused of pandering to any one particular interest. He was from Albany, a small south Georgia city, and was not affiliated with the leadership of the House or the Senate. He, they believed, would lend the bill an independent air. Late in 1959, Ernest Vandiver went on a hunting trip near Albany and gave a copy of the bill to local newspaper editor and Democratic Party executive James Gray, a rabid segregationist, who in turn gave it to Busbee and swore him to secrecy about the governor's involvement. Busbee was reluctant to introduce the bill, convinced that it would be the end of his political career.[31]

Ernest Vandiver and Griffin Bell decided that the Committee on Schools would be made up of prominent citizens from the entire state, but rather than selecting specific persons to serve on the panel, they hand-picked organizations whose presidents would constitute the commission's membership. Bell did not want to "leave it to chance who would be on the Commission." The groups chosen for the assignment included the Farm Bureau, the Press Association, the County Commissioners Association, the Superior Court Judges Association, the Georgia Chamber of Commerce, and the Georgia Municipal Association. Prominent members of the state's educational community also served, including the heads of the Board of Regents and the Educational Cabinet, the chancellor of the University System, and the state superintendent of schools. Key educational committee chairs from the General Assembly rounded out the panel's membership.[32]

Vandiver, determined to name the commission's head, had narrowed the focus of his search to one man, John A. Sibley, former judge, counsel for Coca-Cola, and president of Atlanta's Trust Company Bank. Griffin Bell (who worked for the law firm of King and Spalding, where Sibley was a partner and whose services the firm had "donated" to the governor) approached Sibley with the idea. Sibley expressed reservations about the assignment and was concerned that the committee would be used only to delay desegregation and would not receive the proper support from the governor and General Assembly. Bell assured him that the committee's only purpose was to search for a solution to the school crisis, and Sibley agreed to chair the committee. He told Bell that he was president of the University of Georgia Alumni Association, and that organization was added to the list of groups represented in the committee.[33]

John Sibley represented not only the alumni association but also the interests of the Atlanta business community. By naming Sibley to the head of the commission, Vandiver in effect turned the problem of saving the Atlanta school system and the state's economic growth over to a man who cared deeply about both. It was Sibley's responsibility to find a way to preserve education by convincing the citizens of the state that it was in their best interest to allow Atlanta to desegregate its schools. One member of the commission described Sibley's position. "He was representing the powers that be in Atlanta. That was very obvious. He did not disclaim it when you were talking to him. He knew that Atlanta was a hustling, bustling city and he wanted to promote Atlanta."[34]

The Sibley Commission

The members of the commission, all prominent white citizens in Georgia's political, education, and business communities, were chosen to impress both Judge Hooper and the citizens of Georgia with how serious the state's politicians were about the school crisis. They hoped that Hooper would delay implementation of his ruling until after the commission had made its recom mendations to the General Assembly. This distinguished group of men also reflects the shadow of paternalism that, even in 1960, loomed over Georgia. With its membership of influential, wealthy citizens conducting the hearings and signifying the gravity of the situation, the Sibley Commission represented a brand of patriarchal hierarchy; if these men were concerned enough about the public school crisis, perhaps the state's citizenry should be as well.[35]

No one in Georgia could have symbolized both the southern patriarch and the modern New South businessman better than seventy-one-year-old John Sibley. As Sibley himself put it, "I felt I had been a lawyer and businessman and could see [their] point of view, a city man and could see theirs, and a country boy and could see theirs. With this background I could ask people for their views on the question without making them mad." Sibley, a descendent of Confederate war hero James Longstreet, was born in 1888 to a farm family in Milledgeville, Georgia. He received his law degree from the University of Georgia, paying his expenses by running a small farm. After graduation he practiced law in Milledgeville with his brother Erwin until named judge of the Baldwin County court. During World War I, Atlanta attorney Hughes Spalding asked Sibley to join his law firm. In his first year at King and Spalding, Sibley represented a group of Coca-Cola bottlers who had filed suit against the parent company for an apparent breach of contract. In court, Sibley bested the parent company's attorney, Harold Hirsch, and came to the attention of Ernest Woodruff, president of Coca-Cola, who later offered him the position of general counsel for the company. During the 1920s and 1930s, Sibley led the charge against soft drink companies whose names, Coca-Cola charged, infringed on its trademark. He was a spirited litigator and for two decades fought many legal battles against Pepsi-Cola. Sibley resigned and returned to King and Spalding when Robert Woodruff, Ernest's son who had taken over the company from his father, chose not to continue the fight against Pepsi after mounting losses in trademark cases.[36] In 1946 Sibley took over as president of Trust Company bank when both the president and his apparent successor learned they had life-threatening illnesses. In 1959, Sibley resigned as president of Trust Company, although still serving as a member of its executive council, and was preparing to retire to his farm north of Atlanta when called upon to serve as chairman of the commission that later bore his name.[37]

Perhaps a primary reason for Sibley's selection as chairman of the committee was his stand against integration and the *Brown* ruling. Ernest Vandiver later compared Sibley's views on segregation with those of Herman Talmadge. Sibley once wrote that "throwing the races together" would eliminate racial differences and encourage miscegenation, resulting in "a mongrel race of lower ideals, lower standards, and lower traditions." Sibley believed in what he called "natural segregation" and felt that the Supreme Court had overstepped its bounds. He agreed with jurist William Tuck, who believed in curbing the court's power, and supported Georgia congressman Carl Vinson's 1956 proposal that the United States strengthen the Tenth Amendment to guarantee states' rights. At one point, Sibley considered using that amendment to represent a woman who had been injured by federal troops in the Little Rock melee, basing a lawsuit on the contention that the soldiers had no right to be used in the desegregation of a state's schools. In many ways John Sibley reflected the beliefs of many white Georgians at this juncture in history. He was a man convinced of the validity of states' rights and the sanctity of segregation but not at the expense of ethical legal standards, public education, or a prosperous economic climate.[38]

The rest of the commission presented a cross-section of Georgia and its leaders. If the intent was a blue-ribbon panel of distinguished citizens who would impress Judge Hooper and all of Georgia with the sincerity of the assembly's efforts, it was certainly effective. The chairman, of course, was John Sibley, the president of the University of Georgia Alumni Association. The commission's vice chairman was the president of the Georgia Farm Bureau, John Duncan. The secretary, John Greer, was a well-known leader of the anti-Talmadge faction. He had fought the Ku Klux Klan in an attempt to pass an anti-mask bill in Georgia's General Assembly. A former executive secretary to E. D. Rivers, Greer had also fought against the county unit extension amendment and the private school plan and had lost to Ernest Vandiver in the 1954 lieutenant governor's race. The public schools of the state were represented by state superintendent of schools, Dr. Claude Purcell, who at the age of fifty-three had taken over the highest administrative position in the public school system after a brilliant career as a school superintendent. Homer Rankin, president of the Georgia Press Association, was a former plastics manufacturer in Tifton who at one time was president of that city's Chamber of Commerce. The chairman of the Georgia Education Cabinet, Zade Kenimer, was from Waverly Hall and a graduate of the University of Georgia. The president of the Georgia Municipal Association was Cartersville Mayor Charles Cowan, a farmer and automobile dealer. The Georgia Chamber of Commerce sent its president, John Dent, to serve on the committee; Dent, also of Cartersville, was the director of Fulton Federal Savings and Loan. J. W. Keyton of Thomasville, representing the Georgia County Commissioners Association, ran an ice company in South Georgia. Another member of the anti-Talmadge faction serving on the commission was the president of the Superior Court Judges Association, Judge Samuel Boykin, who had served on the highway board and as state revenue commissioner under E. D. Rivers. The state's Board of Regents sent its chairman, Robert O. Arnold, a former industrialist and mayor of Athens. The chancellor of the University System of Georgia, Harmon Caldwell, rounded out the organizational membership. Caldwell, a graduate of the University of Georgia Law School, also held law degrees from Harvard and Tulane Universities and Mercer and Emory Colleges. He taught law at Emory and the University of Georgia, where he also served as dean of the Law School and as president from 1935 to 1949.

Several members of the Georgia General Assembly also served on the commission. In addition to John Greer, the Senate provided Eulond Clary, a farmer from McDuffie County who had been in the assembly since 1951. Another senatorial member was first-term Senator Wallace Jernigan, a twenty-nine-year-old funeral director from Clinch County. The state House of Representatives sent Howell Hollis of Muscogee County, a decorated war hero and attorney who had received his law degree from the University of Georgia. Hollis had allied with John Greer in the anti-mask fight. Greenville peach farmer, Render Hill, serving his first term in the assembly, celebrated his thirty-eighth birthday during the commission hearings. Robert Battle Hall, who had served in the assembly since 1951, had been active in the massive resistance movement as a founding member of the Georgia Education Commission and had helped draft legislation to bolster the private school plan in 1954. George B. Brooks had served Crawford and Oglethorpe counties since 1937. Lastly there was Walstein Parker, a farmer and first-time representative from Screven County.[39]

The Georgia General Assembly Committee on Schools met for the first time on 17 February 1960 at the state capitol. Its goal was clearly defined by the bill that created the commission: "to make positive recommendations to the General Assembly regarding whether or not to submit the question [on whether or not to change state law to accommodate the court's ruling in the *Calhoun* case] to the people of Georgia for their determination. . . . In order that the General Assembly might be in a better position to make a determination as to the wisdom of presenting this question to the people, the Assembly felt that it should have the advice and counsel of the people, not only as to the desirability of the presentation but also as to its form and content." [40] The language of the bill clearly indicates that Vandiver and those in the assembly preferred a popular vote on the school issue. In addition to relieving those in public office from deciding the school question, a vote in the form of a constitutional amendment (to overturn the private school amendment of 1954) would also put off implementing the *Calhoun* decision until sometime after the next general election in 1962.

The members of the committee knew very early that they faced a very difficult assignment. Render Hill later explained, "what we were hearing out in the political world and hearing from the courts were two different subjects. They were not even close." The commission confronted the task of explaining to Georgians the differences between the court rulings and state law and creating a resolution that could accommodate both public education and segregation. After the committee elected Chairman John Sibley, Vice Chairman John Duncan, and Secretary John Greer, Sibley presented a public statement that explained the men's task. The committee, he said, had to conduct hearings in each of Georgia's ten congressional districts, the equivalent of "six months work . . . in sixty days." He explained that the committee must make its mission clear to everyone and in the course of its hearings must ask the people simple questions so that every Georgian understood the importance of the school issue. Sibley told the members of the committee that it was their responsibility to help Georgia decide whether or not to "abolish public education" and to explain to the state that continued defiance would mean exactly that. From the onset he took the position that Georgia had only two choices: change state law to protect education and preserve as much segregation as possible, or eliminate public schools. He told the members that he understood that, while none of them agreed with the *Brown v. Board of Education* ruling, it was the law of the land, and if the people worked together, they could "modify the evils of the . . . decision." [41]

It seems that everyone in Georgia heard in Sibley's first public statement exactly what they wanted to hear. African Americans, whites, businessmen, farmers, resisters, segregationists, and open school advocates hoped that the commission would give them an opportunity to present their case to the people. Prominent Atlanta businessman Ivan Allen Jr. wrote to Sibley and told him that he agreed with the statement "completely." Abner Israel thanked Sibley for his "clear thinking" as opposed to the "florid oratory" of the resisters, claiming that their speeches "while inflam[ing] the emotions, only freeze the mind."[42]

The creation of the Sibley Commission met with mixed reactions among state leaders. Roy Harris applauded the panel, convinced that it was created to "devise further and additional means for protecting the segregated way of life." Marvin Griffin, on the other hand, believed that the commission's purpose was to "get the governor off the hook from the race-mixing problem facing the public schools" and predicted that it would recommend token integration. Certain members of the media held a common perception that the idea for the hearings and commission was to stall for time and put off implementation of the *Calhoun* ruling. Some members of HOPE believed that the commission's purpose was either to stall for time or to convince the people to maintain resistance. And one politically astute observer maintained that the commission was for "show," allowing the state's citizens to voice their opinion, but that the outcome had been predetermined by both Vandiver and Sibley.[43]

After Sibley presented the commission's first public statement, the committee went to work forming smaller subcommittees to examine various aspects of the task ahead. The men associated with education made up one subcommittee, and the attorneys formed another (Sibley served on both subcommittees). The commission employed two secretaries, to help members in its Capitol office, and constitutional attorney Freeman Leverett, who had been involved with the education and segregation question for quite some time. The members agreed that only Sibley could speak for the commission and that he would give all interviews and reports to the press.[44]

The commission held its next and all further meetings in the boardroom of the Trust Company Bank. "The press was hounding the hell out of us," one member later remarked. "We couldn't have a meeting over at the Capitol without so much press in there we couldn't move around." The elaborate surroundings of the boardroom further impressed the members with the importance of their mission. While the men were seated in high-backed leather chairs, the portraits of former bank presidents, "the real builders of Atlanta," looked down upon them as they conducted their business.[45]

During its meetings, the commission designed a plan for public hearings to convince Georgians to support changes in state law and allow the desegregation of Atlanta's schools. The panel could only accomplish this task by assuring the rest of the state that it would not face a similar situation. To this end, the men submitted for public approval a new form of resistance that adopted every known legal method of preserving segregation. The committee also had to penetrate the silence that surrounded segregation and resistance and make discussion and debate of the issue possible. It could promote such discussion only by borrowing a strategy from HOPE, sharply defining the issue to eliminate any arguments for or against the practice of segregation.

To ensure widespread discussion of the issue, the commission planned each hearing to begin with testimony from representatives of groups that had held meetings, taken polls of their members, or held open forums on the school question. Preference was given to the leaders of civic associations, school groups, farm associations, chambers of commerce, and labor organizations. Individuals speaking only for themselves or their families were heard as time permitted. Encouraging organizational involvement in the hearings assured the commission that many more Georgians participated in the debate than the hearings themselves would allow. People were urged to bring the results of their discussions or polls before the commission or to mail them to its office at the state Capitol. These efforts, as Howell Hollis put it, would give the panel a "systematic cross-section of people's thoughts throughout the state."[46]

Another method of ensuring immense interest in the Sibley Commission's activities was the scheduling of all ten hearings during the month of March. The men did not want to prolong the events and knew that a sense of urgency would generate intense and immediate interest. Sibley wished to move forward "as rapidly as possible," but left the schedule flexible enough to allow for the prospect of additional forums if needed.[47]

The most important task in the pre-hearing meetings of the Sibley Commission was to define the school issue very clearly, explicitly, and carefully so that the average citizen could understand the questions involved. The commission's legal subcommittee assumed this duty. At its first meeting on 18 February, Sibley, Freeman Leverett, George Brooks, Howell Hollis, Samuel

Boykin, Zade Kenimer, and Griffin Bell (whom Sibley requested be present) discussed the best method to create "relevant and simple questions . . . which will elicit the information the commission desires." Sibley assigned Leverett and Hollis to frame the commission's hearing questions to include all the legal options the state possessed. (Sibley had already received from Bell reports on the pertinent federal court rulings and the necessary changes in state laws to allow "placement legislation.") The questions created by the Sibley Commission would narrow the public debate into simple choices that, Sibley hoped, would avoid peripheral considerations of segregation and integration that might obscure the commission's definition of the issues. The chairman planned to offer each witness only two basic options: to continue resistance at the expense of public education in order to preserve absolute segregation, or to change state law to preserve the public schools and the maximum amount of legal segregation. Sibley hoped that narrowing the debate to these simple choices would compel Georgians to see the folly of massive resistance and abandon a private school plan. Restricting hearing testimony to a preference for one of two choices would also allow, as Ernest Vandiver described it, "the hot-heads an opportunity to blow off some steam and frustration" in a controlled atmosphere.[48]

Late in February, Sibley met with Freeman Leverett, Homer Rankin, and Claude Purcell to discuss visits to other southern states and query lawyers and lawmakers about their efforts to contain desegregation. The chairman hoped to determine if other southern lawyers had any new, untested ideas that might be used to preserve segregation. Leverett gathered and examined information on school integration and the failure of resistance. He, Rankin, and Purcell divided the southern states into three categories: those states with no integration, places where resistance had failed, and areas where voluntary desegregation had been implemented to curb the extent of integration. The men examined incidents of violence, the number of students transferring schools, the size and type of schools desegregated, and other pertinent facts. The men planned to incorporate all that they had learned into the structure of the amendment that the commission would submit to the General Assembly. The core of the plan was to permit limited integration in some areas while preserving legal segregation for most of Georgia.[49]

In an effective use of strategy, the Sibley Commission attempted to take advantage of the divisive nature of Georgia's racial population percentages.

The state could be split into three distinct areas. In the Black Belt, which cut a swath down the middle of the state, almost every county had a black population of 45 percent or more. The Piedmont area, which ran from Georgia's northern border to the fall line, had only three counties with black populations of more than 15 percent. In the southern part of the state, or Wiregrass Georgia, which extended from the coastal counties to the state's southwest corner, very few counties had black populations more than 45 percent and most had between 16 and 30 percent. The commission planned to make a time-honored appeal to north and south Georgia not to allow the racial fears of the black belt to control the destiny of the entire state. Throughout the course of the hearings, Sibley reiterated the fact that unless legal action was brought against a local school district to desegregate, its schools would continue as before. Charles Cowan of Cartersville, a Piedmont town, argued before the commission that a local option plan would benefit those from his part of the state because north Georgia would have no problems with integration.[50]

The local option argument played a primary role in the commission's hearings. In addition to holding the events in the separate congressional districts, the commission planned on allowing black testimony to demonstrate that local black populations did not desire integration and would not file suit in a local court. John Sibley based this assumption in part on a speech given after the *Brown* decision by R. W. Greene, a black school superintendent from south Georgia. The chairman was very impressed by Greene's address, making copies of it and sending them to his friends in the summer of 1954. He believed that the speech "develop[ed] a theme which . . . is well worthy of consideration and states the principle of natural segregation." Greene's essay contained the ideas that African Americans preferred separate schools and associating with one another, that southern states were making great strides in equalizing school facilities, and that black schools fostered pride and contributed to racial harmony. Sibley believed that this man represented the beliefs of most of black Georgians. He incorporated Greene's ideas into the commission's plan to allow black testimony to show that black parents preferred "the right to teach, educate, and control [their] own children." Sibley asked Claude Purcell to write a paragraph, to be included in the commission's opening statement, that would show "the advantage of separate schools to the Negro." The chairman ordered George Brooks and Howell Hollis to create a separate set of questions for the hearing's black witnesses. They submitted to Sibley a list of potential questions that included: whether the witness and his associates preferred segregation, felt that black schoolchildren would have the same opportunities to exert leadership skills in a white school, or believed that desegregation would cost parents control over their child's education.[51]

In addition to demonstrating that the state's black population had no interest in desegregating local schools, the commission hoped to convince white resisters that using every available form of legal resistance would prevent integration in all but an infinitesimal percent of the state's schools. Sibley wrote to his brother Erwin shortly after the commission's hearings and explained his reconstructed approach to maintaining segregation. He told Erwin that there were too many legal defenses of segregation available to sacrifice the public schools in an effort to save the futile policy of defiance. He explained that the courts would be much more lenient once the state moved from truculent posturing toward obeying at least the letter, if not the spirit, of the law. If his plan did not work, he assured Erwin, the state could close the schools as "a last resort." The legal defenses of segregation included a strict pupil placement program (as outlined in the Atlanta plan), allowing each community or school system a "local option" of closing its schools or allowing desegregation, and incorporating a "freedom of choice" measure that would enable parents to receive personal tuition grants in the case of school integration. All of these options were built into the Sibley Commission's questions to witnesses.[52]

Sibley hoped to avoid blatant displays of emotion from witnesses by carefully limiting their options to the commission's questions. Sibley's two biggest fears before the hearings were that some ardent segregationists using the hearings as a platform would turn the events into a "circus" and that the passionate nature of the school issue would lead to potential violence. He recalled his apprehension in an interview years later, "We had no police guard, no sergeant-at-arms, nothing to protect us and I thought it could be very easy, with the sentiment as it was, for something to happen and the hearings get out of hand."[53]

In the week before the commission's first hearing, the members attended to the final details and released the hearing schedule to the press. The first hearing would be held in the third district in Americus, deep in the heart of the Black Belt region of the state most committed to resistance, on 3 March.

Sibley and John Greer, who scheduled the hearings, felt that it was important to gauge the amount of hostility toward the commission and its goals from the very start, rather than allow contention to fester while the committee heard from more sympathetic locales. The next week the committee met in Washington on the seventh, Cartersville on the tenth, then moved to La-Grange for the fourth district meeting on the eleventh. Three days later the commission held its eighth district meeting in the Coffee County seat of Douglas. Sandersville was the site for the sixth district meeting on the sixteenth and the following day the committee went to Sylvania in the first district. That district's meeting was originally scheduled for Savannah on the seventeenth, but at the request of Walstein Parker, it was moved to a more central location, Sylvania in Screven County. The town of Moultrie hosted the second district hearing on the twenty-first. Atlanta's Grady High School was picked as the site for the fifth district meeting on the twenty-third. The last scheduled hearing was in Gainesville the next day.[54]

John Sibley spent the week before the hearings making final revisions to the statement he would read before all the commission hearings. The double-spaced, ten-page document (on legal-sized paper) carefully defined the commission's purpose. Sibley claimed that the hearings were to allow the people an opportunity to tell the state government how they felt about the school issue. He very deliberately explained the contradictory nature of Georgia law and federal court decisions and the probable outcome of continued resistance. Sibley asserted that the commission knew that almost everyone, black and white, preferred segregation and that he and the other members of the panel disagreed with the *Brown* decision, but, he added, that it was the law and had to be obeyed. In the document, Sibley outlined the legal options still available to preserve segregation and reminded the attendees at each hearing that unless Georgia law were changed, the state would be forced either to convert its schools to private schools or to completely abandon state-supported education. If the laws were changed, he continued, and other legal measures to preserve segregation were adopted, everything would remain exactly the same for most Georgians unless a lawsuit were brought against a local school district. Then each community would have other options at its disposal, including conversion to private schools or token integration.[55]

Sibley would call witnesses after he read his statement. The commission first planned to allow local political figures to testify, followed by school officials, the leaders of civic organizations, and anyone representing groups that had met and discussed the issue or taken a poll. Witnesses were asked to state their names, addresses, and occupations, and if they had any school-aged children. Next, Sibley asked organizational representatives the results of any voting on the school question. Witnesses were then asked to give their preference for private schools or changing state law. These questions evolved over the course of the hearings, and the emphasis changed according to where the meeting took place, but the basic options stayed the same.

The creation of the Sibley Commission represented a major shift away from Georgia's massive resistance program. Although still dedicated to the continuance of segregation, the commission reflected a rift in Georgia's absolute devotion to the concept of outwardly defying the federal government. Public hearings to discuss the school issue, framed in the language of preserving the public schools, placed the commission within the trend of open school advocacy promoted by HOPE and others. The Sibley Commission also fell into a southern-wide pattern of changing resistance strategy after the events and subsequent federal court rulings in Little Rock and Virginia. The political nature of Georgia's resistance program, the state's early and strident leadership in the massive resistance movement, and Vandiver's precarious hold on the state's political machinery, however, created a need for public approval before Georgia could enact any changes in its position on integration. Whatever the original intent of the commission's creation—a delaying tactic to put off implementation of *Calhoun v. Latimer,* a way to measure the people's devotion to defiance, or a game of political "hot potato" with the school segregation issue—John Sibley planned to do everything possible to change Georgia's laws. Sibley and the commission offered the state a restructured resistance—an elusive plan to preserve public education while maintaining segregation. Before Sibley's program could be carried out, however, he first had to convince the white people of Georgia, devoted to defiance, that Georgia must allow for an evolution in its social structure.

CHAPTER 4

There's Mud on the Backroads

ODE TO SCHOOL STUDY

There's mud on the Backroads,
There's slush in the lane,
There's ice on the high roads,
From the freezing rain.
But wait, Mister Weatherman!
Didn't you know
The Sibley Commission is on the go?
How about it, men
Of the Study Commission
Is the ice going to stop
Your fact finding mission?
No, says John Sibley.
Never, says Greer.
You can quote me, says Rankin—
"We'll let nothing interfere."
So bring on your witnesses,
Call out the press.
We're going to get
To the bottom of this mess.
—Al Kueltne

In the predawn hours of March third, John Sibley and the other members of the commission motored south on an icy Highway 19 toward Americus. For the next four weeks the Committee on Schools held Georgia's absolute attention. It offered the state two choices in the school crisis: to continue with massive resistance and convert the public education system to a collection of private, segregated institutions or to change state law and allow each community to decide its own school question armed with a package of legal segregation strategies. These choices would be repeated countless times by the commission, its witnesses, hearing audiences, and hundreds of social, educational, church, political, business, and school groups when they brought the issue before their members. The power of the issue and the nature of the committee's meetings compelled all Georgians to decide for themselves whether to continue resistance or accept a new brand of Jim Crow. Over the course of that long March, the work of the Sibley Commission prompted the emergence of a fundamental division of opinion.

As expected, the results of the individual hearings mirrored the black population of each congressional district or county represented; the higher the black population, the stronger the segregationist and resistance sentiment (with the exception of some urban counties that had high black populations but also voted for a local option plan), and the lower the percentage of African Americans in an area, the more earnest the support for a local option. Exploiting the state's population differences, the commission pitted the northern Piedmont against the Black Belt and cities against rural areas in the debate over the schools. If support for local option grew strong enough to force the General Assembly to overturn mandatory school closing laws, then the crisis caused by Hooper's decision in the *Calhoun* case would be resolved. Atlanta could move forward with its plan to desegregate its schools with no state interference.

The idea of using black testimony to illustrate that there would be no massive call for integration was not as successful. Black witnesses also followed a regional pattern: those from rural areas testified that they preferred segregation, and urban witnesses supported integration in varying degrees—from calls to obey the *Brown* decision to demands for immediate integration. As the hearing testimony clearly demonstrates, African American witnesses espoused numerous and diverse opinions, both for and against continued segregation. Physical or economic intimidation by local whites certainly played a part in some black pro-segregation statements. The state NAACP called for the dismissal of testimony by black school teachers, principals, and superintendents because they were being pressured by white administrators to defend segregation. Other black advocates for segregation understood that the increasing numbers of new school buildings, buses, and teachers the state had provided in many Black Belt counties to stave off integration would be the first victims of a change in the status quo. Converting to private education, many others reasoned, would be the death knell for all black education in Georgia.

The hearings provided a powerful forum that both massive resistance supporters and open school advocates used to reveal to the world Georgians' true sentiments. Georgia organizations "from Rabun Gap to Tybee Light" represented an array of divergent interests—from chambers of commerce, Lions Clubs, labor unions, farm bureaus, Citizens' Councils, and Rotarians to underwriters' associations, PTAs, county commissions, concerned band parents, and master barbers. Each of these groups either conducted a poll, wrote a resolution, passed a petition, or held a meeting for the sole purpose of sending an agent to the Sibley Commission hearings. The press of Georgia gave unprecedented recognition and exposure to the commission's activities; television and radio stations broadcast the hearings live, and the state's newspapers kept a running tally of hearing results. This public debate over a social question that had previously been the exclusive domain of Georgia's rural politicians revealed in an interpretive judicial setting an intense opposition to the political hegemony of those committed to resistance.

Try as they might, John Sibley, the Committee on Schools, and open school advocates found it difficult to separate the idea of schools from segregation in the public mind. A majority (3–2) of those testifying before the panel preferred to close every public school rather than allow even a single school to integrate. But, by forcing the question of prioritization upon Georgia's white population, the Sibley Commission seized the segregation issue away from the state's politicians. Although for many witnesses schools and segregation were inexorably intertwined, many others understood the difference between segregation and massive resistance. After the commission's tour of the state, Georgians began to comprehend the report's recommendation that the state alter its segregation tactics. This change was not an embrace of any progressive racial moderation, nor a fundamental change in social mores, but simply a subtle shift in the value structure of the state. Its subtlety lay in the elaborate second and third and fourth lines of defense against integration that the commission offered as alternatives to statewide school closings. Although elusive, this slight change in Georgia's attitude destroyed massive resistance in the state and allowed a more pragmatic and defensible form of segregation. The lack of a powerful grassroots movement dedicated solely to the preservation of white supremacy made the toppling of massive resistance much easier than would be the case in other southern states, especially Alabama and Mississippi, whose strong Citizens' Council presence forced showdowns with the federal government. In Georgia, the politicalization of segregation through massive resistance eventually led to its downfall. As Roy Harris lamented, "Sometimes a fellow can be so impolitic as to destroy his own usefulness. I might be a living example of that."[1]

Americus

The first hearing of the Georgia General Assembly Committee on Schools served as a rousing testimonial for the continuation of resistance and the privatization of public schools to thwart integration. John Sibley and John Greer's reasoning that the Black Belt would offer the commission its greatest challenge in presenting an alternative to absolute segregation proved well-founded. The Third Congressional District represented the heart of Georgia's Black Belt. It contained twenty counties and had a black population of 45 percent. All but six of these counties had black student enrollment of 50 percent or more. The district was largely rural farmland and contained only one major city, Columbus.[2]

As people arrived outside the Americus County courthouse, they were guided by twelve city police officers through the heavy traffic and into the parking lots of a nearby supermarket and a recently abandoned bus station. They arrived from all over the third district, some unshaven and in tattered clothing, others in suits, many with written declarations clutched in their hands, all anxiously awaiting an opportunity to speak. Once crowded inside the tiny courthouse, they were instructed to file a written request to appear with the commission's secretary, John Greer.[3]

At the appointed hour of ten o'clock, John Sibley rapped his gavel on the podium and called the meeting to order. He told the audience that there would be no speech-making, that if the school issue were brought to a vote, then would be the time for "debate and argument and eloquence and for thought and emotions." Sibley feared an intense and possibly violent reaction to the commission and its questions and sought to create an atmosphere of calm reasoning. From his seat atop the rostrum he read his thirty-minute prepared statement; the people listened intently to his soft, middle-Georgia accent as he carefully explained Georgia's school situation. He told those gathered in Americus, just as he would tell his audience at every hearing, that the Supreme Court had overstepped its bounds in the *Brown* decision. He called it "devoid of legal reasoning and sociological validity" but, nevertheless, binding upon Georgia. Outlining the events that made the commission necessary, Sibley reminded the crowd of the ruling in *Calhoun v. Latimer,* Judge Hooper's "discretion" in postponing that ruling, the decision in *James v. Almond,* and the possibility of the loss of public education throughout the state. Sibley continued with a reminder that the right to operate the public schools was sacred and should not be taken lightly. He told the crowd that separate schools could still operate and that integration was not an absolute necessity. Speaking to the black members of the audience (seated in a special section of the courthouse), Sibley suggested that the right to educate their own children could be lost and with it a school system that employed thousands of black teachers, principals, administrators, and bus drivers. Then he told the whites in the crowd not to hold "our local negroes responsible for the tensions and ill feelings that are being engendered between the races," arguing that they were "the innocent victims of false leaders, some misguided, some influenced by sinister motives, and many pursuing subversive purposes."[4]

Sibley explained the purposes of the committee and its fact-finding mission; members "were to accurately report the sentiments and desires of the people upon the choices available to them upon the questions involved." He defined certain "universal" facts: everyone preferred public schools; everyone preferred segregated schools, "integrationists are insignificant numerically"; and no one wanted federal intervention in public education. He then presented the people with their options. The first was to do nothing. Atlanta would desegregate its schools, the governor would cut off funds to the school district, the parents of the affected children would probably file suit to reopen the schools, the federal court would force Vandiver to reinstate school funding to the schools or close every school in the state, and the education system would then be converted to a private organization. He reminded the listeners that the state could have nothing to do with the operation of private schools, state property could not be used, and grants-in-aid would be Georgia's only obligation. Private schools, he said, would have to built, organized, and staffed. He asked them to consider whether or not they would want a private school plan if those grants-in-aid were for some reason not available. This scenario was very similar to the one painted by HOPE and was the first public indication of the commission's view on the school issue. Sibley's addendum to the open school argument, the possibility that no grants-in-aid would be awarded, demonstrates the apprehension many in the state felt over the private school plan's legality and reveals their belief that it would be struck down in federal court. Segregationists, familiar with the silence surrounding Jim Crow and the power of that suppression, were taken aback by the severity of the commission's projection. The lack of any widespread public debate on the viability of continued resistance through existing state law hindered resisters from presenting a realistic alternative to Sibley's school-closing scenario. The commission's second option, however, offered segregationists every known legal defense of separate schools, including a pupil placement plan that would limit any school transfers to those students who had passed a very rigorous evaluation, a "freedom of choice" clause that would allow for white student transfers to segregated schools or reimbursement for private school tuition, and a provision allowing every community the right to choose for itself what to do when faced with possible integration. Communities voting to close their schools would be given the tuition grants and an opportunity to establish private schools. After Sibley explained these two options to the packed courthouse, John Greer called the first witness.[5]

Charles F. Crisp, patriarch of an old and powerful Georgia political family and a local bank president, took the stand and listened intently as Sibley meticulously explained each choice. Crisp expressed his opinion that all the schools in the state should be closed rather than for Atlanta to be allowed to proceed with its pupil placement program. He called the Atlanta plan a "snare and a delusion; a subterfuge. Like a little integration . . . it's only a foot in the door." According to one commission member, "Mr. Sibley worked on him harder than anybody else." Undaunted, Crisp explained that he believed most people did not understand the value of a grant-in-aid private school system and opted for resistance.[6]

John Sibley repeated the two options for Louise Hines, president of the local chapter of the Amalgamated Clothing Workers, and she told Sibley that she would prefer a local option plan but curiously and suddenly changed her mind, explaining, "if you put a child into a school where he is not wanted, he develops an inferiority complex. That child is going to fight back with every method he knows how. That's where your juvenile delinquency material is started. And it would be better for both people to be separated, where they will not have that instinct to fight back and start riots and race wars." John Greer next called the superintendent of the Americus city schools, Mr. Clay Mundy, who claimed he would prefer the first option even before any school was allowed to desegregate.[7]

The next witness, Mrs. Robert Robinson of the Marion County PTA, pleaded for a local option plan, explaining that her county was much too poor to convert to private schools and relied upon state funding. She was the only person in the entire morning session of the commission to voice a preference for the second option. After her testimony, Sibley thanked her. "I think that gets what we wanted. We are very glad, indeed, to have your opinion."[8]

Businessmen, farmers, educators, and top school administrators one by one came to the witness stand and testified that the third district would educate its own children before it backed down from massive resistance. One witness explaining this stance drew applause from the crowd, and Sibley banged his gavel down on the podium. "No. No clapping. Gentlemen, we will dispense with approbation or disapprobation on the part of any witness. We want to give the witness an atmosphere of attention, and whether we agree with them, or don't agree with them, is immaterial at this point." B. I. Thornton, a Crisp County lumber salesman, believed state law should be strengthened, making it mandatory for the governor to close down all of the state's schools if even one were allowed to integrate. Sibley could not believe the depths of resistance he was facing; he kept repeating the two options over and over, stressing the fact that the schools in South Georgia would not have to close if only Atlanta were allowed to desegregate. By the time he faced the sixth witness he had explained the two choices twelve times.[9]

Most witnesses represented only themselves or their families, but others brought the results of polls and meetings held in conjunction with the hearings. The results of these surveys mirrored the day's testimony. A Columbus radio station delivered an editorial telling listeners that the school question could not be decided by the Atlanta press, HOPE, or Big Johnny Reb. It asked that local citizens send in postcards with their preference for segregation at any cost or education at any cost written on the card. Of twelve hundred responses, 1,192 were for the segregation option. Thad Gibson explained why he felt that Lee County, which he represented, felt so strongly about maintaining absolute segregation. "We have seen Arkansas, Texas, North Carolina and Tennessee surrender, and we have seen Virginia's massive resistance turn into massive jelly." [10] The pride exhibited by Gibson and scores of other witnesses throughout the hearings in the depths of Georgia's resistance indicates the success of the state's politicians in convincing their constituents of the program's feasibility.

In one eloquent appeal for local option, or at least a private ballot on the subject, Americus priest Father Finian Riley elucidated the problem that public hearings entailed. "I think we all must remember—I am sure you are all aware of it—that there is one factor in all this public testimony that we have to consider, and that is the factor of intimidation. Whether we like it or not, it is a fact. We all recognize it, I am sure. That for someone to speak out publicly, for any type of integration, is to invite recriminations, social, economic, and even physical." [11]

Riley's point was perhaps underscored later in the day in an exchange between Sibley and the press. A local politician, George Matthews, testified on behalf of the county commissioners of Sumter County, who, Matthews claimed, were "all in favor of integration." From the crowded auditorium a voice yelled "What?" Matthews continued, "It's a unanimous vote amongst the commission." Sibley turned to the gathering and addressed the reporters, "Gentlemen, from the testimony we heard this morning, I am sure there was a misuse of the word, and I hope very much it will be treated that way in the press." The chairman turned to explain to a nervous and confused Matthews, "You said 'integration' but evidently you meant segregation." Matthews corrected himself and then read a statement calling for total resistance to integration. [12]

The commission heard from some open school advocates that afternoon but they were a distinct minority. Sibley reached out to anyone he felt might be willing to give the second option a chance. Mrs. Clarence Chambless from the PTA in Clay County expressed some doubt as to the viability of private schools. Sibley asked her if that meant she had some reservations about present Georgia law and perhaps would prefer to try the second option before closing the schools. Chambless told him no, she did not think there was any choice about maintaining resistance. So many others with the same opinion came to the podium that Sibley finally asked for only one person from each county to approach the stand unless there was a person in that delegation with a dissenting opinion.[13]

There was a bright spot for Sibley in the afternoon session; the questions put before black witnesses elicited the response that the commission desired. Howell Hollis, Sibley, and George Brooks had prepared several questions for these witnesses in the weeks before the trial. The questions, designed to show that most local African Americans were content with a segregated school system, revolved around demonstrating the value of black schools in the community and to its children. Like many of the concepts and ideas of the commission, these questions evolved over the course of the hearings. In Americus, however, Sibley did not ask black witnesses to state a preference for option one or two, but asked them if they thought their children should be taught by black teachers, whether or not black schools helped to foster leadership qualities in children, and whether they believed that their children felt inferior because of segregated schools. R. W. Waters of Muscogee County described himself as "a die hard segregationist" but told Sibley that the church groups he represented believed that *Brown* must be obeyed and had asked him to state their preference for integration. Sibley dismissed Waters and called his next witness, minister R. W. Greene.[14]

After the *Brown* decision, Reverend Greene had spoken out against the Court's ruling in a widely distributed speech that praised segregation. Greene called for a continuance of separate education, citing the jobs for African Americans that it created, the opportunities to develop leadership skills, the value of black teachers instructing black students, and the growing equability of the segregated school system. Sibley received a printed copy of the address and admired it so much he made copies and mailed them to his friends in the summer of 1954. When creating questions for black witnesses, Sibley used many of Greene's ideas. On the stand, Sibley allowed Greene a free rein to express his opinions; the witness assured the audience that African Americans did not want integration nor did they believe that it would be beneficial.

He praised the segregated school system and commented that blacks only sought equality in separate schools.[15]

The meeting ended with the commission hearing from black delegations from Sumter, Stewart, and Chattahoochee counties, all of which favored continued segregation. G. W. King told the courthouse crowd that he had "interviewed every Negro school teacher in the county, and every one of them are solid against integration." Joseph Baldwin said, "we are happy, and we are satisfied, and we are asking the continuation of the good will and present friendship that exists between our races. We are happy." The crowd applauded. Sibley turned toward Baldwin and told him that it was "worth the trip down here to meet a man who has done the things you have done, and are now doing. Thank you very much." The testimony of African Americans at the Americus hearing elicited a positive response from segregationists in South Georgia. Marvin Griffin praised the witnesses for having "more sense than the folks in HOPE . . . [or] the agitators in the NAACP . . . [and] the Supreme Court of the United States."[16]

Some white people, however, expressed disdain over the use of black testimony. John Greer remembered that at the hearing in Americus, one of his senatorial colleagues approached him and asked, "what's all these niggers doing in here?" Greer replied that they were there to testify. The unnamed legislator then replied "well, that ain't the way I understood it. I thought we were just going around the state and let the whites talk it over, decide what we'd do and then we'd tell the niggers about it."[17]

According to official Sibley Commission statistics, sixty-six people testified that day. Fifty-two, representing groups whose membership exceeded 12,500, preferred option one or closing the schools.[18] The five proponents of the second option represented only twenty-three people. Nine African Americans testified, and all but one expressed a desire to continue segregation. The testimony by black school officials at the Americus hearing prompted a protest by the state's NAACP. An official statement from the organization claimed that the African Americans who spoke at the meeting had been pressured by local white school administrators to voice a preference for segregation. Continued defiance to the Supreme Court held an appeal for the white citizens of Georgia's Black Belt as was reflected in their testimony in Americus. Almost all the witnesses were willing to sacrifice public education to prevent any degree of integration, clearly illustrating the depths of their commitment to massive resistance and the belief that any change in Georgia law threatened their way of life. This intense reaction startled Sibley, who at first seemed incredulous over this deep-seated reverence for Georgia's resistance legislation.

After the strong sentiment for maintaining massive resistance at the Americus hearing, HOPE's leaders worked to have their ideas represented at the remaining hearings. They were convinced that the commission's hurried hearing schedule was designed to keep open school advocates from organizing a strong presence at the meetings. Frances Pauley complained that HOPE was kept from testifying in Americus and clamored for an additional subcommittee meeting in Columbus to allow residents of the third district's only large city to testify. Pauley and the other HOPE members also spent countless hours on the phone arranging for its representatives to be heard at the individual hearings. She met with Sibley and asked him to "play fair." Pauley told him the group was not asking for special treatment, only "justice." HOPE leadership was convinced that the Sibley Commission hearings were merely a supplement to massive resistance and not a change in policy. However, they agreed that the hearings offered open school advocates a powerful forum to express their views.[19]

Pauley, Muriel Lokey, and the rest of HOPE's membership believed television coverage benefitted their cause at the expense of resisters. "The camera was so plain. . . . It got so when you saw somebody come up on the stage, you'd know whether they were segregationist or not. It was—somehow the picture brought it through. They weren't—I guess it's because they weren't actors. They were real. And the people, the people on our side, were just so nice and so good and so right in comparison with the others, who were filled with hatred. . . . It came across on TV. It did. And so then the numbers [of each side's witnesses] each time, the numbers got more, until when it was added up, we had about as many as they had, in the end. And Sibley was floored."[20]

Media coverage of the hearings from a variety of sources saturated Georgia. The growing influence of television news, however, made the most substantial impact on the public's reaction to the Sibley Committee's meetings. One Atlanta television station, WSB-TV, sent a cameraman to every hearing, and other stations broadcast a few hearings live. In some ways television reporters helped to shape the opinions of their audience. WSB cameraman Joe Fain, who attended every hearing, was responsible not only for WSB's reporting but for providing the NBC network with coverage. Fain's camera only permitted three to eight minutes of continuous filming. This limitation often required the newsman to "create" news. He was compelled to choose carefully which witnesses to record based "on a hunch" as they approached the witness stand. When Fain guessed wrong or missed particularly eloquent testimony, he occasionally asked a witness to retake the stand, during a lunch break or after a hearing, and repeat his statement. After each hearing, Fain drove back to Atlanta and his work appeared on that evening's six o'clock broadcast. After hearings, members of the local or national press corps gathered around the commission members asking them to comment on the days' events. Render Hill recalled several occasions when reporters asked if he had learned something that he did not already know. "The answer was always no." According to Hill, after a few hearings, most of the Sibley Commission members knew what witnesses were going to say by the way they approached the stand and in what part of the state the meeting was held.[21]

National television coverage of the Sibley Commission allowed people from all over the United States to follow the proceedings, and many did so with intense interest. One California woman wrote Sibley, "Ever since the public hearings broadcast over TV, I feel constrained to voice my own opinions in behalf of the South." A Texas man commented on how much coverage the national television news gave the hearings and the "integration-segregation issue and of your committee." And a Tennessee man congratulated Sibley on the "dignified and courteous manner [he] treated every witness regardless of color."[22]

In Georgia, people read the results of each morning session in their afternoon papers and then received full coverage of the hearing in the next day's morning editions. The papers kept a tally of witnesses from both sides as if keeping a contest score. Most of the state's urban papers applauded the work of the commission, but many rural newspapers cast a wary eye on the events and continued to argue for defiance. Committee hearings were broadcast live over the radio, and often people who could not attend listened intently, at home or at work, to their friends and neighbors expressing their opinions.[23] Biographer Elizabeth Stevenson described how the commission's activities crept into the lives of Georgians.

Mr. Sibley let everyone talk; he let no one take over, nor any one element; housewives, city and county officials, farmers, educated men and women, uneducated
men and women, some even with lunches in boxes brought to the hearing as the
sessions grew more and more fascinating; the whole series was televised and
people watched their neighbors for hours expressing wise or foolish opinions.
People who had never done so before wrote out manifestos for their particular organizations and took them along to present at the hearing. It was a typical Southern, particularly low-style Georgia, occasion. All the alarmist dangers alleged
against integration, all the high-minded arguments for it, were blurted out in embarrassing profusion.[24]

Extensive news coverage allowed the commission to create an acute interest among Georgia's citizens. For only through an intense, ongoing, statewide
public debate could the commission untangle the issues of schools, segregation, and massive resistance.

Washington

John Sibley learned many lessons from the Americus hearing, and it is to his
credit that, during the Washington hearing four days later, he quickly recti-
fied some of the more glaring mistakes that appeared at the first meeting. He
changed course very smoothly, because by this time he had taken complete
control of the commission. Only Sibley was permitted to speak for the panel
to the press, and he did not or would not make any public comments other
than his statements and his questions of witnesses at each hearing. One of the
most important things that Sibley learned at Americus was the extent of the
unpopularity of any plan of desegregation. Pupil-placement and token integration were incomprehensible to most Georgians. Although no one wanted
their local schools to close, many would make that sacrifice if they believed it
would stop integration. After Americus, Sibley realized this fact and for the
rest of the hearings emphasized the strength and logic of a local option plan
to decide the school question and the more ambiguous concept of voting on
the measure at some later date.[25]

Sibley also planned to ensure that the panel would hear from more groups
at the rest of the hearings. He had commission members contact as many organizations as possible, extending an invitation to send a representative to the

meeting in their congressional district. During each hearing, Sibley gave preferential treatment to those delegates, both those who preferred the first option and those who fought to preserve public education, whom he felt had a legitimate concern for the school crisis. He permitted group representatives to read statements and offered a more sympathetic ear to those witnesses who had taken the time and effort to harvest the opinions of a large number of people. But his patience wore thin when faced with long, rambling defenses of segregation that were redundant and occasionally embarrassing. Many times during the first few hearings Sibley would simply have the commission secretary record an entire county's delegation away from the witness stand to avoid ceaseless repetition.[26]

As a result of the more aggressive invitations from the commission to group leaders in the tenth district, the meeting in Washington offered a stark contrast to the previous week's hearing. Witnesses revealed the potentially divisive nature of the school crisis. The strength and organization of the open school advocates surprised many and exposed a startling shift in Georgia's public opinion of massive resistance. The school crisis and the attention on the Sibley Commission caused many to reexamine their commitment to the political defenses of segregation, and to its priority, but rarely to its validity. Sibley offered them only the two choices: a conversion to private education, unpalatable at best and a complete failure at worst; and a detailed defense of local segregation that would allow the state's schools to survive. Those who testified at Americus revealed the depth of the Black Belt's commitment to massive resistance; the testimony at the Washington hearing demonstrated drastic divisions of opinion within the tenth district, individual counties, churches, and even households.

In the preface to his statement, Sibley asked the five hundred people who crowded into the recently remodeled Wilkes County courthouse to examine carefully the real options available to them and to abstain from superfluous arguments. He claimed that any "division between the cities and the rural areas" was based on the erroneous "assumption that those in the cities who are advocating keeping open the public schools are really integrationists." Those fighting to save public education, Sibley said, were simply trying to ascertain whether the schools could be saved.[27]

Edward Pope, the mayor of Washington, led off the hearing. Pope, who in addition to his duties as mayor owned gas stations, a cattle farm, and some interests in a timber operation, testified that he would support existing laws. He offered his own views on open school advocacy groups. "I feel that so many of our people who we read about in the Atlanta papers primarily form these organizations to keep the schools open at all costs. I don't believe that these people are completely aware of any alternative other than what they have seen happen in Little Rock. I think that has had more effect on the people than anything else, and I believe that a determined effort, as you outlined at the closing of your remarks, that if we rally about this thing and really want it, that we can have it. We've got to want it; we've got to want it bad, and I'm one of those who wants it bad."[28]

The next witness, Mrs. R. M. Darby, representing the Washington Women's Club, gave that organization's endorsement of local option. Sibley was pleased. "We're so glad to have you here. We are very anxious wherever there is more than one view in a community to get both views, and we're going to get them if we know how to do it, and we have to rely on the people themselves to let us know if they want to speak out on this question.[29] Another woman also expressed her desire for local option: "Honorable Herman Talmadge introduced last year into the House a bill which would give the states sovereignty and give them sovereign rights. I believe that we have that same privilege, that we should be allowed to express our views."[30] Mrs. Bothwell Taylor, representing Georgians for Public Education, told Sibley that she had originally voted for the private school amendment in 1954, but at that time believed that "we would just go on having our schools as we had them except that it would be private." Taylor and her organization, she told Sibley, wanted to preserve the state's public schools and preferred option two.[31]

The Washington Women's Club and Georgians for Public Education were only two of many groups that sent representatives to swear their fealty to education or to testify in favor of a community's right to decide the matter locally. These witnesses often carried to the stand prepared statements or the results of a meeting or poll of their membership. Group meetings extended the commission's influence far beyond the Wilkes County courthouse and further legitimized its authority over the options available to resolve the school issue. Most of the people who chose the commission's second option were from the Athens-Clarke and Wilkes County delegations: the Wilkes County Educational Association; the Elberton County Ministerial Association; the Athens Parents and Citizens' Committee; the Students for Public Education (which submitted a petition containing 838 names of University of Georgia students who supported changing state law); the American Association of University Women; the Junior Assembly of Athens; HOPE; the Sisterhood of the Jewish Temple; the Clarke County Mental Health Association; the Catholic Women's Guild; PTAs from several towns and counties; the League of Women Voters; the Athens Rotary Club; and many others. The hearing inspired two people to spend the day polling their clubs or friends so that they could reveal the results that afternoon. Paul Brown told Sibley that the Athens Exchange Club had held a meeting that very afternoon and voted for local option 33 to 1, and Mrs. Troup Harris had spent the morning collecting names on a petition to give to Sibley asking for the right to vote on the school question.[32]

Witnesses for the second option usually gave the exact results of their group's poll, explained how the vote was taken, and noted if there were any pertinent factors in the decision. A poll of the professors at the University of Georgia revealed that of 279 queried, 252 preferred a local option plan. A member of the American Association of University Women explained that the group's vote was influenced by the abstention of its public school-teachers, a large minority of its members, who had been instructed by their superiors not to participate in any vote on the school question.[33]

An important development at the Washington hearing was the growing support for open schools by business and industrial interests. Sam Chambers, of the Athens Area Industrial Group, testified that he and those he represented, Westinghouse Electric, Chicopee Manufacturing, Anaconda Copper, Dari-Tech, General Time, Southeastern Rubber, Colonial Poultry, Roper Hydraulics, Puritan Cordage Mills, and Thomas Textiles (the top industries in the Athens area), all preferred public schools, even at the cost of losing absolute segregation. Chambers's testimony represents the first organized group of businessmen to come before the commission and express a preference for the panel's second option; it generated a momentum that resulted in an embrace of the open school movement by many of the state's influential business leaders.[34]

Rural Georgia, however, continued to make a case for resistance. The Wilkes County Farm Bureau presented the unanimous results of a poll of its membership, who preferred the first option. The Elbert County Board of Education, the Elberton Bar Association, and an impromptu meeting of seventeen Elberton businessmen all favored standing firm on Georgia's laws. Entire delegations from Hart, McDuffie, Greene, Warren, Oconee, and Lincoln counties as well as the Lavonia Chamber of Commerce, the Tenth District of the American Legion, and the Scrutchin PTA, agreed. Cecil L. Langham tried to offer Sibley biblical references to explain his fealty to segregation. When he began to read the appropriate passages, the chairman stopped him and asked Langham instead to cite the chapters and verses, and he would "ask everybody to read it when they [got] home."[35] In contrast to the voices for open schools, many of the witnesses for continued resistance spoke for no sanctioned groups or offered only vague claims of knowing how the members of their organizations felt. Politicians professed to speak for the beliefs and wishes of all their constituents, and often neighbor claimed to speak for neighbor. Lee Carter, mayor of Hartwell, executive secretary of the Hart County Chamber of Commerce, and president of the Hart-Franklin-Stephens County Development Association, claimed to speak for almost everyone he knew. "Expressing in my opinion, and other opinions, ninety percent of the opinions of Hart county. . . . We are for segregated schools . . . the colored people of Hart County feel the same as I do."[36]

To validate his claim, Carter brought along his maid to testify as a member of Hart county's black delegation. When asked if the two races in her county had amicable relations, Georgia Banks replied, "Yes sir. We have the best white people ever known in our town, and they are interested in us, and we have a beautiful school building—more than beautiful—that the good Lord and the white people have given us. Then we have wonderful buses to ride on. Our people are just wonderful. We are getting along fine. We don't have any trouble in our town. We love each other. The white people are nice to us and we are nice to them."[37] Banks's emphasis on the relations between the races in Hartwell reveals both her employer's influence over her testimony and the fear of potential reprisals against African Americans who might advocate integration.

The afternoon's testimony began with that of a "private citizen from Richmond," Roy V. Harris, president of the States' Rights Council of Georgia and recent Vandiver appointee to the Board of Regents. The author of Georgia's massive resistance sat and faced Sibley, the man determined to destroy his work. Although the two men both believed in voluntary segregation, Sibley would not sacrifice the public schools to attain this goal, and Harris supported the private school plan only if pressure and intimidation did not work to suppress cries for integration. The representatives of the two most powerful forces in Georgia eyed each other carefully. Sibley asked his adversary to state his name and whether or not he spoke as a representative of any group. Harris replied, "My name is Roy V. Harris. I'm from Augusta, Georgia, and I'm never quite sure whether I'm expressing anybody's opinion or not, so I had better express my own." Sibley then attempted to pin Harris to one of the commission's two options. Harris, however, refused to cooperate; he claimed that Georgia had many available options and that the commission had oversimplified the issues of schools, resistance, and desegregation. He explained that the pupil placement plan "was legal if it was used to put Negro children in school with whites." But, he continued, it could not be used "to keep Negro children out of the white schools, and I don't think the Supreme Court would ever hold it." Harris claimed that the only answer available to rural Georgia was voluntary segregation, because the only city in Georgia large enough to allow for residential segregation was Atlanta. Little Rock's problems, he declared, were due to noncooperation between the black and white communities to enforce voluntary segregation and not to the policies of massive resistance. He told Sibley, "I believe if a group of people like you in Atlanta would take the leadership—and that's the only place in Georgia we've got any trouble—if you and other people of your stature would take a lead and ask the white people to come together and work out plans to keep voluntary segregation, and call on the Negroes to join you, I believe it would be done." [38]

Harris brought his own delegation from Richmond County to testify for the continuance of resistance and included the superintendent of the county's schools and the head of the Augusta PTA. Another member of this group was Harris's political ally Hugh Grant, who argued that Georgia should use interposition to fight Judge Hooper's decision in *Calhoun v. Latimer*. [39]

But it was a black witness from Richmond County, William H. Wilburn, the president of an Augusta orphanage, who offered the most stirring testimony of the hearings.

> Well I'm opposed to segregation, not just for segregation in the name, but what it begets, what follows it. In other words, I'm not particular about mixing with white people and I like to mix with them, too. They're a fine group of people, but I [Sib-

ley began to interject], just give me a little time, please sir. I'm eighty-two years old; I won't get a chance to speak no more. I mean this: what follows segregation, I mean, is discrimination, and that's the thing where we suffer, from discrimination. I come from a city, in Augusta, where for more than thirty years . . . the Negroes didn't have a High school. . . . It's just like a one legged man. You've seen them. They buy a pair of new shoes. They can't go out and buy one shoe; they have to buy two. Alright, when they buy the two new shoes they wear one out, the other is new. The separate but equal that we've had in the South, you wore out the separate, but you never put in the equal. Now that's the thing we want.

At this point Sibley tried to stop Wilburn from continuing, to which Wilburn replied, amid a chorus of laughter,

My friend Mr. Harris spoke and I thought I would too. If we do away with this thing [public education], it's going to do the white people more harm than the Negroes. We've done without education for 250 years. And I hate to say this, but I wish you could be a Negro for a half hour; and then hear you say our Governor is coming to town, and I would like to hear the Governor; and they say the public is invited; then they say the Richmond Hotel; I'm not invited; all that kind of stuff. We have so much, so much to contend with; and, listen after all that happens here's what we say to the white folks: "Though he slay me, yet will I trust him."[40]

Other black witnesses disagreed with Wilburn. Irene Zellers of McDuffie County said "I want us to have the same school that the white has, in the same equal [sic], where our children can learn anything just like them, but let's stay in our own school just like we've always done and live lovely, because we've got to die, and we're going to torment if we don't quit fighting over these schools. . . . All of us better get right."[41]

Certain similarities among witnesses appeared that would hold true at almost all the hearings: elected officials, farm bureaus, and small town men's social organizations usually opted for the first choice. When Sibley recognized an exception to this rule, he wanted to ensure that the alternative opinion was heard. When the Oglethorpe County delegation (almost exclusively for option one) filed their names with John Greer, Sibley heard that the county farm bureau supported local option. He stopped Greer and hurriedly called that group's representative, Joe Gorman, to the stand. "Come up, Mr. Gorman; let's get here regularly." Gorman told Sibley that his branch held a meeting, and 95 percent of the organization preferred a local option plan.[42]

Organizations that promoted local option, however, usually consisted of church groups (including most ministerial associations), the League of Women Voters, and any organizations representing institutions of higher learning. Most PTAs and other secondary and elementary school groups split along urban-rural lines. Often during the Washington hearing, these divisions became so plain that Sibley, recognizing a county's pattern of testimony, asked members of that delegation to give their names, organizations, and membership information to John Greer. This information would have important ramifications, as the tally of supporters from both sides was being reported by the state's press. After the hearing in Washington, the newspapers' stories all reported that a majority of people testifying supported local option and pupil placement. The official results of the hearing, however, show that resisters outnumbered open school advocates two to one. The reason for this discrepancy was this timesaving practice. Those supporting open schools were almost always a minority in any county's representation and therefore were heard as an alternative opinion within a county. Another reason they were heard is that so many of those dedicated to the preservation of schools came at the behest of their organizations and the commission made it a practice to hear from anyone representing a group.

The glare of the television lights proved too much for many witnesses to bear; Harold Boggs, mayor of Danielsville and Madison County's representative to the Georgia General Assembly, felt the pressure of the new medium and expressed his steadfastness "for integration 100 percent, regardless of cost." Sibley told him he should think that over. "Segregation—Segregation—Segregation," Boggs responded, realizing his mistake. Sibley turned to members of the press and asked that they, "for the sake of the gentleman's political future, please correct that into the record."[43] Other politicos felt the lure of the television camera and an instant audience. At one point in the hearing a voice called out to the chairman, "we have present two candidates for local representative's race. I wonder if it would be permissible to ask them. . . ." Sibley, perhaps weary of political rhetoric, cut off the voice and answered "No. We'll have to ask them to get their own crowd."[44]

Many in the audience sympathized with Sibley's aversion to political arguments for segregation. Mrs. Kathy Bartow lamented that the hearings seemed to have turned into "a popularity vote between integration and segregation, which [is] not the question at all."[45] And Sibley himself told a witness that the state's political leaders would not solve the problem. When W. T. Ewing stated that "the people of my county places [sic] their utmost confidence in the governor and the house, and at the same time we are going to abide what our governor says without too much opposition," Sibley interrupted. He told Ewing that "the legislature and the Governor sort of put the burden on you; they don't want you to put the burden back on them. Let's hear from you now."[46]

Ninety-nine people testified that day at Washington; fifty preferred the local option plan, and thirty-four opted to continue resistance. The remaining witnesses either refused to express a preference or were among the black delegates not asked the same questions.[47] The disparate testimony given at the first two hearings demonstrates the effects of black population on the opinions of individual districts. The average county's black population in the tenth district was only three-fourths as large as in the third district. Although significant (and this discrepancy would appear in much more dramatic fashion at later hearings), black population figures pale in comparison to the rift between rural and urban areas at the Washington hearing. And perhaps the most important development to come from the Wilkes County courthouse was the popularity of the local option plan and the organization of provincial groups determined to use that plan to save their city, town, or county schools.[48]

Cartersville

Two of the most important developments in the Sibley Commission hearings emerged at the third public meeting, held in the Bartow County courthouse in Cartersville. The Seventh Congressional District, an area of Georgia with a very small black population, presented a strong front for a local option plan. This Piedmont portion of the state refused to succumb to the racial arguments and strong segregationist stance of South Georgia. This pattern, much like the urban-rural split presented at the Washington hearing, would continue to develop as the hearings moved through the state. Business and industry (the seventh district was the center of the state's chenille manufacturing and the burgeoning rug and carpet industry) continued to support the idea of a local option plan, but the meeting at Cartersville also revealed the depth of labor's opposition to any change in state law. Union representatives testifying before the commission brought petitions and resolutions favoring continuing segregation no matter the consequences. Much the way national churches and individual congregations differed in their view on segregation, national labor leaders fell out of touch with their southern membership. Although national labor unions cooperated with civil rights groups, local union leaders testified before the Sibley Commission that they favored resistance. As a result, local labor was often pitted against management over the issue of schools. Labor and farm associations provided most of the early organized support for resistance at the Sibley Commission hearings. The reactionary conservative forces in Georgia (and throughout the South) had always relied on this group of working-class white laborers and farmers for support, and in return promised that there would be no change in the social and economic hierarchy. But in Georgia, the usurpation of segregationist values by the Talmadge faction of the Democratic Party left these men without any method of expressing their affinity for the established social structure outside of politics.[49]

The county courthouse was filled to capacity with four hundred seventh district residents, in spite of a brutal snowstorm that covered north Georgia. They planned to express their disdain for mandatory school closing laws. Sibley's preface to his statement included portions of Judge Hooper's recent decision to forestall implementation of his ruling in the *Calhoun* case until after the Sibley Commission had rendered its report. Hooper praised the committee for "giving the people of this state an opportunity of full and free discussion" and providing a forum that was "conducive to a better understanding . . . of the real issues involved." Sibley devoted much attention to explaining school closing laws that would eliminate all the public schools in Georgia regardless of the number of black students in the school system. Sibley went into some detail on pupil placement and local option plans and their effectiveness in preventing desegregation in other southern states. He pointed out that in the Seventh Congressional District there were five all-white counties and reminded them that, unless some sort of local option plan were implemented, even those counties would lose their public schools.[50]

Also in his prefacing remarks, Sibley addressed some criticisms from the African American community about his questioning of black witnesses and the allowance of testimony by principals and administrators of black schools. At the first two hearings, the chairman continued to ask questions of black witnesses designed to demonstrate that they were satisfied with segregated schools. Several of the state's black leaders charged that school superintendents pressured their black principals to testify in favor of continued segregation. They also suggested that Sibley not "spread the impression that Negroes are satisfied with school conditions in Georgia and are seeking to change them only because of Northern agitation." Sibley answered his critics by claiming that, since the lawsuit to desegregate the schools was brought by black litigants, asking them if they preferred to close the schools under the present system would be pointless, and the only relevant question was whether or not black witnesses preferred integrated or segregated schools. However, Sibley agreed to provide every witness with the commission's standard two options if they preferred.[51]

Sibley's first opportunity to confront this issue came quickly in the Cartersville hearing. Jesse W. Cook, a minister and NAACP representative from Cobb County, confronted Sibley over the options available to white and black witnesses. Urging the chairman not to repeat the questions, Cook stated that "it is better for mixing all of the people for the reason that your separate schools, as have been practiced for a hundred years, have proven to be unequal [in providing] job opportunities."

Sibley asked Cook if he meant that "you believe that Negroes are in a . . ." Cook interrupted Sibley to clarify that he said "Negroes." Sibley responded, "What do you mean? What do you want me to say?"

"It sounds like you are saying 'Negroes' almost like 'niggers,' but I hope you are saying 'Negroes,'" remarked Cook.

Sibley assured Cook that he did indeed say Negroes and asked the minister if he believed that "the Negroes—or *Negroes*—emphasis on the 's' . . . are just as capable, or even more so, to teach and operate their schools; look after their own people; than if they were also mixed with white people to look after them?"

Cook denied that African Americans ever ran their own schools. "These are state schools. There are no Negro officials in the state. The local schools are operated by your superintendents. I know not of a Negro or colored superintendent, so since the Negroes never had an opportunity to operate the schools, I don't know." Cook did, however, express his belief that African

Americans could, if given an opportunity, operate their own schools. The exchange between Sibley and Cook characterizes Sibley's frustration over black testimony that failed to meet his objectives. His paternalistic stance toward Cook also illustrates the attitude the chairman took with most black witnesses during the hearings. It is clear that Cook is advocating immediate integration, but Sibley redirected his questions and began asking about black control over black school systems.[52]

In addition to the increasing bellicosity of some black witnesses, business support for local option dramatically increased at the Cartersville hearing. R. M. Stiles, a farmer representing the Cartersville Chamber of Commerce, supported the local option plan, making his chamber the first such organization in the state to do so. Stiles explained that his group had grave reservations about what a lack of public schools would mean to business and industry. He complained that he could not understand why Bartow County should have to close its schools simply because "one or two other schools were integrated." Mrs. Dan Collier echoed this opinion and asked "what would happen to the labor market should schools close." She answered her own question; "industrial standards would drop." The Rome and Cobb County chambers of commerce also voted for the second option.[53]

The hearing proved to be an unqualified success for those who did not want to see the public education system scuttled by the politics and policies of massive resistance. Testifying to the irreparable harm that losing public education could mean to Georgia, sixty of the day's eighty witnesses preferred the second option. The Reverend Charles Demry stated his "conviction that the crisis we face in our state is more than political; it is moral; for it affects human relations." He continued, "I hate to see this school issue become a political football for those who seek to destroy a living institution, public education, in order to preserve a dying one, segregation. Temperance is one of the words found in our state motto."[54] Other witnesses, however, provided more pragmatic reasoning for choosing the second option. Kanakee Anderson, a teacher and farmer from Polk County, testified that "the way to have the most segregated public education . . . for the longest period of time is to do it locally."[55]

Only five organized groups represented that day preferred the first option: the American Legion of Floyd County, the Polk County Farm Bureau, the Cobb County White Citizens for Segregation, and two labor organizations.

E. K. Grass, of the Rome Central Labor Union, brought the unanimous results of his organization's vote to preserve segregation through resistance. A short time later, James B. Glover took the stand and presented a petition by employees of his machine works that voiced the same opinion. Labor's allegiance to this stand would become the rule at the hearings.[56]

Many people who testified before the commission called on God to support their position or help them in their struggle. One of the most fascinating results of this testimony was the disparate view of God's intentions. Near the end of the day's hearing, a Cobb County minister, W. F. Abernathy, told the crowd that "God is a segregated God. . . . He separated people yonder in days past, and he still wants it to remain that way. I love the colored fellow—I certainly do—but I love him in the place that God gave him."[57] A few minutes later a black building contractor from Bartow County, Henry E. Canty, responded, "fondly do we hope, do we pray, that the mighty scourge of segregation shall speedily pass away. Future generations shall only know by history that this loathsome thing existed, and by the decree of the Supreme Courts of this great nation, has been exculpated."[58]

Another witness reflected white Georgia's refusal to accept the public debate over the school situation. Attorney Rufus B. Jones thought that "there is too much stress; too much fomenting of resentment and emotionalism in this entire subject from unscrupulous people; not only from the state of Georgia, but in the entire United States." He complained that people put "too much stress on a thing that they should shut up about; shouldn't even be printed; shouldn't even be discussed. Leave the question alone," he recommended, "and it will take care of itself eventually."[59] Much to Mr. Jones' chagrin, however, it was too late to stop Georgians from discussing the school issue.

If the hearing at Americus presented the commission with the Black Belt's heartfelt dedication to massive resistance and the meeting at Washington showed them the serious division between urban and rural Georgia on the school question, the hearing at Cartersville demonstrated a genuine split in Georgian's beliefs on the sanctity of segregation through resistance at the state's fall line. The disparate feelings between industrial ownership and management and its employees was also a major factor in North Georgia. These divisions continued to unfold as Georgians came to realize exactly what the Sibley Commission hearings represented.

LaGrange

The hearing on the eleventh of March in the Fourth Congressional District provided John Sibley and the commission an opportunity to clarify and explain some of the precepts and misperceptions that had arisen in the first three meetings. The crowd of seven hundred was sharply divided on the school question, and many times Sibley was driven to define and interpret the problems facing Georgia. He fully realized now that the pupil placement plan, while sure to be an effective deterrent to integration once in place, was extremely unattractive to white Georgians, who found any breach in segregation unacceptable. When explaining the two choices to potential witnesses, Sibley emphasized the right of each community to decide for itself under a local option plan. He also made sure that everyone understood that under current state law, if one school in Georgia was forced to desegregate, there existed the possibility that every school system would close. Once again he explained the difference in his questioning of black witnesses. And in one exchange, Sibley tried anew to separate the school question from segregation; despite all the efforts of the commission and open school advocates, most Georgians saw them as an indivisible issue.

John Duncan opened the meeting (snow had prevented Sibley from arriving on time) and read the official statement. Wearing a tweed hunting cap pulled low over his face and ears, Sibley entered while the vice chairman was reading and took his seat atop the rostrum of the Troup County courtroom. Before addressing the first witness, Edward Gore, head of the LaGrange Board of Education, Sibley elaborated on the flexibility of the second option. He detailed how local option would work, reminding the audience that unless a lawsuit were filed, local school systems would be unaffected and if suit were brought, then every community would have the choice of converting to a private school system or implementing a pupil placement plan. He stressed North Carolina's and Alabama's success using this plan to prevent any large-scale desegregation. After Sibley's aside, Gore explained his organization's preference for the idea, because "under local option, LaGrange would not be affected unless the court ordered LaGrange schools integrated."[60]

LaGrange witnesses demonstrated for the first time a significant understanding and appreciation of the local option plan. Vocal support for the idea reflected the fact that the commission experienced some success in separating segregation and resistance. The superintendent of the Troup County schools did not feel it was fair that another section of Georgia could jeopardize his local schools. And one Clayton County witness opted for the second choice because he did not believe that black parents in his county would bring suit. Previous arguments for the commission's second option had centered on the potential loss of education, but these witnesses emphasized each community's right to choose, based largely on the belief that litigation would not emerge in their district, a subtle but very important difference.[61]

Early in the hearing Sibley explained once again why he presented different questions for black witnesses.

> Their situation is that some of the colored people have brought suit to place colored children in white schools. That is being resisted by the white people. It seems to me that it would be a misplaced statement to ask our colored friends that if some of their own children were placed in a white school at the insistence of some of their own people, would they desire to close the school? I think that would be a question that would be beside the mark. . . . So the question that I am asking them, and asking them to speak their minds, and speak their hearts—because their children are wrapped up in this very serious and grave question—I am asking them say, and say in all honesty: would you rather have your schools with your teachers, or had you rather have mixed schools? Now that is the fairest question I can ask them.

He added that if a black witness wished only to answer one of the two main options, he would be glad to honor that request.[62]

The unexpected reaction of some black witnesses to the Sibley Commission questions surely surprised John Sibley, and could have proved disastrous to the hearings. The chairman based a large part of the commission strategy around the testimony of black witnesses to demonstrate that they were satisfied with segregated schools, thus placating local whites' fears of integration or agitation for integration. More importantly, however, Sibley believed that blacks were content, otherwise why would he permit them to testify, when that could jeopardize his goal of changing state law? This unrealistic belief in the tenets of white paternalism shadowed the chairman's expectations of the hearings. That he was able to adjust his strategy during the commission's schedule demonstrates the quick and sharp thinking that made him an excellent attorney and banker. Sibley recognized that black witnesses in many parts of rural Georgia supported segregation, for a myriad of reasons (pride in new schools, fear of losing black education, among others) and not solely due to the influence of intimidation, as black leaders argued, or his original misguided belief in black contentment. Therefore Sibley continued to pursue his first line of questioning. For the chairman, gaining support for local option from rural whites was worth the risk of exposing potential black discontent. However, as the hearings revealed, Sibley tried to dissuade black witnesses away from two options designed for white witnesses and portrayed those blacks who preferred integration as malcontents and not representative of Georgia's larger African American community.[63]

The LaGrange hearing appeared to be another success for open school advocates when they presented a very strong contingent in the morning session; seventeen of the first twenty-three witnesses preferred the second choice. But the afternoon session went the opposite direction. Witnesses from the fourth district's rural counties expressed an intense aversion to any change in state law that would allow for any type of integration. John Norman, a traveling salesman from West Point, Georgia, tried to explain that most white Georgians saw only two choices, segregation or integration. Sibley interrupted and told Norman, "No; that is not the question. The question is this: I think that you can say fairly that people who wanted the [second] option—they want segregation but they are willing—I want to get this clear, as far as we can determine—that they are of the opinion that maybe changing our system would save the public schools, or at least most of them, without having integration. It is not a question of segregation or integration." He continued, "It's a question of whether or not you can save your public schools without having general integration. . . . And I say that because that is an issue [the belief that segregation or integration were the only two options] that seems to be false issue, and one which sort of arrays the cities against the counties."[64]

Many believed, however, that abandoning education would be less harmful than any potential integration. C. B. Nichols averred, "Private schools would start bad and get better by the month. Total integration would start not so bad and get worse forever."[65] Mrs. W. L. Martin agreed, but pointed to the sacrifices that private schools would entail. "And if we want to educate our children, we can do it . . . we may have to give up having a new car every year, or a new washing machine every time a new model comes out, but we can certainly do it."[66] Another man, Cecil Perkerson, was willing to allow his two granddaughters to "grow up ignorant" rather than permit integration.[67]

The witnesses at LaGrange bitterly divided over the questions. Donald Jenkins, a transplanted Northerner, argued that if Georgia adopted a pupil placement law (which he called a "method of surrendering"), all the "Yankees" in the state would move back North.[68] W. B. Davis, while agreeing that integration was "evil," believed that it was not "nearly the evil that no schools at all would be."[69] But it was not only at the hearings that Georgians discussed the school question. Ardnesa Copeland said "that I don't think you meet very often unless you discuss something about schools. It's so prevalent." She continued, "It is in the air everywhere [and] just seems to float around you."[70]

The meeting ended with forty-seven people testifying that they would prefer to change state law and forty-one people in favor of continued resistance.[71] Once again representatives of groups presented the committee with impressive results of polls and petitions favoring the second option. But resistance supporters caught on to the strength of organizational representation and held their own meetings to present the results to the committee. While PTAs and ministerial associations continued to send their envoys to the meetings, farm bureaus, white supremacy groups, Lions Clubs, Rotarians, veterans organizations, and other male-dominated, rural, sociopolitical associations dispatched their own witnesses in an effort to offset the powerful impact of the open school advocates' representation at the Sibley Commission hearings.

Douglas

John Sibley departed from his normal opening statement at the Douglas hearing to "talk informally about some of the things that . . . we should emphasize and that will maybe clarify and elucidate some of the important features of our hearings." He told the more than seven hundred gathered at the Douglas High School gymnasium that most communities in Georgia, if they agreed to a system of voluntary segregation and utilized the ideas of the commission's second option, would not have to integrate their schools. Sibley strongly hinted that the marked diversity of opinion in Georgia would influence the commission's recommendation. He believed it would be best for each community to work out its problems and that if black and white communities "prefer their own schools we don't have a substantial issue and the matter can work itself out without letting the law take charge of our schools. . . . The white people and the colored people can settle this question outside the law if they want to settle it."[72] This endorsement of the validity and logic of the local option plan gave the public its first look into the commission's eventual inclinations.

The racial makeup of the Eighth Congressional District precluded any preconceived ideas about what the commission could expect in the testimony at Douglas. This extreme southeastern part of Georgia fell below the southern boundary of the Black Belt. No county had more black residents than white, and Berrien, Bacon, and Brantley counties had black populations of less than 15 percent (these were the only three counties below the fall line with these numbers). The economy of the region was largely based on tobacco and timber. There were only two large towns in the district, Valdosta in Lowndes County and Brunswick in Glynn County.

It was at Douglas, however, that those dedicated to the preservation of absolute segregation began to make an organized effort to ensure they would be heard by the rest of the state. If everyone who had registered with the commission at both Washington and LaGrange had actually testified, the public's perception of the state reaction would have been much different. In one sense, the figures presented in the press were an inaccurate portrayal of the sentiment at the hearings, but the reports correctly represented the testimony given at those hearings, for they reported only what everyone at the hearing saw and heard.[73] Realizing this fact, resisters led entire county delegations to the stand to voice their opinion. And many organizations sent representatives to reveal their own polls' often unanimous support of defiance. As one man explained to Sibley, "These little clubs [representing a preference for the second option] . . . they're piling up on you." He said that emphasis on the testimony of groups might conceal the real sentiment of Georgia behind the intent and purposes of the organizations represented at the hearings.[74]

In large part due to the insistence of segregationists to speak for the record, the commission heard 148 witnesses in only five hours, the largest number to date. Most witnesses simply stated their preference and left the stand with little or no explanation for their decision. Local option sentiment was strong in the morning but only because the counties favoring segregation were not heard first. Indeed, the first witness to express a desire to close the schools, rather than integrate anywhere in the state, drew a rousing ovation from the crowd. Sibley expressed his indignant disapproval. "I see that the Chairman doesn't have very much weight with his audience this morning, because I asked that we not have any demonstrations. I think you must realize," he continued, "the importance of these meetings . . . unless people respect us, we can't go ahead." [75]

Two powerful organizations of middle- and lower-class rural whites, farm bureaus and labor unions, continued to offer the strongest support of resistance, but at Douglas they were joined by many county commissions, the Ku Klux Klan, and Citizens' Councils. As the threat of integration escalated, the Citizens' Councils made inroads into many Georgia communities. Unlike Roy Harris's States' Rights Council, they were only loosely affiliated with each other or any national organization and had only limited impact outside isolated communities. The Lowndes County delegation, led by John Langdale, the patriarch of an old, prominent, and very powerful family in Valdosta, insisted on approaching the podium to record an "amen" to continued resistance. Indeed, Langdale desired that his county present a united front for the first option, going so far as to use his position in the county PTA to prevent representatives from the Sallas-Mahone Elementary School from appearing before the commission to reveal the results of a poll that showed a preference for open schools. [76]

Sibley's attempts to separate the school question from segregation appeared to be a complete failure. Witness after witness, when asked his or her preference, stated simply "segregation." Those witnesses dedicated to the perpetuation of Georgia's social structure saw the school issue as a "battlefield." One man testified to his belief that "Atlanta is only the beginning and once they are in Atlanta, they will be in every school—In fact the schools are only the beginning." [77]

Advocates for resistance posted a large majority in the voting at Douglas, but the constant debate, detailed clarification of the school issue, and obvious diversity of opinion slowly eroded the public's staunch support of and brazen confidence in massive resistance. As longtime Georgia politician Downing Musgrove, who gave a rousing endorsement for massive resistance at the Douglas hearing, noted, the commission at "least convince[d] some people of the futility [of resistance]. I know at the Douglas meeting, you could tell when he [an audience member] walked out of the door, that there were some different attitudes than there were when he went in, everybody was just going to say, 'now boy I'm going to give my speech; and we're going to stop this thing dead in its tracks.'" The next day, Musgrove believed, "the people were saying 'Well, you know, maybe we're not as die-hard as we were or maybe I'm not as cocky as I was about this thing.'" The huge buildup of excitement that accompanied each region's hearing was of course followed by decline in the furor over schools, coupled with a more serious reflection on the issue and the realistic options the hearings presented. It was, as North Georgia editor Sylvan Meyer put it, "mind changing time all over Georgia."[78]

The final tally of witnesses revealed a split of eighty-three in favor of option one and sixty-five in favor of option two. This division of attitudes was dramatically presented at Douglas when weather conditions forced a woman to give two conflicting statements to the commission. Mrs. J. Rod Davis was called upon to read a resolution from the Douglas Women's Club supporting local option and also report the official support of unqualified resistance by the local chapter of the United Daughters of the Confederacy.[79]

The Douglas hearing emphasized the growing stature of the Sibley Commission as Georgians realized that the commission presented a new method to address social questions. Those individuals dedicated to both open schools and undisputed segregation scrambled to testify. Sibley began to hint more openly that the only way to get a fair resolution for all the state was through either a local option plan or a statewide vote on the issue. But he also continued to express his belief that only by adopting proven legal techniques to preserve segregation could the state avoid massive social disruption. He believed that segregation could survive and sacrificing public education was wasteful and pointless. Many agreed. Mrs. Neil Yeoman claimed "segregation without education would be damnation." And a young college student, Mary George Dean, lamented on the Douglas witness stand, "It's almost broken my heart today to hear people who are . . . really supposed to care, not care about closing the schools. . . . I don't like all this kick down about the young people going to the dogs and losing all their ideals because it looks like the young people have about as many ideals left about public free education and the real purpose of democracy. A lot more of those ideals than the adults do."[80]

Political leaders and local segregationists reacted to the split in Georgia opinion with their time-proven methods of persuasion—intimidation and political bombast. Vandiver's first speech of 1960 was a rousing "State of the State" address to the General Assembly. He told the legislators,

We are going to resist—and—We are going to resist again and again and again. We will exhaust every legal means and remedy available to us. . . . For the children of Georgia! For our heritage! For our fathers! . . . Future historians will record the actions of this Legislature and this administration. Let it be written that we were men of courage. Let it be written that we were men of faith. Let it be said, yes let it be written, let it ring out through the annals of time that we stood solidly on the rock of that hollowed parchment—the Constitution of the United States. . . . Let it be recorded down through ages that the sovereign State of Georgia has been, is and will forever remain the good land—free from tyranny—a repository of justice—the palladium of liberty.[81]

The following month, while speaking to the States' Rights Council of Georgia, Vandiver promised the crowd of two thousand that he would not allow "them [to] run the flag of surrender over our Capitol city." [82]

The commission hearings set off a wave of posturing among state politicians, including the revival of Bill Bodenhamer's career; he once again accused his 1958 gubernatorial rival of being weak on segregation. He claimed the Sibley Commission represented Vandiver's vacillation on the segregation question and was nothing more than a group of emissaries dispatched by "King Ernie" to raise "doubts in the minds of honest people and [confuse] the real issue confronting us." One high-ranking official in the General Assembly stated that he did not believe that any special session of the legislature would be called to enact an amendment overturning mandatory school closing laws. Basing his claim on the outpouring of segregationist sentiment from rural counties at the Sibley Commission hearings, the assemblyman felt that this organized resurgence was a direct response to the early strength of open school advocates, increasing black protests, and the surprising number of black witnesses at the commission hearings who advocated integration. Indeed, this opinion also reflects the growing dissatisfaction by members of the assembly regarding the commission's activities and conclusions. Sibley asked that legislators refrain from speaking at his panel's meetings, claiming that it would be a conflict of interest, and emphasized this request more and more frequently as the hearings wore on (all the legislators who ignored Sibley's plea questioned the commission's simplification of the questions involved). Prominent members of the assembly attended the last few meetings; and, although most did not testify, their presence could not help but have been felt.

Governor Vandiver, after distancing himself from the commission's creation, would give no opinion on the hearing results or on the commission itself.[83]

Other state political leaders, however, lashed out at the Sibley Commission. Roy Harris accused the panel of spreading "confusion" and warned anyone who would listen that if Atlanta desegregated its schools, "the NAACP, backed up by the federal government and all the money in the world [will] move in against your little county . . . [and] ram race-mixing down your throats." Harris pointed to the "loaded" choices offered by the Sibley Commission in its second option and told readers of the *Augusta Courier*, "if it's race mixing you want, then take your choice between these plans." Marvin Griffin lambasted local option and told his readers that it only meant that "the folks in Atlanta [were] to be free to integrate schools without restraint from the remainder of Georgia."[84]

That March, county commissioners from all over the state met in Augusta and voted to uphold segregation laws. Roy Harris, speaking for the group, again accused the Sibley Commission of muddling the issue and referred to Sibley as "confused." He led an effort by segregationist groups to ensure that an alternative to the open schools position would be heard at the final few meetings. Leaders of local States' Rights and Citizens' Councils as well as representatives of various Ku Klux Klan factions began to appear at the meetings with increasing frequency. Some members of these groups also put pressure on potential commission witnesses, holding rallies at hearing sites the night before a scheduled meeting and many times attempting to coerce PTA organizations either to stay home or to state a preference for segregation. The Ku Klux Klan also held a massive statewide cross burning one Saturday night in March. On the seventeenth of that month, the Metropolitan Association for Segregated Education (MASE) sent a form letter to supporters urging them to overwhelm the Sibley Commission with brief letters expressing their preference for resistance.[85]

Civil Rights

The activities of the Sibley Commission were not the only impetus for the surge toward a more reactionary response from whites. In March of 1960 the black student sit-in movement came to Georgia. This new weapon of protest originated when four black freshmen from North Carolina Agricultural and

Technical College refused to give up their seats in a downtown Greensboro lunch counter. The students demanded that they be served, refusing to cater to the southern custom of excluding blacks from lunch counters. The four students and several of their friends returned the next day to continue their protest. The sit-in movement swept through the South and revealed a heretofore unknown level of dissatisfaction with the Jim Crow system among southern African Americans. The struggles to eliminate separate schools and buses in the South had been attributed by many whites to northern radicals and the influence of the NAACP. Sit-ins, however, could not be explained with the time-honored white supremacist argument that black southerners were satisfied with their position. In February, Ernest Vandiver released a statement claiming he would use the state's full resources to prevent the protests from spreading to Georgia.[86]

This threat did not stop two Morehouse College students, Lonnie King and Julian Bond, from organizing a huge sit-in campaign at downtown Atlanta lunch counters, including the city hall cafeteria, beginning on March 15. The students prefaced their protest by taking out a full-page advertisement in the March 9 Sunday edition of the *Atlanta Journal and Constitution*, protesting separate facilities for blacks and whites in the South. Their action infuriated not only segregationists but also the conservative black leadership of Atlanta. This older generation had cooperated with the white business establishment for many years and had gained numerous concessions, but the students were not under their influence. Vandiver responded to the advertisement and the sit-ins with vehemence, vowing to pass a law prohibiting such actions and claiming that the protest and the newspaper ad were the work of communists "calculated to breed dissatisfaction, discontent, discord and evil."[87]

Black protest spread throughout the state during March 1960. The same week as the Atlanta sit-ins, the Chatham County NAACP leadership called for a boycott of downtown Savannah department stores. The Savannah Movement began when a group of high school students held a sit-in at the lunch counters of eight downtown stores. Three students were arrested that day and twenty-three more over the next few weeks. The NAACP, led by W. W. Law, boycotted the stores that refused to desegregate, and on March 26 began to picket Levy's, a popular department store. This boycott lasted for the next fifteen months. Students held a sit-in at the bus terminal waiting room in Albany, and in Augusta students from Paine College organized a picketing campaign when President Eisenhower came to the city to play golf at the Augusta National Golf Club.[88]

These protests called even more attention to the possibility of a volatile change in Georgia's social structure and the commission hearings reflected the people's reaction to this potential transformation. The results of the first five hearings had enabled Sibley to hint with greater clarity at his intention of supporting a local option plan. But this support met with a fierce determination from segregationists responding to both the black protests and the surprising advocacy of integration among the black witnesses at the hearings.

Sandersville

The Sandersville hearing took place in the middle of a long week for Sibley Commission members who had been to Douglas on Monday and would have to get up early to drive to the hearing in Sylvania the next day. The members of the committee usually drove in groups of two or three to the meetings and tried to stay the night before and after a hearing in a local hotel. The inclement weather and ice storms that plagued the state that March made travel between sites very difficult. After a hearing, the men went to dinner, "had a drink or two," and talked about the day's events or the press coverage. They grew close, in spite of different political beliefs and varying opinions on what Sibley was trying to do. Although certain members of the committee disagreed with Sibley and his plan of action, they kept it to themselves once they saw that the chairman kept the meetings under control and allowed everyone an opportunity to speak his or her mind. They all agreed that "something had to be done."[89]

Although that week's sit-ins took some media attention away from the commission, the students' activities sharply focused hearing testimony. No longer just an exercise in educating the public on the school crisis, the hearings became a means for individuals and groups to express their feelings on the changes taking place in the South. For the first time, Sibley ensured that every member of each county's delegation received an opportunity to place his name and vote on the public record. To save time when confronted by a large delegation that was obviously united in its support (usually for option one), Sibley would have the members stand and speak from the waiting area immediately facing his rostrum. Sandersville testimony revealed the Sixth Congressional District's preference to fight for the status quo; the proponents of option one outnumbered their opposition by a three-to-one margin and posted a majority in twelve of the sixteen counties represented.[90]

Many organizations sent representatives to express a desire to maintain resistance, including, for the first time, large contingents from white church groups. The first witness of the day, Emory C. Gilbert, representing the Washington County Ministerial Association, read a statement that claimed "the present system is best for the Southland. . . . We deplore the work of agitators which have stirred up our people . . . [and] any form of token integration sooner or later will result in total integration. We say abolish the public schools rather than accept any degree of integration." Throughout the day representatives of other church groups, PTAs, Lions Clubs, American Legions, farm bureaus, Rotary Clubs, chambers of commerce, and others, including the mayor of Harrison (W. E. Harrison, who claimed to represent the entire town), all echoed this sentiment.[91]

This organized response, as well as the testimony of many political officials from Washington County, was the work of former legislator and head of the county's Veterans Service, Harvey Roughton. He spent the days before the hearing preparing resolutions for various groups planning to appear before the commission, including the one given by Emory C. Gilbert. An important member of the Georgia General Assembly took the stand late in the morning and verbally sparred with Sibley over the commission's potential scenario of continued resistance and Sibley's disparaging remarks toward a conversion to private schools. Denmark Groover, a former floor leader in the assembly for Marvin Griffin, believed "that we should stand upon the present laws." He questioned Sibley on the logic of the argument that if one school integrated all of the public schools would have to be closed. Pointing to the fact that the decision in *James v. Almond* had never been appealed to the Supreme Court, Groover argued that Sibley's school closing scenario was not the only possible option of continued resistance. Sibley quickly dismissed Groover and prefaced every remaining meeting by reiterating his objection to the appearance of members of the assembly before the commission. Another witness questioned the governor's fealty to resistance. W. C. Brinson, when asked his choice, said he "thought when we elected Vandiver, I voted for it then. He promised in Wrightsville, Georgia, that he'd keep the schools closed if they attempted to desegregate them, and I thought I took a vote then, but it seems that we haven't."[92]

The biggest news at the hearing was not the renewed efforts of resisters but an almost direct endorsement of local option by John Sibley to open the hearing. He explained the North Carolina plan of local option and pupil placement in detail and asserted that the state had been "wise" in developing its strategy to limit the impacts of desegregation. In the weeks before the Sibley Commission began its hearings, Sibley sent Harmon Caldwell and Battle Hall to the Tarheel State to examine and report on the success of the North Carolina plan. Caldwell recounted that only five school districts in the entire state experienced any degree of integration. The number of black students in white schools never exceeded ten or twelve, Caldwell added, and the "number of Negro students attending schools for white students is less now than it was in 1956 when the plan first became effective." Sibley related this information to the crowd gathered at the old red brick courthouse in Sandersville and explained further that federal courts approved the plan. The marked differences in racial population percentages throughout Georgia, Sibley remarked, made a local option plan the most feasible strategy for the state. He pointed out that "in Hancock County, eighty-one percent of the pupils are colored; only five hundred-and-some-odd whites. You could run private schools there if you wanted to without any trouble, but you take over in Bibb County, you see a much more difficult situation." This comment was yet another indication of what the commission might recommend to the General Assembly in its report.[93]

Many present agreed with Sibley's assessment, including large delegations from Bibb and Baldwin (Sibley's home county) counties, the only two counties in the sixth district that had a sizable city or town, once again demonstrating the urban-rural split in the testimony. As one witness observed, "it seems that the majority who have voted for number two live where the streetcars run. Those who have voted for one, most of them live in the country." The Macon chapter of HOPE, the Bibb County League of Women Voters, and the Macon Civic Women's club all voted for option two. Dr. Willis B. Glover testified that he was "not the kind of doctor that does anybody any good. I am a historian." He pleaded for local option because "government which is closest to the people governed is . . . the best. It is when we fail to give the right of self government to all people that we make way for more distance and higher government to come in."[94]

Another witness from Bibb County, John McAffee of the McAffee Candy Company, reiterated the concerns of many business owners. "I think Georgia economically would have to—would suffer a great deal if we go to the extent of closing our schools." And a woman from Jones County, although testifying for local option, found a silver lining in the first choice: "The only possible good that [could] come out of closing the schools is, thank goodness, no more PTA meetings."[95]

John Sibley encouraged comments similar to that of the woman who had grown tired of PTA meetings to provide levity and laughter and offer relief from the tension of the meetings. He treated all witnesses with respect and encouraged them to speak their hearts on the subject but only within the narrowly constructed parameters that the commission's two options presented. He allowed those testifying on behalf of organizations slightly more liberty on the stand to read short statements, but only if they were pertinent to the discussion. The seventy-one-year-old Sibley sat patiently for hour after hour, giving each witness his undivided attention. His focus allowed him to recognize quickly an opportunity to break the tension in a room. At one hearing Sibley inquired from a witness how he might join a "Chittlin Eaters Club." On many other occasions Sibley engaged in spirited banter with witnesses near his age on the subject of grandchildren and lightheartedly refused to allow any grandparent to brag on the number of their grandchildren unless the witness had more than the chairman's eleven.[96]

Sylvania

The day after the Sandersville meeting, the Committee on Schools traveled to Sylvania, Georgia, to host the First Congressional District's hearing. The district extended from the Atlantic coast north to Burke County and west to Wheeler County. Its economy was diverse. The coastal areas engaged in shrimping and shipping, and there was some industry in Savannah, the state's second largest city, but the primary occupation in the area was farming. There were only five counties where blacks outnumbered whites, but the average black population in the district was 40 percent. Savannah's NAACP boasted one of the strongest chapters in the state and, at the time of the Sylvania hearing, was in the first days of a boycott of Savannah's downtown stores. The coastal counties of Long, McIntosh, and Bryan all had much higher than usual black voter registration and were actually a factor in local elections, and Liberty County was the only county in the South where black voter registration outnumbered white.[97]

Sibley opened the meeting with his usual statement and beseeched the audience to avoid demonstrating signs of approbation or disapproval. "We are trying to conduct these meetings orderly—we are trying to conduct them in the atmosphere of calmness—We are trying to conduct them in an atmosphere of friendship and goodwill—and, we are trying to conduct them as fair-minded people recognizing that everybody has a right to their opinions and a right to express it." After reading the statement, Sibley praised the pupil-placement plan as practiced in Mississippi and pointed out that there had been no attempts to desegregate any of that state's public schools. He then recognized Speaker of the Georgia House George L. Smith (who helped create the commission) and thanked him for attending. Sibley finished his opening remarks by allowing the crowd of eight hundred to applaud the mayor of Sylvania for turning off the parking meters for the day.[98]

Segregationists again dominated the testimony; only this time, proponents of massive resistance were well-behaved and moved quietly and expeditiously to the stand to state their preference. Their slogan was "one hundred percent," and scores of witnesses indicated that figure when describing the firmness of their ideals, the vote of their organization, or the amount of segregation they demanded in Georgia's schools. Open school advocates, on the other hand, tried to explain their beliefs in longer diatribes, or what Sibley and the press called "speeches." The development of organized support for massive resistance peaked at the Screven County courthouse. For the first time, groups presenting a preference for option one outnumbered those for continuing public education. Although resisters had outnumbered open school advocates in total testimony several times during the course of the hearings, this hearing marked the first time that segregationist groups were better represented than were option two supporters. Indeed, a great many of those voicing a preference for local option and pupil placement at Sylvania were speaking only for themselves or their families, much like the resister testimony at previous hearings. The groups for option one were, however, the usual white, rural, male-dominated socioeconomic organizations or political groups—farm bureaus, Rotarians, chambers of commerce, city councils, grand juries, bar associations, veterans groups, Lions Clubs, and local boards of education. Also coming out in favor of school closings were some rural church and school groups, and of course, an increasing number of representatives from county Citizens' and States' Rights Councils and the Ku Klux Klan.

These witnesses favoring complete segregation over public education utilized the sheer force of their numbers to make their point. Individuals rarely attempted to explain their reasoning; instead they came to the stand and expressed their vote one right after another with very few dissenting opinions dividing them. The morning session of the hearing was eerily efficient as eighty-six witnesses took the stand in just two hours. There was virtually no applause. Local organizations dedicated to white supremacy were well represented. Two different counties sent local representatives of their Citizens' Councils to testify. And the Chatham County States' Rights Council's president, Mrs. William Roberts, gave a short statement claiming that Georgia would not have to integrate its schools because the *Brown* decision was illegal and it was the state's duty to fight the decision. The commission heard from mainly rural farm counties with large black populations that morning; they included Screven, Bulloch, Jenkins, Treutlen, Effingham, Tattnall, and Emanuel. The number of witnesses can be put into perspective by comparing the morning session at Sylvania with the first hearing, at Americus, where only fifty-seven people testified all day. The deft, quiet morning testimony deviated from the chronic public displays of approval or disapproval that had characterized some of the previous hearings.[99]

The commission heard from a record total of 214 people that day, and 150 expressed their desire to maintain segregation. Most repeated the idea expressed by Judge Henry Howard, representing the Screven County Bar Association. "We prefer to hold on to segregated schools, but if we lose them, we'll make our own arrangements. There has been no agitation among the colored people or the white people over here for integration. We don't have a race problem."[100]

Georgia's political leaders continued to express an intense interest in the Sibley Commission hearings; in addition to Speaker George L. Smith, one member of State Board of Education, Paul Stone, drove down from Atlanta that morning to give a personal endorsement for option one. Hugh Gillis, a former state senator, testified in defense of resistance, representing the opinions of Soperton's City Council, Lions Club, the town's newspaper, the pastor of the Baptist church, Professional Women's Club, the county sheriff, the school superintendent, and the judge of the superior court. And Aubrey Womack, representing the Republican Party of Emanuel County, also voted for option one, to which John Greer remarked "you'd better not let Mr. Nixon hear about that."[101]

The hearing at Sylvania, more than any other, clearly demonstrated the urban-rural split in Georgia over the school issue. Every county represented at the hearing, with the exception of Chatham (where Savannah was located), had a majority of witnesses who preferred to abandon state-supported schools rather than confront desegregation. This division was not limited to the testimony of white segregationists and school patrons but extended to the testimony of black witnesses. The Sylvania hearing felt the strong presence of Savannah's NAACP chapter; the Chatham County black delegation unanimously expressed its preference for integration. This statement directly conflicted with black witnesses from other parts of the district who, for many reasons, expressed a desire for continued segregation.

Despite Sibley's hope that most of these witnesses would state a preference for segregated schools, African Americans free to express their feelings without the restraint of the commission's two basic options offered a far greater variety of opinions than white witnesses. The commission heard from teachers, ministers, farmers, and others who expressed a desire to continue segregation. Others called only for obeying the law and complying with federal directives. Still others demanded immediate integration and compliance with the Supreme Court's decision. Some refused to answer any question other than the choices Sibley offered white witnesses. And others just rambled on until Sibley forced them to answer a question, any question, at which time they would give no public comment.

There were, of course, many reasons for the diversity of black testimony at the hearings. The reasons to support an end to segregation in the public schools are well documented. Many of those testifying fought for many years prior to and after the Sibley Commission hearings for an end to racial injustice. An opportunity to voice their dissatisfaction with state-supported institutions of white supremacy certainly influenced some witnesses' testimony. As a man once explained to Robert Penn Warren, "My boy is happy in the Negro school where he goes. I don't want him to go to the white school and sit by your boy's side. But I'd die for his right to go." Less obvious than arguments for change, however, are the reasons that many black witnesses supported continued segregation.[102]

The *Brown* decision, while a moral and legal victory for southern African Americans, also brought with it enormous increases in state funding of black public schools to preempt any attempts at desegregation. For the first time, many schools for black children were equal or superior to area white schools. Georgia African Americans took pride not only in these new schools but also in the education that black teachers provided their students. A few black leaders continued to promote the idea of equal schools, pointing to the self-reliance and community support of black education. A few witnesses argued for a slow change to integrated education until both school systems were indeed equal. Of course intimidation or a fear of economic or physical reprisal influenced some testimony. More important, however, was the belief that segregated schools were better than no schools, and the looming possibility of a conversion to private education threatened public education for black children. While many white witnesses certainly worried about losing public schools, this fear was compounded in black communities; for if the state adopted a private school plan, black education, tenuous at best before *Brown*, would be the first major casualty of a conversion in the school system.[103]

Other witnesses, however, expressed concerns for the future of black children's education if the public schools desegregated. A deep-rooted apprehension of the unknown raised obvious questions. How would black students be treated in white schools? Where would black teachers, bus drivers, and administrators fit into a new integrated school system? How much community control over education would remain? These fears were not new; a 1956 poll of southern African Americans revealed that only 53 percent approved of the *Brown* decision. All people share an anxiety over rapid or sudden change, and in its midst it becomes easier to defend the status quo; many of the Sibley Commission witnesses—black and white—demonstrated this tension. One cannot simply assume that African Americans testified to their support for segregation solely out of fear of reprisal; such reasoning reduces an entire segment of Georgia's population to a monolithic stereotype with a limited understanding of self-interest. Each individual who approached the stand at the Sibley Commission hearings brought his or her own unique situation and combination of reasons for the testimony given. This public glimpse into the hearts and minds of southerners, black and white, during this time of social upheaval makes the Sibley Commission hearings unique.[104]

Just as the public black support for integration caused concern among resistance leaders, black testimony for segregation raised complaints from the state's African American leadership. These men and women were concerned about whom the commission allowed to testify. Shortly after the Americus hearing, it was reported that black schoolteachers and superintendents were

Testimony before the Sibley Commission
by Congressional District in Georgia, 1960

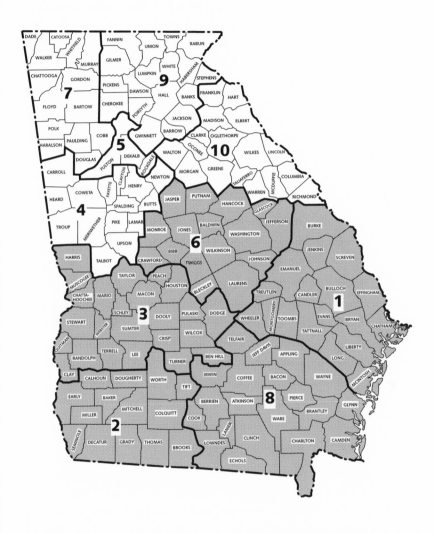

☐ Majority of witnesses preferred
measures other than eliminating
public education to preserve
segregation.

▨ Majority of witnesses preferred
to close the public schools
rather than brook any degree
of integration.

being coerced by their white employers to give testimony in preference of segregation. J. O. Thomas, head of the Georgia Conference on Educational Opportunities, wrote to Sibley and asked him to forswear using testimony from black school officials.[105] Two days later the group reiterated this complaint to Homer Rankin and also questioned the commission's use of different questions for black witnesses and the absence of any large cities (save Atlanta) on the hearing schedule.[106]

Many of the concerns of African Americans were expressed by W. W. Law of the Chatham County NAACP, who had temporarily interrupted his group's boycott in Savannah to lead a delegation to the meeting in Sylvania. The fourteen members of that group came down from the courthouse's segregated balcony en masse and stood in front of the podium waiting for their chance to be heard. Law told Sibley:

> I speak not only for the thousands of colored members [of the NAACP] of Georgia, but for the thousands . . . of Negros and whites who are victims of intimidation. These men and women are silent because they dare not say what is really and truly in their hearts. I even speak for the Negro teachers who were brought before this committee and required to answer questions as to their positions in regard to the maintenance of segregation as the best thing for public schools, in the presence of their white superiors and superintendents who insist [on] segregation."

He then asked Sibley, "What other position do you expect these Negro teachers to take?" [107] Law demanded immediate integration "to guarantee the same educational opportunities for white and negro youths." As Law spoke, murmurs rose and then outright cries of indignation erupted in the courtroom. Sibley squared off with Law over whether the NAACP had held meetings with potential black witnesses to guide them in their testimony. Law denied the accusation. Sibley then asked whether or not Law spoke for many in his delegation (most black witnesses that day had expressed a desire to continue segregation). Sibley instructed Law to take a seat, telling him that he himself would poll the Chatham County delegation. The next witness, Hosea Williams, representing the Morris Brown Alumni Association and the Butler Presbyterian Church as well as the NAACP, told Sibley that his groups "too take the position that the poor thing about the entire hearings—the citizens of Georgia were not given. . . ." Sibley cut him off in mid-sentence and asked him "What do you want?" To which Williams replied, "I want integration." The twelve remaining members of the delegation followed Law and Williams, all but two claiming that nothing less than immediate integration would be satisfactory.[108]

The smooth, quiet morning session gave way to an emotion-filled afternoon. The audience booed Savannah's NAACP members and open school advocates. Sibley repeatedly called for order. He admonished the crowd for allowing the meeting to become sidetracked from its purpose and told them it was unlike any other hearing. "We have had a little disorder [at other meetings], but we haven't had this booing and this attitude that doesn't give a witness the serious thoughts he is entitled to. Now let's not destroy the spirit of this meeting." The situation improved somewhat as the other members of the Chatham County delegation took the stand and attempted to give heartfelt reasoning for their preference for local option. Master Pilot Captain Frank Spencer of the Savannah Bar Pilots Association, a white man whose efforts to improve the status of Savannah's black community had led to a school being named for him, warned the gathering that unless something were done to preserve public education, "our children will be retarded and the state's economic life will be scuttled." Other Chatham County organizations devoted to public schools came forward, including HOPE, the Savannah chapter of the League of Women Voters, B'nai B'rith, the local American Association of University Women, and several ministerial and PTA groups. But Chatham was the only county to show sizable support for the second commission option.[109]

The urban-rural split in voting patterns that developed at the Washington hearing reached its apex at Sylvania. And the organized resistance forces, seemingly caught off guard by the early support for overturning state laws to allow for open schools, now seemed to have most of the momentum. The schedule of hearings provides one reason for the increase in support for continued resistance. After the opening session in Americus, where sentiment for the first option was strong, the group moved north and held its next three meetings in areas where the local option plan met with a more favorable response. When South Georgia (with higher black population percentages) hosted the next four hearings, the region strongly endorsed defiance.

Moultrie

The political and organizational supporters of massive resistance presented another overwhelming show of strength at the Committee on Schools hearing on March 21. All fourteen counties in the Second Congressional District registered a majority of witnesses for option one. Many of the more important political leaders of Georgia came to the meeting and directly influenced the testimony given before the commission. The sometimes unruly crowd, estimated at well over one thousand, packed the tiny Moultrie High School gymnasium (the size of the crowd forced a move from the county courthouse). The panel heard from more than two hundred and fifty witnesses, and all but forty-five preferred resistance.[110]

Some Georgia political leaders orchestrated their county delegation's testimony. Ernest Vandiver's floor leaders in the House and Senate, Frank Twitty and Robert Culpepper, watched as their home county of Mitchell expressed a unanimous preference for the first option. George Busbee of Dougherty County, the sponsor of the bill that created the Sibley Commission, attended and told the press that the local option plan was "hogwash" and a "diversionary tactic." James Gray, State Democratic Chairman, who originally approached George Busbee with the bill, was also there. Leading the Decatur County delegation was representative Cheney Griffin, brother of the former governor. Marvin and Cheney, through their newspaper, the *Bainbridge Post-Searchlight,* even organized a motorcade to the meeting that left Bainbridge at 8:30 that morning. This political presence in the second district should not be surprising; all its representatives in the General Assembly had signed a manifesto the previous month pledging to maintain state laws.[111]

Mitchell County representative Tom Palmer, appearing before the commission on behalf of the county chamber of commerce, expressed the feelings and trepidations of many in state politics. Upon reaching the stand he asked Sibley whether or not the "wisdom and actions of this committee [were] considered above reproach." Sibley told him no, and Palmer continued.

> I would like to take this opportunity to question the wisdom of this committee and decry its action in not allowing the good people of this state the opportunity to express before you gentlemen their decision on the choices now afforded them by the laws of this sovereign state! Your much publicized and famous options one and option two mean one thing and one thing only—they say to the people of Georgia—yes, from Rabun Gap to Tybee Light—do you want to integrate or do you want to close our schools! You can never hear from the people unless you revise your questioning. My fellow citizens say "we have been given no choice!" Gentlemen, only a seriously mentally ill person would wish to close our public

schools or deny equal educational facilities to all the children of this state without provocation.

Palmer went on to explain that the choices that the commission offered were not "ample enough for clear decisions." After complaining about the Atlanta media's coverage of the hearings and their "box score" and "batting average" treatment of the hearing results, he claimed that the press and Georgia would ultimately find the commission a "failure." He then pleaded with Sibley to offer the state "an option three. . . . Hold to Georgia law! If overturned, close the schools and open private schools which the people of this state can use to guarantee separate but equal education to every Georgia child." His statement offers another example of the failure of resistance supporters in Georgia to offer any reasonable alternative to the Sibley Commission options and findings. For all of Palmer's grandiloquence and twisted rhetoric, his "option three" was exactly the same as the commission's option one.[112]

Even the black witnesses who spoke at the hearing seemed to prefer segregation. In spite of the eloquence of W. W. Law at the Sylvania hearing the previous week, rural African Americans with brand new schools were leery of jeopardizing much improved educational facilities. Clinton Tally, a Calhoun County school principal, pointed to the disparate amounts of money spent on black and white schools in his county (black schools received 92 percent of the money in the county school budget) and opted for continued segregation.[113]

Most of the day's witnesses who spoke out for local option came on behalf of PTAs or other school groups and church organizations from the larger cities in the district, Tifton, Thomasville, and especially Albany. John Greer had wired the mayor of that city and asked him to encourage participation from "civic clubs, farm organizations, PTAs and other school groups, veterans' groups, women's groups, and business associations." The *Albany Herald* also encouraged its readers to appear but advised them that Georgia's only real choices were segregation and tuition grants. Dougherty County representative Colquitt Odum, after urging his constituents to testify, promised them that he would follow their recommendations.[114]

Many of those from the larger towns and cities who testified valued the logic of the local option plan. Mrs. Paul Keenan asked if it made any sense for the high schools of Moultrie and Albany to "be empty soon, because of the Atlanta school problem." She argued that each community "be allowed to deal with [its] unique conditions"[115] The Reverend T. J. McCullough argued that "states' rights has [always] been a major platform of southern politicians" and believed that "there should be some room for county rights, or even local community rights."[116] Shirley Freeman, a student at Emory University, scoffed at the idea of a private school plan. "You also know that these politicians who tell you that you can have private schools for your children have no plan." She scolded the crowd. "They say private schools, fine, everything is going to work out all right, but they have no plan; and you should also know that most of you cannot afford private schools because you don't have the money."[117]

Any testimony for the second option, however, was easily diluted by the near constant stream of witnesses from Lions Clubs, Citizens' Councils, chambers of commerce, farm bureaus, and every manner of social, political, or economic organization that supported continued resistance. Tom Jackson swore "with deliberation and determination . . . without reservation, qualification, equivocation or apology" that he was "opposed to integration at anytime, in between times, and at all times, in all forms."[118] Fire-eating segregationists made their final strong stand at Moultrie; the hearings were scheduled to move next to Atlanta and then Gainesville, where local option was sure to be widely supported. But the state's political leaders had seized the momentum away from local option sentiment and drawn clear lines of division on the school question.

Atlanta

The day Georgia's segregationist political leaders were guiding their constituents and their testimony at the Committee on Schools hearing in Moultrie, another state politician, James Mackay, released a statement that presented a significant point to be considered in the school crisis. As many resistance politicians had been quick to point out, the decision in *James v. Almond,* which ruled no state could deny funding to a school solely on the basis of integration, had never been appealed to a higher court (Governor Almond acquiesced, called the assembly into session, and it made the necessary changes in state law to facilitate open schools). Mackay agreed with this assessment but explained the logical consequences of challenging the court ruling. According to Mackay, testing the decision would cause the General

Assembly to decide the issue. He argued that first a school in Atlanta would be integrated, then the governor would close the school and cut off its funding, parents of affected Atlanta schoolchildren would file suit to reopen the school, the court would then order funding restored (saying nothing about other schools) and declare the state's mandatory school closing laws invalid. The legislature would then be forced into restoring school funds to the integrated school or vote to eliminate funding to all Georgia schools. The General Assembly, Mackay averred, simply would never pass a statewide school closing bill. Suddenly, the implications of Mackay's assessment forced Georgia's politicians to face a very ugly proposition. Although they would sacrifice Atlanta's schools and even the entire state's education system—if the court ordered them closed—most could not bear the responsibility of closing the public schools. Mackay's interpretation of a possible school closing scenario was surely meant as a advice for federal judges confronting Georgia's massive resistance. By forcing the General Assembly to vote to abandon public education, Mackay, a longtime open school advocate, hoped to influence the upcoming battle over desegregation in the legislature.[119]

In the week before the hearing in Atlanta, the local press attempted to prepare the city for what it expected to be a contest between HOPE and MASE. In preparation for the meeting, the president of the segregationist sect, T. J. Wesley Jr., sent out letters urging members and supporters to attend. It was important, he said, that they make their views known to avoid "being represented by integrationists such as Mr. Hartsfield and Ralph McGill, who arrogate unto themselves a monopoly on wisdom and virtue and the prerogative of being spokesmen for all the people." Wesley, the vice president of Allen-Grayson Real Estate Company and director of the Atlanta Real Estate Board, claimed his five thousand members were mostly local businessmen. His approach to preserving segregation started with the precept that Georgia must be willing to close the public schools. He argued that if white Georgians expressed absolute dedication to that premise, then "little or no integration would be attempted because the results would, inevitably, work greater hardships on the Negro than the white." [120]

For the first time, Sibley Commission officials were buried with requests to appear before the panel well in advance of the meeting. John Greer made out a schedule of witnesses, deciding that the top school officials from the fifth district's three counties would be heard first. The Committee on Schools expected to hear from most of the city's larger social organizations and many PTAs and other school groups. The Atlanta Chamber of Commerce promised to end its long silence by appearing before the commission hearing at Henry Grady High School. The board of directors for the organization met in a special session on 22 March to draft their response to the commission's options.[121]

Atlanta's newspapers were filled with editorials and letters lauding the wisdom of a local option plan. This public embrace of the plan was one of the most important accomplishments of the Sibley Commission. It was, quite simply, the best method of presenting the idea of desegregation to Georgia. While occupying a minor role at the first hearing in Americus, the idea had grown to represent the commission's second option. This basic appeal to local democracy offered the best hope to overturn mandatory school closing laws in order to allow Atlanta to desegregate its schools peacefully. Local option also appealed to many segregationists who understood that integration could be indefinitely delayed in their counties. Newspaper editors throughout the state clutched at the plan and beseeched the state's political leaders for at least an opportunity to decide the measure by secret ballot. J. Roy McGinty of the *Calhoun Times* pointed to the commission hearings and the diversity of the opinions presented as proof of the need for local choice. However, Cooper Smith of Waycross warned, the hearings had changed and had become forums for "extremists and professional agitators." He thought that a referendum would give the "rank and file of plain people" a voice "in this awesome issue." He continued by saying that education in Georgia was too important to be "manipulated like a puppet on a string by a bevy of big-mouthed politicians and a few narrow-minded hotheads who can't see two inches in front of their noses."[122]

On the morning of the twenty-third, with school let out for the day, uniformed Atlanta police officers guided witnesses into the parking lot of Henry Grady High School. A bald man in a plaid sportscoat passed out handbills outside the gymnasium that featured a picture of a black man and white woman dancing together with the caption, "Do you want this to happen in Georgia?" The man, representing the U.S. Klans, was removed from school property. Once inside the gym, witnesses registered at a long table manned by three state employees. State troopers then led them to their seats. Plainclothes Georgia Bureau of Investigation officers mingled with the crowd. Realizing that a smoking ban would be fruitless, fire officials ignored the closeness of the room and concentrated on keeping exits clear.[123]

Sibley and the commission entered the room a few moments before ten o'clock. He, Duncan, Greer, and Freeman Leverett sat elevated at one end of the basketball court, behind a table lined with red, white, and blue bunting. They were difficult to see over a solid line of television and movie cameras. TV news reporters from all over the country were in attendance, and one local station broadcast the hearing live. Sibley rapped his gavel down three times on the table and welcomed everyone. He explained that the gavel had been given to him that morning by his daughter and requested the audience of well over one thousand to maintain their decorum lest he break his gift. Nevertheless, several times during the course of the Atlanta hearing, Sibley had to bring down his new gavel, not only to stop witnesses from rambling on about the importance of maintaining Georgia law but also to stifle their supporters, who engaged in the discordant but organized displays of clapping, cheering, and whistling that had become prevalent at the hearings.[124]

However, the witnesses at the Atlanta hearing, as expected, gave a rousing endorsement of the second option. Eighty-five of 114 witnesses, most representing some Atlanta group or organization, voiced a preference for changing state law to accommodate local option and the Atlanta plan. Some of the city's most important leaders, including those from the black community, school systems, and churches, called for the right of self-determination. And the Atlanta Chamber of Commerce finally spoke out and presented their official endorsement of local option.

The first witnesses to appear before the commission were school officials from Fulton and DeKalb counties. A. C. Latimer, the defendant in the Atlanta desegregation suit due to his position as president of the Atlanta School Board, was the first to testify. He pointed out that Atlanta would face a much more serious problem if the state converted to private schools than would a small county; the city could hardly be expected to make adequate provisions for Atlanta's one hundred thousand school-aged children. He then explained the Atlanta plan in detail and told the audience that "geography is the one single pattern that will deter any mass mixing of the races more than any other single factor." Urban geographical segregation, as Latimer pointed out, was yet another defense of segregation available under the Sibley proposals. The chairman, intent on winning the support of *rural* Georgia, had neglected to promote this strategy because, as Roy Harris pointed out in the Washington hearing, it could only be used in large cities. Murphy Candler, the attorney for the DeKalb County Board of Education, followed Latimer and detailed his county's local option plan, which offered each district, school, and parent an opportunity to choose private schools in the case of desegregation. Jim Cherry, DeKalb County's superintendent, then gave his endorsement for the second option. Cherry's views were well known; he had repeatedly voiced his opinion that the schools were simply the first clash in a battle to dismantle the Jim Crow system. He averred that sacrificing public education and the future of Georgia's children simply to win a temporary victory in this fight could serve no purpose. In a speech before the Georgia Education Association annual meetings (also in March), Cherry outlined his faith in local option. Cherry offered yet another utilitarian defense for changing state law. It is far more likely that most Atlanta open school advocates chose the commission's second option using the type of reasoning exhibited by Latimer and Cherry rather than because of any racially enlightened views or absolute devotion to public education. The next witness, Fulton County Superintendent Paul West, said that the diversity of opinion "in this critical issue" mandated local option. "Boards of Education are split. Families are divided and even close friends dread to meet one another on the street for fear that the subject of the public schools will be brought up. In this framework of division it seems only fair that the people should have the sovereign right to settle the issues since it is they to whom the schools belong." [125]

During the morning session of the hearing, the committee heard from many witnesses representing only themselves and their families, but the majority of those who testified came at the request of a particular group. The Fulton County Women's Republican Club, HOPE, PTA organizations from DeKalb County, and the Georgia League of Women Voters all preferred the second option. And Tom Linder, 1954 gubernatorial candidate, resurfaced, coming out in favor of local option. He prefaced his support, however, by reiterating his solution to the problem. He suggested to Sibley that the state poll everyone on their choice in the matter, and then the state could build schools for those who preferred integrated education. He had obviously reconsidered the plank from his 1954 campaign to commit all those who preferred integration to the state's mental hospital. [126]

Witness Testimony by County in Georgia, 1960

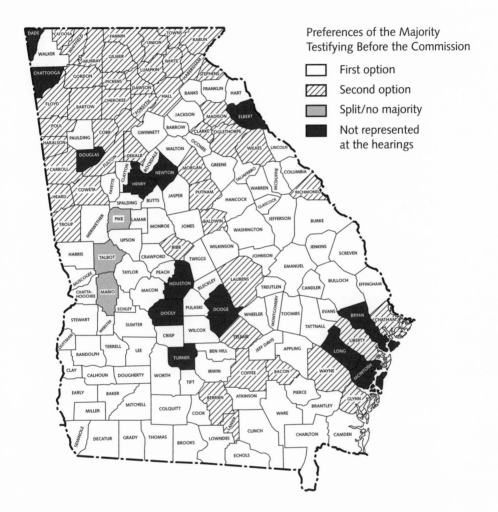

This particular map, although an effective measure of sentiment in many areas of the state, does not reflect the true feelings of every county. For example, Walker County, in the extreme northwest corner of the state (a region that overwhelmingly preferred a local option plan), produced only one witness due to a heavy snowstorm; he opted to close the public schools rather than face any amount of integration. Telfair County, the home of arch-segregationists Eugene and Herman Talmadge, sent a large delegation to testify, but the members of the Telfair group grew tired of waiting and returned home. Ironically, the only Telfair resident to remain was an African American man who testified a preference for option two and Telfair County was represented in the next morning's papers as choosing local option over absolute segregation.

Opposition to local option in the morning session included MASE President, T. J. Wesley Jr., who claimed that some people's priorities were skewed. "Some of our people are saying, save our schools. We say, save our children first." He went on to describe a conversion to private education that involved public auction of school facilities and supplies to private individuals.[127] Wesley Morgan of the U.S. Klans as well as several other individuals spoke out in favor of maintaining state law.[128]

Shortly before the lunch break, Greer called on the first of the black witnesses. Austin T. Walden, a prominent attorney and member of the black civic elite, came to the stand and explained in calm, concise terms why segregation must end. He read a short statement from the Negro Democratic Voters League. "We do not believe in segregated education for the reasons that the Negroes have learned by long and bitter experience, long before the announcement of the Supreme Court . . . on this subject, that there is no such thing as equality in segregated education on the basis of race. In fact, if Georgia, in good faith, attempted to provide separate but equal education for its Negro children, it would go bankrupt overnight."[129] Walden was followed to the stand by a few other members of the black delegation. They did not testify en masse as had been the case in other hearings but in small groups scattered through the day. In all cases they presented their testimony with a calm appeal for peaceful integration or an endorsement of option two. The contrast between the black delegations from Atlanta and Savannah clearly shows the difference in the race relations of each city. Atlanta leaders had learned to work with the representatives of the city's black community in solving problems, and men like Sibley and Walden had met many times to smooth out friction between the two communities. Savannah, on the other hand, was run by a political machine based on unequivocal Democratic control. The lack of clear communication between black and white leadership helped to create a powerful black civil rights movement led by the local NAACP.[130]

After an hour-long lunch break, Sibley gavelled the crowd to silence and told them that "Our Mayor, Honorable William Hartsfield, called me this morning and said that he would very gladly come down and welcome the people and express his views. . . . I wanted you to know that I told him that if the Committee needed him we would not hesitate to call him."[131] Hartsfield's preference for a local option plan was well known, and the audience chuckled appreciatively at being spared a certain speech by the longtime mayor. After the testimony from many of the expected witnesses, the hearing in Atlanta more closely resembled its predecessors. Individuals favoring each option gave eloquent, dull, persistent, or even irrelevant testimony to support their choices. Union support for massive resistance ran high. Ernest Lazarus of the UAW Local 34 said segregation must be maintained at any cost: "when I say any cost, I mean any cost—the cost of lives if necessary." [132] One man, a descendant of Stonewall Jackson, claimed that if his grandfather had heard "the testimony of some of our people here this morning he would have us shot at sunrise as traitors." [133] Later that afternoon, however, a woman, also a descendent of Civil War veterans, claimed she testified for local option not on behalf of her grandfathers but for her children. [134] Lester Maddox, who identified himself as a restauranteur, urged the crowd to fight against communists and integrationists who were creating the "greatest tragedy occurring in America." [135] And Mrs. May Andrews stated that integration "leads to the Communist goals of amalgamation of the races [and] promotes centralization of power and uses the Negro to set up a police state with the federal government policing the situation." Loud cheers and applause erupted among the proponents of resistance, and the open school advocates responded with boos. Sibley brought down his gavel repeatedly and threatened to move the questioning into a classroom and away from the "whooping and hollering and clapping contest." [136]

The meeting ended with the testimony of another group of black witnesses, including Jesse O. Thomas, Whitney Young, William Holmes Borders, and John Wesley Dobbs, who bantered with Sibley over whether his granddaughter, the opera singer Mattiwilda Dobbs, was the greatest singer in the country, the world, or the universe. These men were all associated with the black leadership of Atlanta; Thomas was vice president of the Atlanta Life Insurance Company, Borders was pastor of the Wheat Street Baptist Church, Young represented the Atlanta NAACP, and Dobbs was the head of Georgia's black Republicans. All the men testified for integration. Donald Hollowell, the attorney representing the plaintiffs in *Calhoun v. Latimer*, read their statement to the commission: "We, the ten parents who filed the suit against the Atlanta Board of Education, want you to know why we did it. Our children never got, they don't get now and we don't believe they will ever get equal education under a separate system. Therefore, the only thing to do is to do away with segregation like the Supreme Court said to do. Then all children, white and colored, will get the same education." [137]

Sibley realized that the number of witnesses who still wished to testify was far greater than the time they had allotted. He took a short break and came back with two announcements: the commission would adjourn until 31 March at ten A.M. and John Greer would read the statement from the Atlanta Chamber of Commerce. The chamber fully supported the local option plan as outlined by the Sibley Commission as the "most practical" method to decide the school question. The statement pointed to the great variances of opinion among the state's citizens and sections and professed that everyone should be given the right to decide for himself. [138]

Gainesville

The last full meeting of the Sibley Commission took place in Gainesville on 24 March. Everyone in the state expected that the Ninth Congressional District would vote for a local option plan. The area had one of the state's smallest black populations, and anyone keeping up with the hearings could guess what the outcome would be. The meeting produced no radical or unusual results; the district echoed its Piedmont neighbors and fully supported local option. But a perceived foregone conclusion did not deter the 141 witnesses who came bearing the customary petitions, polls, and meeting results. Among the groups represented were the Metropolitan Life Insurance Company Underwriters Association, the Rabun County Farm Bureau, the Hall County Junior Chamber of Commerce (which had polled its members in January), the Gainesville Business and Professional Women's Club, and dozens of PTA and educational organizations. [139]

Much like those from the other industrial centers of the state, the witnesses at Gainesville were concerned about the potential economic impact that the school question could have on their particular communities. William Jarrett, of James Lees and Sons, spoke in favor of local option because of the difficulty inherent in recruiting skilled technicians to an area where the public schools were in jeopardy. And the mayor of a small Piedmont town, Mrs. Charles Graves, brought a petition, signed by the top "merchants and industrial leaders, clergymen, doctors, and business men or business people in Clarksville," that demanded local option.[140]

Resisters comprised a definite minority; only thirty-six witnesses chose option one, and most spoke solely for their families, although a few brought petitions signed by friends and neighbors. But they were adamant about their beliefs. Bill Williams said, "I don't believe if I knew Webster's dictionary word for word, that I could possibly express as strong as I feel how much I desire to continue 100% segregation in everything." And another man expressed disdain toward the flurry of polls and resolutions by the state's ministers: "If they would start to preaching the Bible instead of having all these polls, I think it would be a lot better off. If one of them comes down to my Baptist church, we are going to poll [pole] him." Only Jackson and Barrow counties produced any large number of resistance supporters. Located on the southern edge of the district, they had sizable farming operations and the two largest black populations in the ninth district.[141]

The Subcommittees

The intense lobbying effort by the citizens of Columbus and the HOPE representatives of that city paid off when the Sibley Commission held a subcommittee meeting on 31 March, the day the Atlanta hearing resumed. Columbus was the only large city in the Third Congressional District and was, as John Duncan who acted as chairman for the meeting pointed out, inadequately represented at Americus. He told the crowd of three hundred gathered for the event that the opinions of the residents of Muscogee County were the primary reason for the additional meeting, but the commission would hear from other counties or individuals who had previously testified if time permitted. To prepare for the day's hearing, the *Columbus Enquirer* had printed the two Sibley Commission choices in that morning's paper, but by the end of March, most Georgians could have surely recited them from memory.

Acting chairman John Duncan opened the meeting with a new, shorter version of the traditional opening statement that he and John Sibley had prepared for the two subcommittee hearings. He and Sibley (at the Atlanta meeting) explained that the philosophy behind the second option was an aversion to "compulsory association and [a desire] to permit on the part of the parents and local community absolutely free choice in selecting schools in conformity with the parent's desires. The plan," they said, "is designed to effectuate voluntary association and to avoid compulsory association among the races." Sibley crafted the final statement to explain once again the local option plan and how, with voluntary segregation, no radical changes would take place in most school systems.[142]

The Columbus hearing was a microcosm of the others. There was a serious urban-rural split in the testimony, with most representatives of church, women's, or school groups voting for the second option. The biggest victory for open school advocates came when the Columbus Chamber of Commerce joined its Atlanta brethren and supported open schools.[143]

Farm and labor organizations continued to provide strong support of resistance. Local Machinists Union 1870, and the Columbus Association of Master Barbers presented the commission with their unanimous vote in favor of segregation at all costs.[144] And of course the local branches of the Citizens' Councils and the U.S. Knights of the Ku Klux Klan testified to their preference for the continuation of resistance.[145] Duncan could not resist poking fun at Klan representative Martin Adams by asking if the group had taken a poll of its members.[146] Most segregationists at Columbus, however, represented only themselves or their relatives. Zeke Calhoun from Alabama, claimed to represent "perhaps the youngest person being spoken for here today. Pamela Diane Calhoun . . . is five weeks old and I will say this, that Pam Calhoun shall attend an all white segregated school six years hence, whether it be private or public." [147] As they did at every hearing, many of those speaking in favor of the first option explained that school integration was only the first step in the unraveling of southern white society. M. C. Elmore told the meeting, "God made the colored man and he made the white man and that any form of token integration would lead to whole integration, which would destroy both races God made, my conscience forbids me from supporting the second option because of the fact that I think if I do that, I would be destroying what God made and I would want to keep both of them where they are." [148]

Columbus also boasted the largest contingent of black witnesses at any of the hearings. A group of seventy-five persons gathered to give support to the seventeen that testified. Eleven spoke in favor of integration, and all but one chose the second option. Albert W. Thompson told the hearing: "I believe in integration; I think that we are all citizens; I think that the future of this country lies only in utilizing the full resources and materials of this country. It cannot be done in a segregated society."[149] R. W. Greene, who had not only testified at Americus but also attended every commission hearing, once again spoke out passionately for the benefits of segregation. This time, however, he was booed by the African Americans in attendance.[150]

On this last day of public hearings, perhaps no one expressed the views of many in the state better than the white minister James Webb.

> I would like to say that I do not come as a representative of my church because the people of my church, similar to those of any large denominations, are divided on this issue. There are many that would prefer segregation and private schools, and there are many who would prefer continued public education with what they believe would be a minimum of integration. So, I can not speak for our people or for the church. I wish to express my personal opinion only and that is that if these hearings have brought anything, it has brought forth the divided nature of the opinions of the people of this state and therefore to me, there ought to be a plan which would be flexible enough and adaptable enough to meet the needs of our whole state, and I feel that the second plan with pupil placement, would offer hope of being flexible enough to work out our differences.[151]

John Sibley and the rest of the commission met in Atlanta the same day to continue their suspended hearing. Sibley's considerable patience had by this time reached its end. Witness after witness, believing that this was his last chance to speak on the subject, badgered the chairman for one more minute, sentence, or thing to say. Sibley halted a great number midway through their diatribe, forcing them to immediately state a preference for one of the two options and eyed warily anyone approaching the stand with a lengthy prepared statement. Seventy-one people at the Atlanta hearing chose option two and forty-nine opposed that view.

Representatives of schools dominated the testimony for local option and included Carl Renfroe, of the Decatur city schools; M. D. Collins, the state school superintendent emeritus; representatives of the Agnes Scott College and Oglethorpe College faculties; the Georgia Tech mathematics department; and students from Atlanta University Center, many of whom had participated in the sit-ins two weeks earlier.

Segregationists were well represented by numerous individuals, each beseeching their fellow Georgians to support segregation through massive resistance. One man, C. F. Craig, lamented the harmful effects the school crisis had on the state and asked Sibley for permission to lead a silent prayer to guide Georgia through the situation. Sibley asked the audience to bow its heads for a few moments of contemplation and then asked Craig to close with a few words. Craig asked for the Lord's blessing in preserving segregated schools. The use of a prayer to express an opinion for the preservation of segregation shocked and angered John Sibley and most in attendance. However, by the end of March some people were willing to use extreme measures to make their point.[152]

During the month, the Sibley Commission heard from more than 1600 witnesses from 148 of the state's 159 counties. For hour upon hour John Sibley sat patiently and intently listened to each witness. His remarkable attention span allowed him to recognize quickly when a "short point" or "just one more thing" or a "short statement" meant a long harangue or defense of a person's testimony. He cut many off in mid-sentence and gavelled many others to silence. His behavior at the hearings was reminiscent of the paternal society of the Old South. Sibley's firm, unequivocal control of the hearings combined with this calm, patriarchal presence were the two main reasons the General Assembly Committee on Schools became known as the Sibley Commission.

Sibley took control of the committee from the day Griffin Bell approached him to be its chairman; Sibley wrote and released the panel's first public statement before the group ever met. He ran every meeting of the commission in the month preceding the hearings, including the education and legal subcommittees. No one else on the committee was allowed to release information to the press and indeed, other than John Greer, who controlled the flow of witnesses at each hearing, and John Duncan, who read the statement when Sibley was late to one meeting (and later chaired the subcommittee hearing in Columbus), the other members of the committee seemed to be only audience members with better than average seats. Render Hill recalls that many of the commission members did not agree with their chairman but remained silent until after the hearings.[153] Sibley wrote and read the group's statement that introduced every meeting, often interjecting it with his own thoughts. During the questioning of witnesses, he occasionally interpolated a more detailed explanation of the two options available. This absolute control of the hearings allowed Sibley to restructure Georgia's resistance.

The limited permissible responses to John Sibley's questions carefully focused the school-segregation-resistance question. They were designed to present the people of the state the only logical conclusion of continued resistance. But as many who testified before the panel suggested, there was no precedent for mandatory school closings in the face of a court order. Sibley's (and most open school groups') projection of an abandonment of statewide education based on the *James v. Almond* decision, while a logical deduction, was not necessarily a foregone legal conclusion. Through constant repetition, however, Sibley convinced many Georgians to consider the possibility of a loss of the public schools. The second option, although hardly original (Hamilton Lokey, James Mackay, HOPE, and others had suggested most of the alternatives before), nevertheless was reinforced and reiterated by the prestige of the commission.

The judicial setting of the hearings provided the commission with a paternalistic certification that few people would dispute. John Sibley's conduct and the fairness in which he approached every witness, combined with the seemingly moderate choices he offered the public, enabled the commission to emerge from the hearings as *the* expert on the school question. Resisters and segregationist politicians, who had no real alternatives to the Sibley Commission's options, could respond only by refuting the panel's work or resorting to name-calling. In the months after the hearings, however, many of these same men spoke out in favor of local option, calling it the best method to preserve segregation. The governmental sanction of the commission and the intensity of the its schedule forced the school issue upon Georgia. The hearings and the famous two options were the primary topic of discussion at the barbershop or beauty parlor, the fishing hole or the stands at Little League games, the feed store and Rotary meetings, but more importantly, the school issue was the subject of hundreds of polls, resolutions, and petitions that took the school issue far beyond the gymnasiums and courthouses of the Sibley Commission hearings and into the hearts and minds of all Georgians.

CHAPTER 5

Bulwarks of Protection

What happened between the winter of our discontent in 1960 and the present
spring of our hopefullness was just a variety of talk, talk that thawed the sullen
set of mood, cracked it into floes, and washed it away on a flood of words. And
it was not always polite talk, but talk about sore things and troubled things,
out-loud talk, with enough real difference of opinion to get people used to
the fact that not everyone took everything the same way.
—Elizabeth Stevenson on the Sibley Commission hearings

The Sibley Commission accomplished its primary goal of unravelling the
cord that had been used to bind Georgia since 1946. The hearings and the
widely published two options enabled most of the state, for the first time, to
distinguish the five separate strands of that cord. As the public meetings exposed white supremacy, segregation, schools, defiance, and massive resistance as separate issues, resistance as the unifying element of segregation
loosened, then fell away. Due directly to the commission hearings, open
school advocates, the first to recognize that schools and segregation could be
two distinct issues, were joined by many others. But more importantly, the
local option plan created a differentiation between segregation and massive
resistance and offered a way to preserve local education *and* segregation.

Moreover, the plan's basic appeal to allow each community to decide for itself what to do in case of desegregation (which in most Georgia counties did
not happen until the Supreme Court became more aggressive in promoting
full integration) became more widely accepted *after* the hearings. The commission convinced many white people that the preservation of white supremacy could exist independently of the political tools of massive resistance
and defiance. The Sibley Commission's public and political sanction as the
authority on the school segregation question effectively removed the issue
from political control. Without political participation, massive resistance
could not survive, because in Georgia it had always been primarily a political
and not a social movement.

The March hearings uncovered and created clear divisions among Georgians as individual and county statistics attest. According to the official committee results (different from news accounts) seventy-nine represented counties testified to uphold resistance by at least a four-to-one margin and only
seventeen preferred the second option by the same ratio. Other counties' testimony was more closely divided. Newspaper accounts of the testimony reveal that 831 individuals and the groups they represented preferred maintaining resistance and 731 chose the committee's second option. The panel's
official count was 1,003 to 575.[1] Georgia's ten congressional districts were
equally divided in their Sibley Commission testimony. The first, second,
third, sixth, and eighth congressional districts all came out in favor of segregation at all costs. The fourth, fifth, seventh, ninth, and tenth preferred a local option plan. This division parallels the fall line and the border of the Black
Belt of the state. The average black population in the districts voting to maintain massive resistance was 41.26 percent with a black student enrollment of
41.8 percent. The five districts that voted to change state law and allow for local option and pupil placement had an average black population and student
enrollment of 24.4 percent. The summary of official Sibley Commission statistics offered a quite different picture because John Greer recorded many
votes for option one from people who did not actually take the stand. According to its findings, seven of the ten districts voted to maintain Georgia
law and close the schools. But, as John Sibley pointed out time and time
again, the testimony was designed only to gain a sampling of public opinion
through the state, and the official results would be used only to guide the
commission in its report to the General Assembly.[2]

The Sibley Commission's conclusions, however, were foreordained. John Sibley's command of the commission and hearings enabled him to narrowly focus Georgia's options in the school dilemma. He had openly suggested that the local option plan was the only fair answer to any question regarding segregated schools. It was also the only resolution that allowed Atlanta to move forward in its desegregation without the pandemonium that had accompanied events in Little Rock and New Orleans. But more importantly to Sibley and most Georgians, it was the superior method to preserve the greatest degree of segregation. The individual hearings and testimony supplied Sibley and the commission with the requisite breach in resistant sentiment among white Georgians to offer an acceptable alternative to existing segregation laws.

The sampling of public opinion, however, marked the first real discussion of the school issue; its publicly sanctioned setting, official atmosphere, and testimonial constrictions freed many to express their opinions within relatively safe confines. Before the hearings, debate over the school segregation issue, while certainly one of the most complex predicaments Georgia had ever encountered, was limited, among white people, to echoes of the defense of segregation and resistance (southern liberals and open school advocates, while vocal, were a small minority). The choices presented at the hearings divided Georgia not only along traditional political lines at the base of the Piedmont and city limits, but also within counties, communities, social organizations, churches, and families. Those counties above Georgia's fall line contested the idea that massive resistance was the best defense of segregation and refused to sacrifice their public education to placate the fears of the Black Belt. The division between urban and rural counties centered on larger towns and their commitment to education versus the fear of white rural residents that geography could not preserve segregation in farming communities. Opinions differed from one county to the next, based primarily on black population percentages. These divisions grew after the hearings, further paralyzing state politicians who could not keep up with rapidly fracturing public opinion. The idea of measuring sentiment through the hearings ricocheted toward the capitol as the meetings unleashed a cacophony of determined and diverse voices. Two camps emerged, one dedicated to segregation "one hundred percent" and the other determined to save public schools. Both groups anxiously waited for the Sibley Commission report, hopeful that it would recommend the preservation of the doctrine they cherished.

The Sibley Commission hearings also revealed divisions among the black communities in the state. Most welcomed the day that the hated Jim Crow system and state-supported institutions of white supremacy were no longer accepted in Georgia. But many others, mostly in rural areas, feared not only an end to the large amounts of money that the state was spending on black schools but the destruction of all black public education. It was black testimony favoring segregation that Sibley valued and believed would lead to acceptance of a local option plan. He told his brother Erwin, "You may note that our policy has been to let the Negroes speak freely, though sometimes irrelevantly to the main issue, the reason being their attitude may have considerable impact on how the question is determined ultimately."[3]

Over the course of the hearings, resistance politicians grew leery of the commission and its goals and tried mightily to rebind the issues of resistance, segregation, and schools in order to retain their control over a central issue in Georgia politics. Their supporters, spurred by surprising black testimony and increased militancy, followed blindly, muttering the mantras of states' rights and white supremacy. But faith was all the resistance disciples could rely upon, for the authors of the program could offer no realistic alternatives to the commission's proposal of a local option plan. Furthermore, the lack of any established grassroots movement to preserve segregation foiled resisters efforts to curb the appeal of local choice in the school question.

The Sibley Commission report demanded the termination of the political authority over segregation, an end to massive resistance, and the relinquishment of control of school systems to local communities. The report, while philosophically a plea for public education, was a blueprint for the defense of legal, locally controlled segregation. Its proponents called it "defense in depth" and it soon caught on with many segregationists who encouraged the plan as a more logical defense of segregation. Throughout the summer and fall, leading to the assembly's 1961 session, the number of supporters of local option grew, and the state's business leaders took positive steps to ensure its incorporation. In addition, certain commission members, including John Sibley, toured the state and gave speeches that convinced many Georgians that the only alternative to continued resistance and the abandonment of public education was the commission's proposal. The showdown between the defiant politicians and the federal government unexpectedly changed venue in January 1961, when the University of Georgia, rather than the Atlanta public schools, became the site for the state's first defense of massive resistance.

Georgia's political leaders turned to the Sibley report to avoid closing the university, and the General Assembly, following Governor Vandiver's suggestion, disassembled the state's elaborate resistance program.

The Report

Immediately after the last two subcommittee meetings, John Duncan and Sibley directed the members to remain silent and arranged for secret meetings of the commission to ensure privacy. Sibley and Duncan planned the first two private sessions to be for discussion and analysis only and no vote among commission members was taken. In addition to reviewing testimony and responses to the hearings and the committee, members examined the results of a research trip to Virginia (which had abandoned massive resistance that January) taken by Battle Hall, Render Hill, and Harmon Caldwell. The three men met with Governor Almond and the state school superintendent to learn all they could about how the state's new pupil placement plan worked and how it was adopted in the Virginia General Assembly. They also visited Prince Edward County, which had closed its schools to prevent integration, to see "the lay of the land." The men decided that a private school plan could only work in an "old close-knit community" where social and economic pressure would force everyone to contribute to the local private schools.[4]

Between the hearings and the first closed-door meetings of the commission, its members took a week off to absorb carefully and reflect on they had seen and heard. They scheduled a full meeting of the panel for Tuesday, 12 April. The men agreed not to speak publicly about the hearings until after they had met and held discussions so that they could work in an atmosphere free from outside pressure. Freeman Leverett, the commission's legal advisor, spent this time preparing a copy of an amendment that would allow the ideas expressed in the commission's second option to become Georgia law. As he explained to John Sibley, he favored a constitutional amendment that would "satisfy both factions" (resisters and those seeking to save the schools) that the Sibley Commission could present to the General Assembly, which would in turn pass on to the people. He explained that this amendment would satisfy rural county unit proponents, because the legislative body was elected by the system, and urban dwellers, whose voices would be heard in a popular vote of the people. John Sibley gave this assignment to Leverett before the post-hearing meetings because he wanted to be able to present it to the panel during its discussions. Leverett's responsibility was to offer an opinion on the potential constitutionality of the group's recommendations.[5]

The first post-hearing meeting of the commission was attended by the full complement of its members. John Sibley led the discussion of the school issue in a seven-hour session. He explained his unavoidable conclusions. The people were critically divided. Almost everyone preferred segregated schools, but they split over their preferences for massive resistance or allowing the schools to remain open. He suggested that the committee recommend an amendment vote to allow the people to decide by secret ballot. The committee members, however, could agree only that everyone preferred segregated, public schools. But since the *Brown* decision had eliminated this option, the only way to maintain completely segregated schools was through a conversion to private education. This indirect but important difference meant that many in the group still held out hope for massive resistance. At the end of the day's spirited debate, Sibley left the panel members with four questions to consider before their next meeting on the fifteenth: whether or not the members believed that the General Assembly would close the schools; whether private schools would work; how the public would react to the privatization of education; and whether the commission should recommend that a plan of local option, pupil placement, and tuition grants be implemented instead of the conversion to private schools. Sibley strongly advised the members to consider this last option very carefully for he felt that it was the only legal defense of segregation. After the meeting Homer Rankin faced the press and read a brief statement: "The committee began an examination and discussion of the evidence and of the specific problems involved in the over-all issue."[6]

Three days later the commission met for the last time and discussed further Georgia's options. The panel however, much like the people it was chosen to represent, was divided. Most of the representatives from the General Assembly had preferred continued resistance all along and believed the hearings clearly demonstrated that most Georgians agreed. But the majority of the committee preferred changing state law. The two groups agreed to submit majority and minority reports, each with its own recommendations.[7]

On April 28, John Sibley walked alone into a packed State Supreme Court Chamber, sat at the head of a long table, and placed the Committee on Schools majority report before him. The room was filled with press representatives, and the intense lights of the television camera crews picked up the dark red flecks in his blue tie. One by one the other committee members entered and stood around the table. John Sibley read the report in his deliberate, soft Georgia accent. He described the difficult decision the state faced, pointing to the division within the commission itself as evidence of the complexity of the situation. The chairman explained that the public schools were a fertile training ground and taught citizens their responsibilities in a democracy and that the state should adopt measures to guarantee the continuance of that instruction.[8]

The philosophy behind the report was that the public schools must be maintained. Sibley claimed that the decision in *Brown v. Board of Education of Topeka* was wrong and that the separate but equal doctrine had been upheld on eight separate occasions by the court. Southern states maintaining separate schools, he continued, had spent billions of dollars in "reliance of that doctrine." Sibley claimed the ruling was "utterly unsound on the facts" and "contrary to the clear intent of the fourteenth amendment; a usurpation of legislative function through judicial process; and an invasion of the reserved rights of states." But he warned that the decision "is binding on the lower federal courts; and that it will be enforced."[9]

The hearings, while showing clear division of opinion among Georgia's citizens, Sibley explained, also revealed fundamental beliefs that all but a small minority shared: the "deep conviction that separate school facilities for the white and colored races are in the best interest of both races, and that the compulsory association of the races in the schools through enforced integration will be detrimental to the peace, good order and tranquility of the state," and that most citizens "prefer tax-supported, segregated public schools." But if "total segregation" could not continue, the people were divided "as to the course that should be followed." Sibley divided the state into three groups: those who would brook no integration anywhere in the state and preferred to close all the state's schools, those who believed every locale should decide for itself (many believing that their district would experience no call for desegregation) because conditions in the state were so varied that every community deserved an opportunity to handle its situation locally, and those who were willing to accept a small "degree of integration rather than to sacrifice their public schools."

After a careful explanation of the exact legal situation, Sibley argued that segregation could be maintained for most of Georgia and that closing the schools in an attempt to avoid the *Brown* and *Calhoun v. Latimer* rulings was "a useless gesture and [would] cause nothing but confusion, great economic loss, and utter chaos in the administration of the school system." He claimed that the private school plan was unworkable and impracticable, pointing to likely astronomical start-up costs, potential losses in accreditation, and the state's surrender of curriculum control if a conversion to private schools were initiated. While the original plan to close schools or districts one at a time seemed feasible in 1954, Sibley explained, subsequent rulings by the federal courts circumvented the viability of the program and threatened the state's entire education system. Besides this, Sibley suggested, "even if a system of private schools [were] adopted, the state, having no control of such schools, would be powerless to prohibit integration in them if some private schools voluntarily integrated. Those who want to mix voluntarily [could] mix under the law and the state [would be] powerless to stop it."

Sibley then outlined a plan to preserve segregation; for if the philosophy of the report was a plea for the protection of public education, its underlying structure was an elaborate design to protect *separate* schools. He contended that most of the state would never need tuition reimbursement or pupil placement or any other freedom of choice measure. There were few Piedmont counties that would confront a suit calling for integration, and most localities in the rest of the state could preserve separate schools using techniques other than massive resistance.

Voluntary segregation, Sibley explained, was the answer for most communities. After all, the Supreme Court had not ordered the states to integrate their schools; it simply forbade them from mandating racially segregated schools. If an individual community agreed to a separate education system, then that school district would not be affected if the massive resistance laws were overturned. Sibley beseeched the people to accept the inevitability of some integration and to work to limit its impact on the state. He then outlined his plan to "establish a system of education within the limitations of the Supreme Court decision, yet one which will secure the maximum segregation possible within the law, which will vest the control of its schools in the people of the community, and which will ensure the parent of each child the greatest freedom in protecting the welfare of his child."

The majority report recommended a "freedom of association" amendment to the constitution that guaranteed each student the right to transfer schools or receive from the state a tuition credit for private school if his or her school were forced to integrate. A second amendment would offer each community an opportunity to choose for itself through a local election what to do when faced with possible desegregation. The report further suggested that the General Assembly enact legislation that would provide for tuition grants that would be applicable under the first proposed amendment or if a community opted to close its local school system, ensure retirement benefits to teachers of public schools (a law passed in 1955 threatened those benefits to teachers of public integrated schools), and adopt any other needed pupil placement, local option, school transfer, or tuition reimbursement laws. Sibley believed that, as he explained later to Coca-Cola attorney Pope Brock, "A few wise legislators, guided by able and far-sighted counsel ... could get this question behind us on a workable basis if steps are taken ahead rather than after an adverse court decision." The majority report was, therefore, primarily an attempt to preserve both public education and the maximum amount of legal segregation.[10]

Ten other men on the panel agreed with this assessment and joined John Sibley by attaching their names to the document. They were: Homer Rankin of the Georgia Press Association; the committee's secretary, Senator John Greer; the chairman of the Board of Regents, Robert O. Arnold; state representative from Columbus, Howell Hollis; Cartersville's Mayor Charles Cowan; Zade Kenimer of the Georgia Education Cabinet; chancellor of the University System of Georgia, Harmon Caldwell; the state school superintendent, Dr. Claude Purcell; Judge Samuel Boykin; and the president of the state's chamber of commerce, John Dent of Cartersville.

A sizable minority within the commission disagreed and submitted its own report, calling for the continuation of massive resistance as the majority of people who testified had requested. John Duncan, the committee vice chairman and president of the State Farm Bureau (an organization that had voiced its almost unanimous preference for massive resistance throughout the hearings), wrote the minority report with the help of arch-segregationist and Vandiver executive assistant Peter Zack Geer. The other members of the minority were J. W. Keyton, representing the County Commissioners Association, whose members had also expressed their devotion to defiance at the hearings; members of the Georgia General Assembly's House of Representatives Walstein Parker of Sylvania, Robert Battle Hall of Rome, Render Hill of Greenville, and George Brooks of Crawford; and state senators Eulond Clary

of McDuffie County and Clinch County's Wallace Jernigan. The minority report argued that the pupil placement plan could not work and that statewide
school closings were not preordained. The report called for an end to agitation for desegregation by "communist-inspired organizations" before they
had an opportunity to "inflict incalculable damage." These men derided the
majority report, claiming "it is nothing less than an intolerable affectation of
superior virtue for us now to proclaim to them [the citizens of the state that
voted for option one] 'Well, notwithstanding that you have made clear your
sentiments, we think that you are wrong and that we know what is best for
you.'" They recommended that an amendment to the state constitution be
enacted that would "guarantee that no Georgia child shall be forced . . . to attend any public school wherein a child of the opposite race is enrolled." The
minority report asked that the state streamline the private school plan even
further to ensure the provision of grants-in-aid to the parents of affected
children. It called for "the public school system [to] be preserved on a segregated basis as far as it is possible to do so unless closed by unprecedented federal court decree and recommended that the system of grants be instituted
only as a last resort." [11]

Render Hill, a member of the minority, released a separate statement to
explain that the division of Georgia was too close to justify changing state
law. He argued that although almost everyone polled desired both segregated
schools and public education, the narrow margin of the 55 percent to 45 percent split in opinion required the state to examine other options. Hill did not
believe that either of the submitted reports adequately described the situation
or offered viable solutions to the school crisis. He beseeched each incoming
member of the General Assembly "fully [to] inform himself concerning the
school situation in the State of Georgia and carefully determine the wishes
of the people of his county, so that each may properly and fully present these
views at the 1961 session." He then challenged the legislature to "resolve the
issues." [12]

Sibley sent a copy of all the reports and statements to Governor Vandiver
with a note explaining that although it was his "deep desire to have a unanimous report . . . [because] it would simplify future considerations on the part
of all concerned . . . [it] turned out to be impossible, although a strong effort
was made to obtain it." Copies of the document were also sent to senators
Richard B. Russell and Herman Talmadge as well as Dugas Shands, the

attorney general of Mississippi, who had written to Sibley requesting a copy. In fact copies of the report were widely available and much used by open school advocates in the ensuing months.[13]

The report was a bombshell in Georgia. For the first time, a government-sanctioned body advocated abandoning massive resistance and accepting the inevitability of integration. The split within the committee offered only more proof of the deep division of opinion within the state. Governor Vandiver, who had created the elaborate poll-taking measure to offer some hint as to public opinion on the subject, was paralyzed. He refused to call for "any specially convened, extraordinary session to consider" the report, referring to a "universal recognition" that to do so would be "fruitless." He, like most members of the assembly, refused comment on either the majority or the minority report and would only praise the committee members for the efforts. Charles Pou, political reporter for the *Atlanta Journal,* claimed that the report allowed no politician to profit and indeed frustrated those at the Capitol because "politicians do not relish choosing sides on the 50–50 issues in this life."[14]

The state's newspapers also divided in their opinion on the majority report. Both major Atlanta papers enthusiastically praised the document. The *Macon Telegraph* called it "an honest, helpful approach to Georgia's school crisis." And the *Macon News* lauded the report for recognizing that the court's ruling in *Calhoun v. Latimer* and the potential for school closings were not "nightmares but facts to be dealt with." Citizens should take the responsibility to "inform themselves on the issues," advised the *Moultrie Observer,* because surely the question would come to the people. Others, however, including two Augusta newspapers (three if one counts Roy Harris's statewide political mouthpiece, the *Augusta Courier*) and the *Albany Herald,* edited by James Gray, disagreed. The Albany paper called the report "disappointing and contradictory in that it clearly cuts across the expressed will of a majority of Georgians" and would lead the state to "wander in search of a will of the wisp with the beguiling but false label of 'local option.'" The *Augusta Herald* did "not believe that the majority recommendations were in line with the wishes of most Georgians, those of the rural areas in particular." The *Augusta Chronicle* compared the committee to the "mountain that labored and brought forth a mouse" and claimed the "commission majority chose to express its own opinions rather than those of the majority of Georgians whose feelings were heard from them." It blamed the group for leaving the state even more divided than it had been before the hearings. The headline of Roy Harris's account of the report read "11 of Sibley's Committee Make Silly Impossible Report to the Legislature." Harris, with almost no responsible journalistic objectivity to restrain him, claimed that the report's recommendations would make Georgia schools the laughingstock of the nation.[15]

A few days after the release of the report, Judge Hooper made his ruling on a request by the plaintiffs in the *Calhoun v. Latimer* case that he implement his decision to desegregate the Atlanta schools for the fall semester of 1960. The plaintiffs made their original request during the hearings, but Hooper, desiring to give the state another opportunity to change its laws, elected to wait until after the Sibley Commission had given its report. On May ninth he denied the request of the plaintiffs and charged the General Assembly to take the majority report's advice and overturn massive resistance laws. He ruled that the Atlanta schools should be desegregated in the fall of 1961. Hooper praised the work of the Sibley Commission for its education of "the people of the state as to the dangers which threaten our public schools." Sibley thanked Hooper for his "wise and helpful" decision and promised "within the year the good sense of Georgia should take charge of the situation." After Hooper's ruling, Robert Arnold wrote to Sibley congratulating the committee for its "real accomplishment in getting a year's delay for the Atlanta schools." He felt that the panel's work "aroused people to thinkin [sic] about a subject which they were willing to 'brush off' or run from, in the hope that it could never happen in Georgia." As Sibley wrote to Howell Hollis from his hospital bed while recovering from a minor automobile accident, "I expected our report, maybe before it is over with, to put others in the hospital besides me. I believe we turned loose a document that will be hard to get rid of, and in fact should stand up against the most severe test." And to his brother Erwin, Sibley wrote,

I hope the report will have educational value and will result in the adoption of a wise legislative and legal policy. After making a thorough study of the situation, I am convinced that wise leadership in the legislature, guided by lawyers of good sense and character, could create conditions that would soon put this integration question at rest upon an entirely workable and livable basis. My view is that we have much room within the Supreme Court decision to build up legitimate bulwarks of protection; I also believe that when we begin to operate within the Supreme Court decision, recognizing that we cannot enforce our state statutes, the courts will take a very lenient view in developing effective safeguards. Certainly, if this is not true, the schools can be closed as a last resort and only as a last resort should they be closed." [16]

The postponement of any potential desegregation of the Atlanta schools gave the supporters of the majority report seven months to sell the state on its proposals. Some of the Sibley Commission members used this opportunity to speak throughout Georgia and explain the defensive philosophy of the majority report and how it could be used to preserve segregation and education. On May first, Harmon Caldwell and John Greer appeared on *Press Gallery*, a television program hosted by Ralph McGill. They explained to McGill and the television viewers why they felt the majority recommendations were best for the state. Later in the month, John Sibley was interviewed on national television by Edward R. Murrow. He was joined by Governor Vandiver on the program "Who Speaks for the South?" Sibley explained Georgia's unique situation and how the state would benefit from the adoption of the commission's recommendations. Vandiver felt that the "committee proceeded in good faith and, regardless of the differences in opinion expressed . . . they acted in what they believed to be the best interests of this state." He still refused to make any public comment on the advisability of following either the majority or minority recommendations. [17]

That autumn, Sibley, certain other members of the commission, and many former resistance politicians spoke throughout Georgia in support of changing state law. Homer Rankin told the Chula PTA that the recommendations of the Sibley Commission were the only way to provide "public schools and maximum segregation possible under the law." He was joined on the dais by none other than Bill Bodenhamer, who told the gathering that the Sibley proposals were "defense in depth" and that the state must "withstand the [Supreme] Court. We must be respectful but we must circumvent them [court rulings]." The defense attorney in the *Calhoun* case appeared before the state bar association urging its members to support the majority report. Buck Murphy and Jim Peters, authors of much of Georgia's massive resistance legislation, also publicly supported Sibley's recommendations. Two prominent members of the General Assembly, Carl Sanders and Frank

Twitty, went on a speaking tour of the state that fall, and though they did not publicly endorse the Sibley report, they encouraged open discussion of the school question. On September sixteenth John Greer released a press statement defending the report and the commission. "Now I am not a moderate on segregation. I'm a segregationist, period. . . . I think that the people of various counties, if they are given the chance, can preserve segregation in 95 percent of the counties in Georgia." The following month Greer appeared before the Macon Rotary Club and gave a speech that was reprinted in several newspapers. He responded to a recent federal court ruling in New Orleans that forbade the state from interfering in a local school's attempt to comply with a federal court order to desegregate. He prefaced his explanation of the school situation to the Rotarians by telling them "every member of the [Sibley] committee, both those who signed the majority report and those who signed the minority report, are segregationists" and differed only in their *methods* of defending segregation. He warned the gathering that something must be done because federal law would overturn state law every time. "We do not like it, but it is true. And we simply cannot secede again from the Union, no matter how attractive the idea sometimes seems to be." Any solution to the problem, he continued, must "maintain every bit of segregation that is possible in our state or we will face a catastrophe that would be nearly unpalatable as closing the schools." Since massive resistance cannot work, he concluded, "we should turn to another battleground where we certainly can win over ninety percent of the battles instead of losing them all." The Sibley Commission report, he told them, was "the best and only workable blueprint that has yet been offered to the people in an effort to keep our public education and our system of equal but segregated education from being completely destroyed." Much like the witness testimony that evolved during the hearings, politicians and segregationist leaders slowly caught on to the value of the majority report's value as a defense of segregation. Since the report offered a means to protect education and segregation, proponents of the Sibley recommendations promoted the report for often very different reasons.[18]

On 10 November, at West Point, Georgia, John Sibley gave a speech entitled "The Urgency of Education and the Georgia School Situation." In it he stressed the unprecedented value of education and knowledge in the modern world. He framed his statements in the language of the Cold War, telling the crowd gathered at the West Point–Pepperell Mill that it was upon the "scientists that our hope of safety and survival and even peace depend." Sibley's use of Cold War rhetoric offers an interesting contrast to politicians who attempted to link their resistance politics to the anti-Communist crusades of other conservative groups; he pragmatically insisted that any interruption in public education would do far more harm in the fight against Communism than slight changes in the racial status quo. Sibley also sympathetically recounted the rise of massive resistance in Georgia after the *Brown* ruling. "It is not hard to justify the loud and vigorous protest of the people affected by the decision and their reluctance to accept it," he declared, "or to understand why the governors, legislators and state officials . . . moved quickly to avoid the force of the blow that the decision dealt to the power of the state to enforce separate schools." However, Sibley categorically denied the practicality of resistance as a method to preserve segregation. The federal courts, he explained, would not allow a slow conversion to private schools, and if one public school was forced to close, state-supported education would have to be abandoned. "Georgia must not make the mistake of holding to trying to enforce her school laws that have been voided by the Supreme Court decision. These laws give no protection; they merely open the way for successful litigation by the professional agitator and the political demagogue. These laws offer a fruitful field for profitable litigation and for political exploitation," he warned. Sibley claimed that if the state could repeal these laws, it would "strike the hardest possible blow to the effectiveness of the professional integrationist and race agitator." He further argued that the state must change its laws to incorporate the recommendations of the majority report or Georgia would "experience a period of hesitation in its growth and development and unless settled wisely and speedily, hesitation may develop into stagnation." [19]

HOPE and Business

The Sibley Commission report was an obvious boon to HOPE and the other open school advocates. After its release, the leaders of the organization created a new program, "Operation Last Chance," to exploit the ideas and recommendations of the document. In a May 1960 meeting, the group's leadership brainstormed on the best way to create public support for open schools using the majority report's suggestions. Atlanta state senator Muggsy Smith

suggested that the group utilize outdoor advertising, stressing the theme
"Your schools will close too" throughout South Georgia. Harold Fleming
added that buttons, posters, advertisements, and cartoons could also be used
and that Helen Bullard should handle the campaign. William Hartsfield suggested that the group publish and mail a cheap newspaper, similar to Roy
Harris's *Augusta Courier,* emphasizing the report's proposals. But the main
thrust of the campaign involved pressuring business leaders and assembly
members to accept the recommendations of the report and overturn massive
resistance laws. Athens businessman H. Edsel Benson, the brother of HOPE
leader Beverly Downing, spent the fall of 1960 gathering the names of 986 of
the state's prominent business leaders on a petition that he sent to Governor
Vandiver. HOPE members from all over the state were given the phone numbers of their state representatives and were urged to call and express their
views in the days preceding the 1961 session.[20]

HOPE leaders were, however, divided on their opinion of the Sibley Commission and its growing prominence. Some recognized that their support of
the committee's report might taint the public's opinion of the panel. Fran
Breeden, writing to John Sibley after his West Point speech, told him "I'm
afraid the newspaper stories today have put us in the same pew, regardless of
your desire to stand alone. I, for one, am proud that our statements were so
similar in content. However, if you feel that the paper's implication that you
are hand-in-glove with HOPE has damaged your considerable effectiveness,
then I am truly sorry."[21] But other members expressed dismay at the usurpation of the open school ideal by the committee and John Sibley. As Muriel
Lokey put it almost thirty years later,

> I don't really mean for it to sound that way [sour grapes], but [Sibley] was simply
> a vehicle. It was at no personal risk to himself. He was nice to give the time. It was
> wonderful that he did. . . . The questions that were asked were totally loaded—in
> the 'Have you stopped beating your wife' category. . . . He just simply presided at
> these hearings and kept order at those hearings, but I don't believe he ever said or
> indicated anything about what he thought about it one way or the other, which di-
> rection they should go to. It was a useful thing, then they gave a report that the
> people of Georgia generally prefer not to have the schools integrated. So what—
> you know? It bought time. He gave his time. I would like to know what it is that
> people think that the Sibley Commission did to save the schools except the idea of

it was a useful time-buying device and kept the state calm, calmer than it would have been, but I don't see any ideas coming out of it.[22]

The ideas that did come out of the Sibley Commission hearings quickly caught on in the business community. Business leaders from all over the state, especially Atlanta, continued their support of open schools. In June, Robert Woodruff of Coca-Cola wrote to his old friend John Sibley: "I have followed with satisfaction the growing community interest in the effort to solve our pressing social problems. Some of us ought to know more about this movement so that, if it proves to be as promising as it now seems, we can encourage its growth and effectiveness." He invited Sibley to a small luncheon and "orientation" discussion of the school problem. Sibley and Woodruff were lifelong friends and associates, and Sibley had been a powerful leader in each member of Georgia's ruling business triumvirate: general counsel for Coca-Cola, a partner in King and Spalding (Coca-Cola's law firm), and chairman of Trust Company Bank (Coca-Cola's bank). Although speculation exists about Woodruff's involvement in the creation of the Sibley Commission and its results and strategies (very few events in Georgia of any importance escaped the "Boss's" attention and surely the Sibley Commission was not an exception), no hard evidence of Woodruff's involvement has been found.[23]

Atlanta's business leaders also confronted the growing problem of the student sit-ins at the downtown lunch counters. In June they negotiated a temporary reprieve with the protesters until after the school crisis was resolved. In October, however, the sit-down strikes resumed when the students grew impatient waiting for the Atlanta establishment to resolve its problems before attending to student demands.[24]

The corporate hierarchy, of course, did not rely solely upon petitions and meetings to secure the economic future of the state. John Sibley orchestrated a plan to introduce an open schools amendment drafted by Freeman Leverett in the 1961 assembly. Working with Atlanta Chamber of Commerce President Ivan Allen Jr., Sibley planned to have rural members of the assembly introduce "House Bill number eight" in the next session. By January he had procured twenty-eight signatures on the legislation, including the entire delegations from Fulton and DeKalb counties. Allen asked Sibley to contact his bank officers in Rome and Columbus and ask them to approach their assembly delegates and demand passage of the bill. He told Sibley that Mills B. Lane, president of Citizens and Southern Bank, one of the state's largest banks, planned to ask his bank directors in Savannah, Augusta, and Athens to contact their delegates. Allen expressed confidence in the plan, predicting it "should move forward rapidly from this point." Sibley himself, in a letter to Howell Hollis, voiced his reservations about the upcoming General Assembly session. "If the legislature refuses to act until after the final judgement is obtained, much of the flexibility in controlling the situation will be lost." It was, as Robert Sherrill described in *Gothic Politics in the Deep South,* as if "the money kings of Atlanta stepped in to quietly wipe out Herman's nonsense [the private school plan]. . . . The men who owned the legislature went ahead and ordered what they had in mind to begin with: public schools, permanently, and no funny business."[25]

Vandiver's Quandary II

The main reason behind the intense pressure to convince the General Assembly to overturn massive resistance was an increasingly growing belief that Governor Vandiver did not know how to proceed in the school crisis. Hoping that the hearings, by offering the people a clear understanding of the issues, would result in a mandate either to continue resistance or to preserve public education, Vandiver instead received a massive division of opinion and an aroused populace. In addition to his political troubles, the governor was not in good health. He suffered a heart attack during March, and his recovery lessened his effectiveness as governor. Vandiver spent the autumn of 1960 preparing for either contingency: to oppose the federal government when the fall school year opened in 1961 or, if public sentiment allowed, to overturn resistance laws in the next assembly. There existed a faint hope that he would have to do neither. If John F. Kennedy won the presidential election, the governor hoped to be appointed to a federal post (most probably secretary of the army); or if the General Assembly could be convinced to allow the people to decide the issue in the form of a constitutional amendment, and if Judge Hooper allowed for one more long delay, that vote would not take place until the general election in November 1962, three months before Vandiver would leave office. And so Vandiver used the time-honored tactic of public officials—he stalled. The governor avoided public comment on the school crisis and the commission recommendations, assuming a defiant stance without actually having to defy the federal government.

Vandiver spent the early part of the summer actively campaigning for John F. Kennedy's presidential nomination. Robert Troutman, a partner in King and Spalding and former roommate of Joseph Kennedy at Harvard, had pushed Kennedy for the vice presidential nomination in 1956. That summer he introduced the Massachusetts senator to several influential Georgia leaders, including Ernest Vandiver. The two men kept in contact during the last four years of the Eisenhower administration and discussed the future of Georgia's Democratic Party over breakfast in November 1959. Vandiver led the Georgia delegation to the Democratic National Convention in Los Angeles the following July. Upon arrival, Vandiver, James Gray, George L. Smith, Griffin Bell, and Robert Troutman met with Robert Kennedy and discussed Georgia's sit-in movements and how John Kennedy would respond to such events as president. The future attorney general assured the men that he and his brother supported such movements only if they were lawful and that since they were illegal in Georgia, the protesters could expect no support from a Kennedy administration. With this assurance and a belief that Kennedy would work with the South in the arena of civil rights (and the failure of Lyndon Johnson to generate enough momentum to capture the nomination), the delegation backed Kennedy.[26]

Upon returning to Georgia, Vandiver discovered that many political leaders in the state opposed Kennedy's candidacy because they were unsure of his civil rights platform. Among those politicians who adopted this "wait and see" attitude were Roy Harris and senators Russell and Talmadge. Their belief was that the state should use unpledged electors so that the South working together might deny either candidate, John F. Kennedy or Richard M. Nixon, the required number of electoral votes and throw the election into the U.S. House of Representatives, where a unified Dixie could influence the outcome of the election. This strategy would also prevent Kennedy and Johnson from voting for any civil rights legislation that might come up in the August session of Congress.[27]

When that session began, Vandiver traveled to Washington with James Gray and Bob Russell to meet with Kennedy. The men talked with Kennedy and Johnson in the latter's office and explained the fears and apprehensions of many Georgia leaders. Vandiver then asked Kennedy for a private meeting, and the two men excused themselves and went into the Senate Majority Leader's bathroom. There, Vandiver exchanged his support of the Kennedy campaign and the likelihood of Georgia's electoral votes for the promise that, if elected, Kennedy would not send federal troops to Georgia in the event of an integration crisis. "I wanted to have the assurance from him that we wouldn't have a situation in Georgia the way that Arkansas had to confront the federal troops and the National Guard," Vandiver explained. "The National Guard firing on their neighbor, well, that was just unheard of. You couldn't have a situation like that."[28]

Long before his trip to Washington, Vandiver had been preparing for potential defiance to the federal government in case the General Assembly refused to take appropriate measures to overturn mandatory school closing laws. He had suspected what the Sibley Commission would propose long before its report was read on April 28. Griffin Bell talked to Sibley at the King and Spalding offices many times during the hearings and reported the results of these conversations to the governor. Vandiver had hoped that Sibley could convince all the commission members of the viability of his suggestions but feared the panel would be divided in its opinion. Vandiver was convinced that Claude Purcell, Harmon Caldwell, Charles Cowan, Homer Rankin, and Robert Arnold would join Sibley and surmised that Eulond Clary, John Duncan, Walstein Parker, Render Hill, Battle Hall, J. W. Keyton, Wallace Jernigan, and George Brooks would support continued resistance. And although he was unsure about John Greer, Howell Hollis, Zade Kenimer, and John Dent, he believed that they would side with Sibley.[29]

Some of the men closest to the governor worked to make overturning resistance law possible. Carl Sanders and Frank Twitty, on a speaking tour of the state that fall, realized that public support for resistance was waning and hinted that some amount of integration was inevitable. In Augusta, Sanders claimed that he preferred open schools. Vandiver's key consultant on the segregation and massive resistance question, "B" Brooks, spent the last two months before the forthcoming assembly session preparing strategy to overturn mandatory school closing laws. At the end of November, Griffin Bell suggested to Brooks that the amendment to abandon massive resistance, a local option bill written by Freeman Leverett and Robert Battle Hall (who signed the Sibley Commission's minority report), be introduced in the

House. The next day Leverett sent Brooks a copy of the amendment. In the early days of the new year, on the eve of the assembly's first meeting, the men, much like their business counterparts, recruited several rural representatives to help them; among delegates were R. E. Cannon of Clayton County, Ed Goble of Gilmer County, Marvin Moate of Hancock County, David Newton of Colquitt County, and Henry Payton of Coweta County.[30]

Vandiver, however, still publicly maintained that he would uphold Georgia law, perhaps because he hoped to be offered the secretary of the army position under the new John F. Kennedy Administration. The governor had certainly done his part to help elect the new president. Besides helping with the Kennedy campaign, Vandiver had surreptitiously arranged for the candidate to receive credit for the release of civil rights leader Martin Luther King Jr. from a Georgia prison in the week before the election. Kennedy and his brother Robert had made some well-publicized phone calls after King was sentenced. John phoned King's wife to offer his moral support, and Robert called the judge that sentenced King to state prison for a parole violation (stemming from an earlier traffic violation) and asked that the judge order King's release. Vandiver had cleared the way for Robert to call the judge and ensured that the younger Kennedy would have a receptive listener. This event garnered Kennedy huge support from African American voters.[31]

In the days before Kennedy's inauguration, Georgia's newspapers reported that the governor and president-elect had worked out all but the final details of a Vandiver appointment. The press gathered outside the home of Lieutenant Governor Garland Byrd, waiting for his reaction to Vandiver's appointment and his succession to the governor's office. Byrd's segregationist beliefs were known to be even stronger than the governor's, and conjecture about his possible response to the state's school crisis swirled around the capitol. But on 5 January, Vandiver announced that Georgia's problems were too immense for him to leave office and he withdrew his candidacy for the federal position.[32]

From Courthouse to Campus

On 6 January, the Friday before the assembly was to meet, a federal judge in Macon, William A. Bootle, ordered the University of Georgia to immediately admit and enroll two African American students, Hamilton Holmes and

Charlayne Hunter. Holmes and Hunter then drove from the Macon court-house to the Athens campus. Along with their attorneys Donald Hollowell and Constance Motely, they entered the registrar's office with a copy of the court order. The students filed new applications (the originals were still with the federal court), drove to their homes in Atlanta, and spent the weekend, packing, choosing classes, and preparing to register the following Monday. No one knew what to expect when black and white Georgia met in the class-room for the first time. The university was in an uproar; that night a group of students burned crosses on the track field. The following day Governor Vandiver sent Attorney General Eugene Cook to Macon to request a stay in Bootle's order.[33]

On Monday the ninth, Judge Bootle granted Cook's petition stopping Holmes' and Hunter's registration. Hollowell and Motely immediately phoned Elbert Tuttle, the senior judge of the Fifth Circuit Court of Appeals, and asked him to overturn the stay. Tuttle granted their request, claiming Bootle had no reason to prevent the registration other than the state's request. That night, Eugene Cook flew to Washington, D.C., and asked Supreme Court Justice Hugo Black, who was responsible for the Fifth Circuit Court of Appeals, to overturn Tuttle's decision. Black denied the request on the morn-ing of the tenth. That afternoon, Ernest Vandiver ordered the university closed. Years later, Vandiver lamented his hopeless situation. "These students had been carefully screened and were obviously well qualified. The order of the judge said now, and since this was the last day of registration, no time was left to appeal. Under the laws of Georgia I had no choice but to order the Uni-versity of Georgia closed." [34]

Earlier that day, in the midst of this school crisis, Vandiver gave his annual state of the state message to the assembly. In it he deviated little from his pre-pared remarks to address the plight at the university. He said only that the sit-uation would require hourly attention and pledged that when the students entered the school he would suspend funding. He would not, however, be "party to defiance of the law, as a few would wish, or do anything which might foment strife and violence in an explosive situation." Members of the assembly expressed ambivalence towards the governor's address. Pierre Howard of DeKalb County said, "I never heard one man talk about so many things that don't need immediate action and so little about things that do need immediate action. He didn't tell us what his remedy is for the school

situation." James Mackay expressed concern over the governor's unwill-
ingness to call for "uninterrupted public education." Freshman legislator
Thomas B. Murphy sighed relief that Vandiver finally comprehended "the
theory that we cannot afford to close our public schools." And Render Hill,
of the Sibley Commission, defended the governor, claiming it was the best
"speech as could be made under the circumstances."[35]

The next day, the eleventh, Judge Bootle ordered the school opened and
filed an injunction against Vandiver forbidding him from cutting off funds to
the school until a hearing on school funding laws could be held the next day.
Hamilton Holmes and Charlayne Hunter went to class at the University of
Georgia. It was, as the *Atlanta Journal* described, "the first time that Negroes
and whites have sat down together in the same classroom in a tax-supported
school." The *Albany Herald* called the situation "an ugly abuse of federal
power" and predicted that the General Assembly would turn to the Sibley
Commission recommendations in the face of the crisis. The *Athens Banner-
Herald* called for an immediate end to resistance. The paper asserted that,
even though limited integration was "contrary to the wishes of state leaders
and thousands of Georgians," it was "tolerable" because "closure of the University and the resultant damage to the culture and economy of the state
[was] intolerable."[36]

That night, following a Georgia-Georgia Tech basketball game, riots
erupted on the campus. Students stood outside Charlayne Hunter's dormi-
tory and hurled rocks through the windows. One rioter clobbered a television news reporter's face with a brick. According to one witness, the large
crowd moved "like wheat blowing in unison and there wasn't any straggling.
Whichever way the wind blew, . . . they all went that way." The Dean of Men,
William Tate, waded into the crowd demanding student identification cards
and screaming at individual students. He punched anyone inciting violence.
Many of the rioters were led by Eldon Edwards of the U.S. Klans, and he and
seven other members were arrested—all were armed. Governor Vandiver
called out some units of the state patrol to quell the riot, but according to
Athens Mayor Ralph Snow, by the time they arrived, the situation had grown
much less dangerous. Some observers believed that the governor wanted to
allow the extreme segregationists to make their point, an assertion he denied.
That night, Vandiver suspended Holmes and Hunter to maintain the peace.[37]

Roy Harris praised the rioters. "They had the courage and the nerve to stand up in the face of federal court decrees and to defy the police and the army of Deans and get the Negroes out of the university." He asserted, "these students are entitled to your encouragement." In another statement, he claimed that when the "students found the governor, the legislature, and the school administration didn't have the nerve to deal with the situation they took it in their own hands." Vandiver responded by joining "that rapidly growing group of citizens who do not want to engage in trading statements with Mr. Roy Harris." [38]

On Thursday, the American Association of University Professors held a meeting among the faculty to protest the suspension of Holmes and Hunter. History professor Horace Montgomery wrote up a resolution demanding the students' reinstatement—four hundred faculty members signed the document. Vandiver felt the pressure from other organizations that urged him to reinstate the students, keep the school open, and end massive resistance. [39]

At the hearing on the suspension of funds to the university later that afternoon, Judge Bootle ruled unconstitutional Georgia's 1956 provision that denied state money to an integrated public school. In response to Vandiver's suspension of the students, Donald Hollowell asked Bootle to reinstate Holmes and Hunter. Freeman Leverett, the state attorney, asked that he be given time to prepare a defense of the suspension. Bootle advised Hollowell and Motely to make a written request for reinstatement and then he would make a ruling. On Friday he responded to the written request and ordered that the students be reinstated to the school on Monday. [40]

Years later, Ernest Vandiver recalled his feelings when he realized that weekend that he finally had to choose between direct defiance of a federal court order or compliance and an acceptance of integration. "There was a feeling of impending doom. Had a case been filed against Georgia Tech, I think there probably would have been a difference because Tech had so many out of state students and didn't have ties to every family in Georgia that the University of Georgia has. I mean, the University of Georgia is just part of the fabric of Georgia." He continued: "I had to make the fundamental decision of whether I was going to do what George Wallace later did in Alabama and stand in the school house door. The popular thing to do would have been to go to jail, and make a big media event out of this thing. . . . I figured that if I made the decision to go along with the court order that I would be finished politically, that I would be through. . . . As a governor, I was sworn to uphold the constitution and laws of this country, and if I violated them, it might be smart politically, but it would have thrown the state into the kind of turmoil that they had in Arkansas, Alabama, and Mississippi. I figured it as worth sacrificing one man's political ambitions to go ahead and take whatever flak was coming."[41] After two years of avoiding and vacillating on the school question, the situation at the university forced Ernest Vandiver into a decision. He could not close the University of Georgia nor would he directly defy the federal government. When constrained to choose Georgia's final direction in its resistance movement, he relied solely upon his practicality and pragmatism. He knew that any truculent posturing over the university's desegregation would end in failure and harm the state's and the university's reputation.

That weekend, representative Charles Pannel of Murray County (one of Sibley's and Allen's "rural" legislators) told reporters that he would sponsor a House bill to allow for public education and that he had much unpledged support for the bill in addition to twenty-eight signatures already affixed. Pannel urged every citizen to contact his representative to ensure the bill's passage and the continuation of public education in Georgia.[42]

On Monday, the day Hamilton Holmes and Charlayne Hunter returned to the university, Vandiver called together "fifty or sixty people, leaders, state department heads, legislative leaders, and others to the executive mansion to discuss the situation."[43] During the deliberation, only Carl Sanders and Frank Twitty recommended the abandonment of massive resistance and urged that the university be kept open. Near the end of the meeting, Vandiver went around the room shaking hands, thanking everyone for their efforts, and telling them that he had enjoyed working with them. The members of the gathering asked Vandiver what was going on. He told them that he planned to recommend the repeal of not only the mandatory school closing laws but all massive resistance legislation, and he knew that if he did they would feel compelled to resign.[44] He announced his intention to call the General Assembly into a special night session on Wednesday to overturn the resistance laws. After most of the men left, the governor met with a smaller group of his principal advisors including Render Hill and Peter Zack Geer, and sat down with "B" Brooks to prepare his Wednesday night speech. When they were finished, Brooks walked out of the door of the governor's mansion, turned to the small gathering of interested onlookers and reporters, and in his best Neville Chamberlain impersonation, opened his umbrella and said, "Gentlemen, there will be peace in our time."[45]

The next day Governor Vandiver called for a joint session of the assembly to meet at seven o'clock on Wednesday evening, marking the first night session of the legislature in the history of the state. He wanted to ensure that a large television and radio audience understood "that we just could not afford to have a generation of children without any education at all, and could not close the schools." He believed that television coverage "would be more helpful than just talking to the legislature. At least people could put pressure on their legislators to support this legislation." Griffin Bell, seeking a favorable response from the *Atlanta Constitution* and *Journal*, kept the papers' editors Gene Patterson and Jack Spalding apprised of the events at the governor's office.[46]

Speaking to a packed session of the assembly, Vandiver finally but firmly announced his decision on the desegregation crisis at the University of Georgia and the conflict between massive resistance legislation and the federal government. The speech outlined for the state a plan to adopt the measures of the Sibley Commission report. He told the legislators that "public education will be preserved." He described the events of early January as "days of shock, frayed tempers, anger, shouting, even violence, but" he continued, "over in the distance, through it all shone a steady light—the light of Georgia character, the innate inbred integrity of our people." He criticized the federal government and the courts for transforming Georgia laws from "instruments of defense to instruments of doom" and warned the legislators that if something were not done, the confrontation between Georgia and the federal courts would spread "like a cancerous growth, it will devour progress—consuming all in its path—pitting friend against friend—demoralizing all that is good—stifling the economic growth of the state and denying the youth of Georgia their proper educational opportunity." He called for an end to the "futile defiance of federal force and authority" but hoped to continue the maintenance of segregation. He then turned to the recommendations of the Sibley Commission majority report and asked that the General Assembly adopt a "freedom of association" amendment that would be accompanied by three bills: the first to suspend massive resistance laws and guarantee a grants-in-aid and pupil placement plan, the second to allow for local option, and the third to turn control of schools over to their local school boards.[47]

Legislative reaction to the speech and the plan set forth by the governor was surprisingly positive. It was, as news reporter Celestine Sibley described it, as if "the scales . . . fell off their eyes. . . . I sort of felt an undercurrent of acceptance mainly because they loved their schools and loved the prospect of having their own children [attend the University."][48] Frank Twitty and Carl Sanders expected the bills to be passed within the week, and Speaker George L. Smith called it "realistic and most heartening." Two members of the Sibley Commission agreed: Wallace Jernigan commended the governor for "taking the initiative to present . . . a package of bills [that] has a good chance of passage," and Battle Hall thought "it represents the best thinking available on the subject." Freeman Leverett later wrote John Sibley and told him, "You would probably find the behind-the-scenes maneuvering on the 1961 school bills interesting."[49]

Shortly before the governor spoke, Hugh Grant, Roy Harris's longtime political ally, climbed the steps of the capitol, knowing what was about to take place inside the chamber. The creator of the States' Rights Council of Georgia addressed a small group of ardent segregationists and lambasted Roy Harris and the state's politicians for precipitating the end of segregation. He realized, all too late, that the politicalization of segregation had accelerated its downfall.[50]

Harris denounced Vandiver for "throwing in the towel" and tried in vain to convince the assembly not to accept the governor's proposals. He appeared before the House Education Committee and beseeched to hold to defiance, but to no avail. The headline of the 30 January edition of the *Augusta Courier* read "BYRD, SANDERS, SMITH, TWITTY, ALSO JOIN IN IRREVOCABLE PLOT TO RACE MIX SCHOOLS." He lashed out at the Sibley Commission, which Vandiver and others had promised him was only a plan to stall for time, and described Vandiver's speech as "absolute proof that behind the Sibley Commission was a deliberate scheme to lay the foundation to surrender Georgia to the race mixers in 1961."[51]

Two of the state's other most committed resisters echoed Harris's indignation. Marvin Griffin directed most of his attacks at his old enemy Ernest Vandiver. "Georgia has long been looked upon by other southern states as the capstone and the bulwark against the insidious onslaughts of the NAACP and others to force integration and destroy our way of life. When we needed a man to stand up and be counted in the governor's chair of this state, we got a weakling, who first tried to run away from his responsibilities of office by getting a Washington appointment, and then when he failed in this, threw in the towel." Griffin described Vandiver's speech as "a sell out . . . all preamble and no punchline . . . a surrender speech dressed up in pretty phrases." James Gray scoffed at the notion of "defense in depth" and said saving public education was not worth the price of "principle and Southern tradition." [52]

Despite objections from those still committed to resistance, Vandiver's bills sped through the assembly with little difficulty. The governor signed the bills into law on 31 January. Hamilton Lokey explained the assembly's actions. "The legislature might have been willing to close all of Atlanta's public schools rather than permit integration, [but] it was unwilling to destroy the University, so we yielded." Jesse Hill, the vice president of the Atlanta Life Insurance Company, agreed. "The Governor might have closed Georgia State or the Atlanta High Schools if they had come first, but the University of Georgia with all those legislators' sons over there and the way everybody in the state feels about it was different. He wouldn't dare close it." In addition to the love that Georgians from all over the state felt for the University of Georgia (with pride they will explain that it was the first chartered state institution of higher learning in the United States), it was also the alma mater of a majority in the assembly and most Georgians with a college degree. More importantly however, Judge Bootle had followed the pattern predicted by James Mackay the previous spring. He ordered the university's funding restored and decreed that Georgia's mandatory school closing laws were unconstitutional. The judge said nothing about other schools. Members of the General Assembly confronted the inevitability that if the state were to convert to private schools they would have to vote to end public education in Georgia.[53]

Atlanta

With massive resistance legislation removed from the state statutes, the way was cleared for Atlanta to comply with the decision in *Calhoun v. Latimer*, and the city prepared to desegregate its school systems. Atlanta ministers spoke to their congregations and told them that the desegregation of the schools offered them an opportunity to apply Christian precepts in their lives. HOPE, the NAACP, and other groups formed the Organizations Assisting Schools in September (OASIS) and cooperated with the city's government and school officials to make the transition go smoothly. Ralph McGill donated advertising space to the new organization and in his editorials appealed to Atlantans' civic pride to help desegregation efforts. But this did not mean that Atlanta was embracing the spirit of the *Brown* decision, for that was not the case. School officials applied rigid and complex admission procedures that were designed to stymie the flow of applications to white schools. Atlanta's black parents who wished to transfer their children to white schools could only apply for a transfer from 1 to 15 May and were required to have their application notarized. The children were then subjected to psychological and placement tests. During that first year, only nine students in the entire system received approval to change schools.[54]

As the first day of school approached on 30 August, the city prepared for every possible contingency. City leaders were anxious to avoid any ugly confrontations like those that had erupted in New Orleans and Little Rock. One television news station sent reporters to New Orleans and Charlotte to observe their school desegregation efforts. Mayor Hartsfield furnished the onslaught of reporters from all over the country with a central information center at City Hall designed to squelch rumors and hearsay by offering the newsmen instant access to city officials. The chief of police, Herbert Jenkins, kept a close eye on the schools and arrested anyone found on school property who could not offer a legitimate reason for being there. Known segregationist leaders were conspicuously watched by police and kept far from the four Atlanta high schools that were to be desegregated, one of which was Henry Grady High School, site of the Atlanta Sibley Commission hearing.[55]

The preparation of the city's leaders reaped the expected dividends. There were no fervent protests, and Atlanta became the first Deep South city peacefully to integrate its school system. President John F. Kennedy offered his congratulations to Governor Vandiver, Mayor Hartsfield, Herbert Jenkins, and the citizens of Atlanta for their efforts. The nation watched on its television screens as the "city too busy to hate" lived up to its reputation live on the *Today* show.[56]

The overturning of resistance law that permitted the Atlanta schools to desegregate without incident was largely the direct result of the efforts of John Sibley and the commission that bore his name. Its report and recommendations offered a blueprint for changing Georgia law and making token desegregation palatable for the citizens of the state. The day before the governor signed the new school bills into law, Erwin Sibley wrote to his brother congratulating him "for incubating the plan and progress of the lately adopted education laws in the effort to control desegregation in this State and which but for your wise and patient hearings as chairman of the State-wide Committee several months ago, could not be realized at this time."[57] The actions of certain committee members speaking publicly on the merits of the report and the efforts of others affiliated with the panel working within the confines of government allowed for the necessary changes in the state's massive resistance legislation to create a reconstruction of resistance and permit the continuity of segregated education.

Business leaders' adoption of open school advocacy permitted the state's economic future to grow unchecked by the strategies of politicians who had staked their futures on the precepts of white supremacy. The effective methods of the fiscally motivated partners in the open school crusade provided the necessary catalyst to allow uninterrupted public education.

This usurpation of the ideas and ideals of HOPE and others by those dedicated to economics or even continued segregation rather than racial equity created some resentment among the original champions of open schools. They felt that the commission did little and offered no real new ideas or solutions to the school crisis and questioned the governor's original motives in creating the panel. Nan Pendergrast, HOPE's primary public spokesperson, believed that the governor was surprised at the commission's results and final report. "I don't think that when Governor Vandiver appointed him [Sibley], he had any idea that Sibley was going to come up with what he did. And I know that when I heard he was appointed, I wasn't all that hopeful. I knew that he was a very prominent man and a very intelligent man. But it is hard to judge him. He was a very cold fish."[58]

Indeed, she was correct; Vandiver did not know what to expect from the commission, its hearings or its final report when he originally considered the idea. He only hoped that it would give him some indication of public opinion. Years later Griffin Bell reflected on the hearings: "This was an open thing. The Governor was hoping that Mr. Sibley's side would win, but it was tough going to know that. The people . . . were stirred up, particularly in South Georgia. They just raised hell at these meetings. That's why I think that if we had a vote on it by the people, they would have voted to close the schools."[59]

The Sibley Commission provided a vital link between community involvement in open school advocacy and political commitment to massive resistance. Although the panel's message was remarkably similar to that of HOPE, the commission's government sanction, judicial setting, and public forums allowed it to reach many more Georgians than HOPE could have ever achieved. The commission also linked itself to segregationist politicians by promoting open schools as the best way to preserve separate schools.

The unexpected court order to admit Hamilton Holmes and Charlayne Hunter to the University of Georgia left the governor and state political leaders with only the Sibley Commission's recommendations to guide them. During this period of chaos and confusion, the commission's proposals seemed the only viable option to closing the school. It is fortunate that Georgia's initial experience with desegregation occurred at the university and during the General Assembly session; this timing enabled Vandiver to immediately turn to the legislature to dismantle massive resistance and eliminated the need to call for a special session, as would have been the case in the fall. The University of Georgia crisis also forced many resistance leaders in the legislature to realize that defiance would affect them and their constituents in a way that closing the Atlanta schools would not. With the Sibley Commission's recommendations to ensure maximum segregation under the law to guide them, they and the governor shifted their stance and accepted Sibley's restructured resistance that enabled them to defy the spirit of the *Brown* decision much longer than massive resistance could possibly permit.

A Nice Refreshing Pause

In October 1961, shortly after the desegregation of Atlanta schools, HOPE sent an invitation to its supporters to help celebrate the preservation of public education. The invitation came in the form of a poem written by Nan Pendergrast.

> The air is full of fall out;
> the woods are full of spies.
> The courts are full of lawsuits;
> the Russians full of lies.
> Berlin is full of tension,
> and Africa's aflame.
> But Georgia, bless her heart, has made herself a name.
> She's run HOPE out of business,
> in the best way we could ask.
> Now each of us is free to choose another noble task.
> But before we launch ourselves
> into the next consuming cause,
> We need a brief hiatus—a nice refreshing pause.[1]

This backhanded acknowledgment of Coca-Cola's involvement in resolving the school crisis is indicative of the major role that business and industrial

leadership played in settling the issue. The man that the state's corporate hierarchy depended upon in this resolution was one of its most influential associates, John A. Sibley.

John Sibley led the state out of the quagmire of contention between federal law and state resistance using time-honored, paternalistic conventions.
His wise, grandfatherly image allowed Georgians to maintain a link with their
ancestors as they preserved education for their children. Sibley represented
the new image of Georgia, one dedicated to the principles of modern education, political tolerance, and above all economic growth, but not at the expense of tradition. He reflected all the positive tenets of the paternal figure—
good sense, intelligence, and a firm but fair hand—wrapped in the guise of
the gentleman-businessman-farmer. He presented living proof that Georgia
and its citizens could accept the modern world and still maintain their southern heritage and culture. This image helped Sibley compel Georgians seriously to consider which principle they held most dear, public education or
resistance to the federal government. He did not force them to choose between education and segregation but rather between education and resistance, for the chairman made everyone well aware that it was quite possible
to forge a new system of legal segregation removed from the political control
of massive resistance; thus preserving Georgia "tradition" without sacrificing
education and the future of the state's children.

The governmental sanction of the commission and the judicial setting
helped form a widespread public acceptance of the Sibley proposals. The
hearings, an excellent portrayal of modern paternalism, allowed any citizen,
rich or poor, black or white, man or woman, to express his or her views
within the carefully calculated framework of the commission's options. John
Sibley, acting as a moderator, listened intently to everyone, casting no judg-
ments on individual opinion. He was a man who, according to one observer
who attended every hearing, "had a look of somebody that if you walked in
and said 'Judge, Jeff and I have a disagreement, and we would say that whatever you say Jeff and I have decided that we will accept it; that one of us is
wrong.' I mean he was the kind of guy that when I looked at him I thought he
would tell you the truth."[2] After hearing Georgians speak their minds, Sibley
released his report, symbolically walking alone into the state supreme court
chamber to render his decision. His recommendation to overturn resistance
was palatable to many of Georgia's white citizens, not because of any adop-

tion of progressive racial attitudes but due to a subtle conservative shift in priorities. Most of these people simply did not want to surrender public education in a futile political battle with the federal courts. The Sibley Commission hearings and report helped the populace understand that a small retreat from Georgia's defiant stance would not only preserve the schools but also empower each community with the future of its own local education system, removing it from the control of the state's politicians. This movement, though conservative and pragmatic, represented a significant shift from previously held conventions. The committee hearings ended the silence that surrounded the sanctity of segregation and forced Georgia to answer difficult questions about societal priorities that few people living within the vacuum of a strictly segregated society dared to ask.

After the hearings, Sibley's reputation continued to grow in stature. He was the first recipient of Georgia's Distinguished Service Medal for his actions in the spring of 1960. In 1961 he received the annual "Brenda" award, given by a journalism sorority to the person who had done the most in the field of communications during the previous year. And in February 1975 he received the "Shining Light Award," given to Georgia citizens whose work contributed immeasurably to the progress of the state. On 30 April 1977 Herman Talmadge praised Sibley when presiding over the unveiling ceremony of his portrait at the University of Georgia Law School. "He listened with patience, sympathy and understanding to the diverse opinion, the frustrations, and the bitterness," Talmadge reminded his listeners. "And he affirmed the ultimate supremacy of the law, illuminating the inevitable choice before the people of Georgia. . . . John Sibley's commitment to the value of education and its place in the welfare of our state tipped the balance in favor of preserving public education in Georgia."[3]

Georgians from all stations in life credited John Sibley and the commission for saving the state's public schools. Senator Sam Nunn, speaking at Griffin Bell's confirmation hearing for United States Attorney General, told his fellow senators that the Sibley Commission "is universally, by black and white, credited with being the vehicle that saved the Georgia public school system during those tumultuous and potentially explosive times." This sentiment was echoed by many of Georgia's leaders, including Herman Talmadge, Ernest Vandiver, Griffin Bell, and Osgood Williams. Noted Atlanta African American leader A. T. Walden told Sibley in a letter shortly before the

Atlanta schools were desegregated, "I am sure that the crowning achievement of your fruitful life shall prove to have been the Sibley Report authored by you and interpreted with such crystal clarity that it might be understood by the man in the street." Erwin Sibley wrote to his brother and told him that he believed "it is not unreasonable to presume that its influence [the majority report] may be reflected in the national attitude of sobering up the emotional pressure that has been engendered in dealing with the situation under many misapprehensions." And John Sibley himself thought "from the standpoint of the public interest and historical significance of the questions involved, it was certainly the most important single thing I've ever had any connection with." He was extremely pleased with the results of his work. "I think it's had a very happy ending. The public school system has been preserved, law and order maintained and the reputation of the state and its people enhanced all over the world."[4]

John Sibley's reputation extended outside Georgia, and his advice and counsel on the conflict between the federal government and southern segregation laws was sought by many during the heady days of the civil rights movement. He continued to justify his belief in locally controlled, voluntary segregation and the futility of resistance. In an interview with *U.S. News and World Report,* Sibley responded to a question on the slow movement of integration in the South by saying that most black southerners were satisfied with and appreciated the value of their own schools. In 1963, Sibley spoke to the Birmingham, Alabama, Kiwanis Club on the dangers of maintaining resistance. "Such resistance will prove futile, humiliating and degrading. It will open the way for further harsh, punitive and oppressive legislation to be fostered by the successors of Thaddeus Stevens in the Senate and will give the self-righteous politicians of other sections of the country a platform upon which to perpetuate their political power." Sibley, no racial progressive, recommended taking appropriate measures only to preserve public education and economic security. In 1964 he publicly came out in opposition to the Civil Rights Act in a speech to the Southern States Conference of Certified Public Accountants. In his remarks he called for the people to move ahead with desegregating public facilities, claiming that continued defiance toward civil rights legislation could lead toward a police state.[5]

As time separated the commission and the atmosphere that created it, detractors appeared. One ardent segregationist, Carolyn Hansen, wrote to

Sibley after he received an award in 1975. "Rather than a Shining Light Award for you, a far more fitting [sic] would be the present degenerated condition of the schools. Remember, our schools were of excellent rating until you broke them down by forcing blacks and whites. You were in good company with old Benny Mays [longtime president of Morehouse College]. You will have to answer for this some day. You destroyed the God-given rights of people to comply with the communists [sic] plan for racial degeneration." She included with her letter newspaper articles on "white flight," Sibley's award ceremony, violence in the Atlanta schools, and an enumeration of Benjamin Mays' alleged communist leanings.[6]

While some staunch segregationists lamented the results of the commission, a far more compelling complaint arose from the African American community. After Jimmy Carter was elected president in 1976, he named Griffin Bell his attorney general. During Bell's confirmation hearings, he was forced to answer for some of his actions while acting as Ernest Vandiver's chief of staff. He claimed to have acted moderately given the extremely volatile circumstances that surrounded the Vandiver administration. To prove his point he offered the Sibley Commission as proof of his temperate reaction to Georgia's school crisis. But many who testified in the confirmation hearings attested that the commission was only a validation of Bell's, and indeed Georgia's, racial conservatism. The NAACP's Clarence Mitchell called the panel and its suggestions "a more sophisticated attempt to evade the court's decision." Joseph Rauh, of the Americans for Democratic Action, claimed that the "Sibley Commission was set up at the very moment when massive resistance died. It was reborn again massive resistance." He called the committee's recommendations "massive recalcitrance" and said that Griffin Bell and John Sibley orchestrated, not the preservation of the public schools, but "a simple retreat to the next stage in segregation, a stage they thought would win." Rauh is correct, of course, in part of his assessment. The Sibley Commission was designed to preserve local segregation—and both subtle and overt segregation exists in many forms to this very day—but it was also planned to save the public schools. A prominent member of Atlanta's black community during the 1950s and 1960s, Walter Cochrane, explained to the Senate panel that "in spite of the bad report, and I have read the Sibley report, but that was the best that could be gotten out of it at that time. You don't look at the report alone; you look what was done."[7]

What was done was a restructuring of resistance, but another result was a new configuration in Georgia politics. As Numan Bartley has argued, the chief political legacy of massive resistance was the breakdown of any New Deal alliance between urban progressives and poor rural whites as the politics of massive resistance lured the wool hat boys toward the pure racial politics of Talmadge, Griffin, and Vandiver. It also fractured the courthouse-boardroom alliance. When resistance threatened economic growth, a new alliance was formed between the business conservatives (who had always quietly favored the frugality of neo-bourbon governors like Eugene Talmadge), urban progressives, and African Americans. This alliance severely weakened the economic support of the racially conservative politicians who relied upon corporate funding for their election coffers.[8]

The Sibley Commission showed everyone in Georgia the serious division over the school question and made many in government realize that it would be very perilous for any politician to stake too firm a claim with either side of the issue. By effectively removing race from its central position, the commission permitted a new political power to emerge in the Piedmont and urban areas, two sections of the state that had always been stifled by racial politics, especially during Georgia's romance with resistance. In 1962, when the Fifth Circuit Court of Appeals and its newest judge, Griffin Bell, dismantled the county unit system, the decentralization of the Black Belt's political power entered its final phase. That same year the gubernatorial election featured Carl Sanders running against Marvin Griffin. Each planned to use the end of massive resistance as a major campaign issue. Griffin wailed about the failure of Ernest Vandiver to maintain complete segregation and averred that only with a devout white supremacist in office could the state withstand massive integration. Sanders pointed to the progress of Georgia as the fundamental issue and called himself a segregationist "but not a damned fool." He promised Georgia "while I am governor we are going to obey the laws, we are not going to resist Federal court orders with violence, and we are not going to close any schools." And in this race, the first gubernatorial election in the modern era not controlled by the county unit system, Sanders handily defeated one of the principal authors of massive resistance.[9]

Although it deserves much of the credit it receives for saving the public schools in Georgia, the Sibley Commission was only the physical manifestation of the political, social, and economic revolutions taking place in the state and throughout the South. Calvin Trillin once described the commission's hearings as part of the "ritual" of accepting change. One commission member believed that the panel acted as a "catalyst" in promoting the acceptance of desegregated schools by getting "out into the boondocks and talking to people." He is proud of the committee's accomplishments for "making the people think" and for creating an acceptance for change that helped to "avoid the bloodshed" that accompanied the same transformations in other parts of the South.[10]

We can credit John Sibley and Ernest Vandiver for recognizing the potential for violence and the importance of allowing the people to express their opinions with words and not rocks, spittle, or guns. Because of the Sibley Commission's work, when the moment of truth came for Georgia, massive resistance, always only a political movement, faded quickly. The state's citizens and its leaders had enough time to reflect on the changes in their society and come to terms with them. The commission's hearings provided an open conduit of communication and information for all Georgians—politicians, business leaders, segregationists, resisters, open school advocates, and African Americans—to express their views on the future of Georgia.

NOTES

Introduction

1. "Opening Statement," John A. Sibley, Papers, Georgia General Assembly Committee on Schools Collection, Robert W. Woodruff Library, Emory University, Atlanta, Georgia (hereafter cited as Sibley Papers). Since I finished the research for this project, the Sibley Papers have been processed by the staff of the Woodruff Library Special Collections Department. Because the box and file numbers have all changed, citations will include as much information as possible without the exact location within the collection. However, all citations, unless otherwise noted, refer to the Committee on Schools Collection, which is housed separately from Sibley's other papers that are also located in Woodruff Library's Special Collections. Time, distance, and expense prevented me from returning to the collection to match my notes with the recently processed collection. I apologize for any inconvenience this might cause future researchers.

2. For an insightful look at the changes the South faced after the Second World War and the challenges they offer historians, see Numan Bartley, "Writing About the Post–World War II South," *Georgia Historical Quarterly* 68, no. 1 (spring 1984): 1–18. For Bartley's masterful synthesis of the period see *The New South: 1945–1980* (Baton Rouge: Louisiana State University Press, 1995). For an extensive look at the civil rights movement in the South and its effects on society, see David R. Goldfield, *Black, White, and Southern: Race Relations and Southern Culture, 1940 to the Present* (Baton Rouge: Louisiana State University Press, 1990). And for a class and economic analysis of the movement, see Jack M. Bloom, *Class, Race, and the Civil Rights Movement* (Bloomington and Indianapolis: Indiana University Press, 1987). Examinations of the transformation of the agricultural economy during the postwar period include: Pete Daniel, *Breaking the Land: The Transformation of Cotton, Tobacco, and Rice Cultures*

Since 1880 (Urbana: University of Illinois Press, 1985); and Jack Temple Kirby, *Rural Worlds Lost: The American South, 1920–1960* (Baton Rouge: Louisiana State University Press, 1987). James C. Cobb has written two excellent works on the southern economy during the twentieth century, *The Selling of the South: The Southern Crusade for Industrial Development, 1936–1980* (Baton Rouge: Louisiana State University Press, 1982); and *Industrialization and Southern Society, 1877–1984* (Lexington: University Press of Kentucky, 1984). See also Bruce J. Schulman, *From Cotton Belt to Sunbelt: Federal Policy, Economic Development and the Transformation of the South, 1938–1980* (New York: Oxford, 1991).

3. For a thorough examination of southern massive resistance, see Numan Bartley, *The Rise of Massive Resistance: Race and Politics in the South During the 1950s* (Baton Rouge: Louisiana State University Press, 1969). For more on southern political trends during this era, see Dan T. Carter, "Southern Political Style," in *The Age of Segregation: Race Relations in the South, 1890–1945*, ed. Robert Haws (Jackson: University Press of Mississippi, 1978), especially 56–57, and Dewey Grantham Jr., "The South and the Politics of Sectionalism," in *The South and the Sectional Image: The Sectional Theme Since Reconstruction* (New York: Harper and Row, 1967).

4. Render Hill, telephone interview by author, 3 September 1995.

5. Elizabeth Stevenson, "A Personal History of Change in Atlanta," *Virginia Quarterly Review* 41 (April 1965): 594.

6. For more on national political changes after the failures of massive resistance, see Dan T. Carter, *The Politics of Rage: George Wallace, the Origins of the New Conservatism, and the Transformation of American Politics* (New York: Simon and Schuster, 1995). Carter persuasively argues that Alabama's George Wallace effectively utilized resistance political strategy and rhetoric to gain a nationwide appeal. Since Wallace, Carter contends, other political conservatives have recognized and copied Wallace's message and guided the strategy of the New Right.

Chapter 1

Augusta Courier, 7 June 1954.

1. Interview with Roy Harris, 29 July 1947, in Calvin Kytle and James Mackay, "We Pass . . . On Democracy: Who Runs Georgia," unpublished manuscript, Special Collections Department, Robert W. Woodruff Library, Emory University, Atlanta, Georgia. "We Pass" is scheduled to be published by the University of Georgia Press. Hereafter references to the manuscript and accompanying interviews will be cited as Kytle and Mackay, "We Pass."

2. The whites-only primary was used in many southern states, including Georgia, to disfranchise African American voters. In states where the Republican Party was almost non-existent, the winner of the Democratic primary usually ran with little or no opposition in the general election.

3. Judge Elbert Tuttle quoted in Jack Bass, *Unlikely Heroes* (New York: Simon and Schuster, 1981), 26. Alterations in Georgia's social and economic landscape left the state's leaders grappling with the best method to deal with them. As Randall Patton has noted, Georgia had three main options: the "Talmadge" option of hanging on to the existing social order, using white supremacy to ensure social stability in the face of a changing economic infrastructure; integrating its economy into northern industrial concerns; or pursuing "an anti-colonial policy, promoting southern industries and economic growth." Randall L. Patton, "A Southern Liberal and the Politics of Anti-Colonialism: The Governorship of Ellis Arnall," *Georgia Historical Quarterly* 74, no. 3 (fall 1990): 609.

4. The county unit system, enacted at the turn of the century, was designed to prevent the possibility of urban political machines dominating the then largely rural state. Counties were represented by two, four, or six votes based on population, and the candidate receiving the plurality of votes in that county received its unit votes. In the years following the Second World War, the county unit system rewarded those in the least populated county with a vote worth almost eighty times that of a voter in the state's most populous county. See Numan Bartley, *From Thurmond to Wallace: Political Tendencies in Georgia, 1948–1968* (Baltimore: Johns Hopkins University Press, 1970), 15, and V. O. Key, *Southern Politics in State and Nation* (New York: Vintage Books, 1949), 117–19.

5. Ellis Arnall, interview by Jane Walker Herndon, 24 July 1971, Georgia Government Documentation Project, Pullen Library, Special Collections, Georgia State University, Atlanta, Georgia (hereafter cited as GGDP).

6. Ivan Allen, *Notes on the Sixties* (New York: Simon and Schuster, 1971), 9. For more on race relations in the South before World War II, see John Egerton, *Speak Now Against the Day: The Generation Before the Civil Rights Movement in the South* (New York: Knopf, 1994); and for an excellent examination of race relations in Georgia for the first third of the twentieth century, see John Michael Matthews, "Studies in Race Relations in Georgia, 1890–1930" (Ph.D. diss., Duke University, 1970).

7. See Numan V. Bartley and Hugh Graham, *Southern Politics and the Second Reconstruction* (Baltimore: Johns Hopkins University Press, 1975), 18. See also Harold P. Henderson, *The Politics of Change in Georgia: a Political Biography of Ellis Arnall* (Athens: University of Georgia Press, 1991), 142–43; and Michael J. Klarman, "How *Brown* Changed Race Relations: The Backlash Thesis," *Journal of American History* 81 (June 1994): 97.

8. For a thorough account of the election, see Numan V. Bartley, *The Creation of Modern Georgia* (Athens: University of Georgia Press, 1983). Also see Harold P. Henderson, "The 1946 Gubernatorial Election in Georgia" (master's thesis, Georgia Southern College, 1967); Henderson, "M. E. Thompson and the Politics of Succession," in *Georgia Governors in an Age of Change: From Ellis Arnall to George Busbee,* ed. Harold P. Henderson and Gary L. Roberts (Athens: University of Georgia Press,

1988); and his *Politics of Change*. And see Joseph L. Bernd, "White Supremacy and the Disenfranchisement of Blacks in Georgia, 1946," *Georgia Historical Quarterly* 66, no. 4 (winter 1982): 492–513.

9. Bartley, *Creation of Modern Georgia*, 184.

10. Many contemporary observers believed that Ellis Arnall's reform efforts and national ambitions limited his political appeal and power within the state's borders. See Kytle and Mackay, "We Pass."

11. For more on the organization of the Talmadge camp, see William Anderson, *The Wild Man From Sugar Creek* (Baton Rouge: Louisiana State University Press, 1975), 213. Billy Bowles and Remer Tyson, in *They Love a Man in the Country: Saints and Sinners in the South* (Atlanta: Peachtree Publishers, 1989), 49–56, provide an entertaining look at Talmadge's campaign style.

12. Besides his frugal economic philosophy, Talmadge had proved himself no friend to labor. During a 1934 national textile strike, Talmadge sent state troopers to break the strike in Covington and Newnan. He later pardoned eight men convicted of flogging organizing members of the CIO. Donald L. Grant, *The Way It Was in the South: The Black Experience in Georgia* (New York: Birch Lane Press, 1993), 350–52, 354. See also Ralph McGill, "How It Happened Down in Georgia," *New Republic* 116 (26 January 1947): 12.

13. Interview with Mrs. Henry Nevins, 9 June 1947, in Kytle and Mackay, "We Pass."

14. Interview with Fred Hand (Speaker of the House, 1947–54), 14 July 1947, in Kytle and Mackay, "We Pass." During the 1947 session of the General Assembly, Harris, although holding no elected office, used Speaker Fred Hand's office in the Capitol to conduct his political business. J. Roy McGinty, the influential editor of the *Calhoun Times* and a stanch anti-Talmadge man described Harris as the "most dangerous man in the state." Interview with J. Roy McGinty, 30 May 1947, in Kytle and Mackay, "We Pass."

15. Interview with John Bell Towill and Henry Eve, two leaders of the Independent Party, 24 June 1947, in Kytle and Mackay, "We Pass."

16. Charles Boykin Pyles, "Race and Ruralism in Georgia Elections, 1948–1966" (Ph.D. diss., University of Georgia, 1967), 94; Bartley and Graham, *Southern Politics*, 25; Bernd, "White Supremacy," 493; Bartley, *Rise of Massive Resistance*, 43; Robert Sherrill, *Gothic Politics in the Deep South* (New York: Grossman Publishers, 1968), 45; Henderson, "1946 Gubernatorial Election," 33.

17. Registration totals from Bernd, "White Supremacy," 492; Pyles, "Race and Ruralism," 16; and Henderson, "1946 Gubernatorial Election," 61. See also James Charles Cobb, "Politics in a New South City: Augusta, Georgia, 1946–1971" (Ph.D. diss., University of Georgia, 1975), 37–38; Anderson, *Wild Man From Sugar Creek*, 222, 228–32; and Grant, *Way It Was*, 364.

18. Although some in the South believed that the end of the white primary might actually de-emphasize the role of race in southern elections, politicians like Talmadge

and Theodore Bilbo in Mississippi made white supremacy central planks in their platforms in 1946. See Dan T. Carter, "Southern Political Style," in Haws, *Age of Segregation,* 48; Dewey Grantham, *The Life and Death of the Solid South: A Political History* (Lexington: University Press of Kentucky, 1988), 119; and Klarman, "How *Brown* Changed Race Relations," 92.

19. Talmadge, quoted in Henderson, "1946 Gubernatorial Election," 48, 43, 46. For the Klan's ten-dollar offer, see Clement Charlton Mosely, "Invisible Empire: A History of the Ku Klux Klan in Twentieth Century Georgia, 1915–1965" (Ph.D. diss., University of Georgia, 1968), 142.

20. Eugene Talmadge, quoted from a speech in Columbus, Georgia, on 13 July 1946, in Calvin McLeod Lougue, ed., *Eugene Talmadge: Rhetoric and Response* (New York: Greenwood Press, 1989), 282–83.

21. Interview with Lillian Smith, 4 June 1947, in Kytle and Mackay, "We Pass."

22. Apparently the fervor Talmadge raised during his campaign lingered. Three days after the primary, Macio Snipes, the only African American who voted in Taylor County, was shot and killed while sitting on his porch. A hand-painted sign appeared on the door of a local church that read, "the First Nigger to Vote Will Never Vote Again." See Grant, *Way It Was,* 366; and Kytle and Mackay, "We Pass," 88. Another historian has attributed a 1946 Walton County lynching to white feelings toward African Americans registering to vote. Wallace H. Warren, " 'The Best People in Town Won't Talk,' " in *Georgia in Black and White: Explorations in the Race Relations of a Southern State, 1865–1950,* ed. John C. Inscoe (Athens: University of Georgia Press, 1994). See also Egerton, *Speak Now Against the Day,* 383.

23. For a detailed look at this aspect of Eugene Talmadge's 1946 gubernatorial campaign, see Bernd, "White Supremacy," 494–506; Mosely, "Invisible Empire," 142; and interview with Dr. R. W. Gadsen, 10 July 1947, in Kytle and Mackay, "We Pass." Grant, *Way It Was,* 365.

24. The effort to split the anti-Talmadge vote is recounted in Arnall, interview, and in Bernd, "White Supremacy," 508. See also Henderson, "1946 Gubernatorial Election," 65–66. Another common perception held by many state political leaders was that Fred Wilson, the chief lobbyist for the Georgia Power Company, supported Rivers's candidacy and efforts to split the anti-Talmadge vote. See Kytle and Mackay, "We Pass." James Carmichael won the popular vote in the Democratic primary 313,389 to Talmadge's 297,245 and 69,489 for Rivers. Talmadge, however, won the county unit vote 242 to Carmichael's 130 and Rivers's 22. Talmadge won one six-unit county, Chatham, largely due to the split of the anti-Talmadge vote and Johnny Bouhan's polling place slowdown, fourteen four-unit counties and ninety of one hundred and twenty-one two-unit counties. Carmichael won seven of eight six-unit counties, fifteen of thirty four-unit counties and twenty-two two-unit counties. Rivers won one four-unit county and nine two-unit counties. Election results can be found in Henderson, "1946 Gubernatorial Election," 63.

25. James Mackay, interviews by Cliff Kuhn, 18 and 31 March 1986, transcript, 32, GGDP.

26. Interviews with Tom Morgan, 12 June 1947, and Mrs. Henry Nevins, 9 June 1947, in Kytle and Mackay, "We Pass."

27. Henderson, "1946 Gubernatorial Election," 83, 90. See also McGill, "How It Happened."

28. Henderson, "1946 Gubernatorial Election," 91.

29. Carey Williams, interview by Cliff Kuhn, 23 February 1989, transcript, 13, GGDP.

30. Interview with William T. Dean, 31 March 1947, in Kytle and Mackay, "We Pass." Only 381 bills were signed into law during the 1947 session, including 301 pieces of "local" legislation. The remaining eighty contained more than thirty laws for the benefit of special corporate interests. The assembly passed only five tax measures: one to tax "fortune tellers" out of business and the remaining four to grant tax exemptions to businesses. See Kytle and Mackay, "We Pass," 25.

31. Pyles, "Race and Ruralism," 18.

32. Interview with Joe Rabun, 7–8 July 1947, in Kytle and Mackay, "We Pass."

33. Talmadge rewarded the Klan support by appointing the head of the Association of Georgia Klans, Dr. Samuel Green, as an aide-de-camp in his first administration. David M. Chalmers, *Hooded Americanism: The First Century of the Ku Klux Klan 1865–1965* (Garden City, N.Y.: Doubleday, 1965), 329.

34. Interview with O. W. Coffee, 12 June 1947, in Kytle and Mackay "We Pass," 65–66; Grant, *Way It Was,* 368.

35. For a wide variety of responses to the 1946 election and Herman's write-in victory, see Kytle and Mackay, "We Pass." Henderson, "M. E. Thompson," 64. Herman Talmadge is quoted in Sherrill, *Gothic Politics,* 48; M. E. Thompson, "Thompson Recollections," interview by Gene Gabriel Moore, in Henderson and Roberts, *Georgia Governors,* 68.

36. As political scientist Earl Black noted, before the decision in *Brown v. Board of Education,* race and segregation were rarely key issues in southern gubernatorial races. Herman Talmadge's campaigns in 1948 and 1950 were two of the primary exceptions. Earl Black, *Southern Governors and Civil Rights* (Cambridge, Mass.: Harvard University Press, 1976), 29.

37. The Court's June 1950 decision in *Sweatt v. Painter* stipulated that the state of Texas had to admit qualified black applicants to the law school at the University of Texas because the black equivalent was not equal. During the same session, the Court ruled in *McLaurin v. Board of Regents* that a student could not be segregated within the graduate program. Both these cases were built upon the Supreme Court's 1938 decision in *Missouri ex rel. Gaines v. Canada,* which ruled that states practicing segregation must provide equal facilities or allow black applicants into white schools. For more on Talmadge's response to these decisions see Thomas V. O'Brien, "Georgia's Response to *Brown v. Board of Education*: The Rise and Fall of Massive Resistance,

1949–1961" (Ph.D. diss., Emory University, 1992), 60–65, 70–71. Talmadge is quoted in Black, *Southern Governors*, 29.

38. Roger Panjari, "Herman E. Talmadge and the Politics of Power," in Henderson and Roberts, *Georgia Governors*, 90–91; Bartley, *Rise of Massive Resistance*, 41; Thompson, "Thompson Recollections," 71.

39. The attempt to equalize school facilities reflects one of the tenets of white supremacy—the claim that black southerners were basically happy in their station and that only a few agitators and malcontents were responsible for civil rights objections. Herman, and many other southern leaders, ignoring the trend of the Supreme Court toward an eventual reversal of the *Plessy v. Ferguson* decision (that allowed separate but equal segregation), believed that the basic objection to Jim Crow laws was that black facilities were unequal. They refused to consider that the separation of the races was the main focus of the civil rights movement. To this end Talmadge believed (and convinced rural Georgia he was correct) that if the disparities in school facilities and spending were alleviated, the agitation against segregation would stop.

40. Herman Talmadge, *You and Segregation* (Birmingham: Vulcan Press, 1955), introduction; *Southern School News*, September 1954; Panjari, "Herman E. Talmadge," 82; Frederick Allen, *Secret Formula* (New York: Harper Collins Publishers, 1994), 314; Jack Bass and Walter Devries, *The Transformation of Southern Politics* (New York: Basic Books, 1976), 137; Sherrill, *Gothic Politics*, 50; O'Brien, "Georgia's Response," 60–65, 71, 94.

41. Talmadge feared what might happen if a strong opponent in the primary, like Thompson, challenged the validity of the county unit vote by transforming his faction into a rival Democratic Party and running against him in the General Election, which did not use the unit system. In an election with a low voter turnout, the strength of Georgia's urban areas combined with the popularity of an opponent like Thompson or Carmichael could defeat Talmadge or a member of his faction.

42. Paul Mertz, "'Mind Changing Time All Over Georgia': HOPE Inc. and School Desegregation, 1958–1961," *Georgia Historical Quarterly* 77 (spring 1993): 48; Sherrill, *Gothic Politics*, 51–55.

43. Bill Shipp, interview by Cliff Kuhn, 22 April 1987, transcript, 40, GGDP. Bartley, *Rise of Massive Resistance*, 54–55; O'Brien, "Georgia's Response," 82–88, 108.

44. Susan Margaret McGrath, "Great Expectations: The History of School Desegregation in Atlanta and Boston, 1954–1990" (Ph.D. diss., Emory University, 1992), 66–70; Herman Talmadge, interview by Harold P. Henderson, 17 July 1987, transcript, 90, GGDP; O'Brien, "Georgia's Response," 128–33; Bartley, *Rise of Massive Resistance*, 55; *Southern School News*, October and December 1954.

45. For more on *Brown v. Board of Education* see Richard Kluger, *Simple Justice: The History of Brown v. Board of Education and Black America's Struggle for Equality* (New York: Vintage Books, 1975); and Bass, *Unlikely Heroes*.

46. Charles Longstreet Weltner, *Southerner* (Philadelphia: Lippincott, 1966), 21.

47. Klarman, "How *Brown* Changed Race Relations," 117.

48. Governor Cherry, quoted in *Southern School News,* September 1954. Roy McCain offers two explanations for the moderate stance of many political leaders, editors, and other molders of public opinion: Foremost they had seen Jim Crow dying a slow death, and they knew it was only a matter of time before it ended; and secondly they were convinced that segregation in residences would preserve the segregation in schools. Roy McCain, "Reactions to the United States Segregation Decision of 1954," *Georgia Historical Quarterly* 52 (December 1968): 372, 378.

49. Bartley, *Rise of Massive Resistance,* 261; *Southern School News,* September 1954. For more on Virginia and the massive resistance movement, see James W. Ely, *The Crisis of Conservative Virginia: The Byrd Organization and the Politics of Massive Resistance* (Knoxville: University of Tennessee Press, 1976), the Gray Commission's Plan is discussed on 38–39. See also R. C. Smith, *They Closed Their Schools: Prince Edward County, Virginia, 1951–1964* (Chapel Hill: University of North Carolina Press, 1965); Benjamin Muse, *Virginia's Massive Resistance* (Bloomington: Indiana University Press, 1961); Robin L. Gates, *The Making of Massive Resistance: Virginia's Politics of Public School Desegregation, 1954–1956* (Chapel Hill: University of North Carolina Press, 1964).

50. For a detailed look at Eisenhower and the *Brown* decision, see Michael S. Mayer, "With Much Deliberation and Some Speed: Eisenhower and the *Brown* Decision," *Journal of Southern History* 52 (February 1986): 43–76; and Bartley, *Rise of Massive Resistance,* 58–65.

51. Mayer, "With Much Deliberation," 70; *Southern School News,* October and December 1954; Reed Sarratt, *The Ordeal of Desegregation* (New York: Harper and Row, 1966), 207.

52. Bartley, *Rise of Massive Resistance,* 120; Herman Talmadge, *You and Segregation,* 3. Providing ideological and political links between the civil rights movement and communism became a common tactic among resisters throughout the 1950s and 1960s. On many occasions, southern politicians and politically active private citizens allied themselves with conservative organizations less preoccupied with race. As Dan T. Carter has cogently argued, the influence of southern racial conservatives has had a direct and lasting influence on modern right-wing conservatism (Dan T. Carter, *Politics of Rage*). Also see Carter's *From George Wallace to Newt Gingrich: Race in the Conservative Counterrevolution, 1963–1994* (Baton Rouge: Louisiana State University Press, 1996). For other examinations of race and the right-wing, see Edward G. Carmine and James A. Stimson, *Issue Evolution: Race and the Transformation of American Politics* (Princeton: Princeton University Press, 1989); Thomas B. Edsall and Mary D. Edsall, *Chain Reaction: The Impact of Race, Rights, and Taxes on American Politics* (New York, 1991).

53. David Daniel Potenziani, "Look to the Past: Richard B. Russell and the Defense of Southern White Supremacy" (Ph.D. diss., University of Georgia, 1981), 71, 126, 132.

54. McCain, "Reactions," 373. Louisiana's amendment passed 217,992 to 46,929 (*Southern School News,* December 1954). Alabama's amendment passed in December

of 1954, 91,903 to 40,875 (*Southern School News*, January 1955). White is quoted in *Southern School News*, September 1954.

55. Talmadge is quoted in McCain, "Reactions," 371, 381; "Talmadge and Segregation: He Makes His Stand," *Newsweek*, 31 May 1954, 31; Sherrill, *Gothic Politics*, 60; Eugene Cook, "The Georgia Constitution and Mixed Public Schools" (Pamphlet, Georgia Attorney General's Office, October 1954). Sibley Papers.

56. Klarman, "How *Brown* Changed Race Relations," 98; Key, *Southern Politics*, 117–19.

57. *Athens Banner-Herald*, 19 May 1954; *Augusta Courier*, 24 May 1954. For other reactions see *Athens Banner-Herald*, 18 and 21 May 1954; *Bainbridge Post-Searchlight*, 18 May 1954; *Albany Herald*, 18 and 19 May 1954.

58. The newspapers' reactions can be found in *Southern School News*, June 1955.

59. Stevenson, "Personal History," 587.

60. Dewey Grantham, "The South and the Politics of Sectionalism," in *South and the Sectional Image*, 53.

61. As earlier noted, the near constant migration of both black and white farmers from rural areas to urban centers since the Depression further strengthened rural political power. By 1960, more people lived in cities than in rural areas. This divisive rural-urban split would prove prevalent during the hearings of the Sibley Commission that year. Bartley, *From Thurmond to Wallace*, 11.

62. Bartley and Graham, *Southern Politics*, 47; Black, *Southern Governors*, 49–50; Bartley, *Creation of Modern Georgia*, 192.

63. Marvin Griffin, interview by Gene Gabriel Moore, in Henderson and Roberts, *Georgia Governors*, 132; Talmadge, interview, transcript, 71; Bass and Devries, *Transformation of Southern Politics*, 139.

64. Grace W. Thompson was the only woman in the field and the only candidate to endorse the *Brown* decision. She received less than one percent of the primary vote. Grant, *Way It Was*, 125–26, 370.

65. Bartley, *Rise of Massive Resistance*, 68; *Southern School News*, September 1954; Osgood Williams, interview by Cliff Kuhn, 2 June 1988, transcript, 28, GGDP; O'Brien, "Georgia's Response," 125–26; Roy Harris, interview, 20 August 1972.

66. Griffin quoted in *Albany Herald*, 19 May 1954. Sam M. Griffin and Roy F. Chalker, "S. Marvin Griffin: Georgia's 72nd Governor," in Henderson and Roberts, *Georgia Governors*, 125; Pyles, "Race and Ruralism," 97–98; Weltner, *Southerner*, 24. For more on Marvin Griffin's political style, see Bowles and Tyson, *They Love a Man*, 57–71.

67. Vandiver, Moate, Groover, and Griffin are quoted in *Southern School News*, June 1955; Herman Talmadge is quoted in *Southern School News*, May 1955.

68. Grant, *Way It Was*, 373. For more on the Dixiecrat revolt, see Dewey Grantham, *The South in Modern America: A Region at Odds* (New York: Harper Collins Publishers, 1994), 200–204; Bartley, *New South*, 81–96; Grantham, *Life and Death*, 126, 136; and O'Brien, "Georgia's Response," 106.

69. Bartley and Graham, *Southern Politics,* 26; Bartley, *Rise of Massive Resistance,* 51, and his *New South,* 163; Grantham, *Life and Death,* 134–48.

70. Grantham, *South in Modern America,* 210. For more on the massive resistance in the entire South, see Bartley, *Rise of Massive Resistance,* and his *New South,* 159–222.

71. Stephen A. Smith, *Myth, Media and the Southern Mind* (Fayetteville: University of Arkansas Press, 1985), 38–39; Francis M. Wilhoit, *The Politics of Massive Resistance* (New York: George Braxiller, 1973), 74; Talmadge, quoted in *Southern School News,* January 1957. *Southern School News,* February 1956. The phrase "second reconstruction" was coined by noted historian C. Vann Woodward in a lecture given shortly after the *Brown* decision. Although Woodward did not mean for the phrase to invoke a feeling of sentimentality for the past or contemporary anger toward the North, many southern politicians including Talmadge used the comparison between Reconstruction and federal support of the civil rights movement to justify southern resistance.

72. Marion Gressette, quoted in Sarratt, *Ordeal of Desegregation,* 33–34; for more on the idea of interposition during massive resistance, see Bartley, *Rise of Massive Resistance,* 126–50.

73. McGrath, "Great Expectations," 20–21; Robert W. Dubay, "Marvin Griffin and the Politics of the Stump," in Henderson and Roberts, *Georgia Governors,* 111. In one of the commission's largest coups, it infiltrated the Highlander Folk School in Monteagle, Tennessee. The school promoted integration and civil rights. The agent of the commission took pictures (one of which featured Dr. Martin Luther King Jr.) that soon appeared in a pamphlet titled "Communist Training School," which was distributed all over the South. Roy Harris remembered, "We published one million copies of that paper at state expense." Bartley, *Rise of Massive Resistance,* 182. Harris is quoted in Howell Raines, *My Soul is Rested: The Story of the Civil Rights Movement in the Deep South* (1977; reprint, New York: Penguin Books, 1983), 395–96.

74. Bartley, *Rise of Massive Resistance,* 237. Lewis quoted in Grantham, *South in Modern America,* 212. Francis Wilhoit in his *Politics of Massive Resistance,* 58–61, identified the ten main tenets of white supremacy: blacks and whites are different psychoculturally; blacks are inferior to whites; blacks are lazy, thriftless, immature, criminal, ignorant, unreliable, and hypersexual; God predestined white superiority; it is man's duty to God to keep the races separate; segregation is race consciousness, not racism; segregation is Christian, democratic, and compassionate; blacks prefer segregation; whites are purer because of segregation; if integration occurs, it will be followed by miscegenation and lead to a decadent race.

75. Ralph McGill, *No Place to Hide,* 2 vols. (Macon, Ga.: Mercer University Press, 1984), 226; *Southern School News,* January 1955, October 1954; Bartley, *Rise of Massive Resistance,* 177. For more on the Citizens' Council movement, see Neil R. McMillen, *The Citizens' Council: Organized Resistance to the Second Reconstruction* (Chicago: University of Illinois Press, 1971); Hodding Carter, *The South Strikes Back* (1959; reprint, Westport, Conn.: Negro Universities Press, 1970); Bartley, *New South,* 199–207.

76. Harris is quoted in Raines, *My Soul Is Rested,* 395. For more on the history of

the Ku Klux Klan in Georgia, see Mosely, "Invisible Empire," 167–68, 175. Most historians contribute the lack of Klan growth during the fifties to the growth and popularity of the Citizens' Councils; this theory does not hold true in Georgia. The Klan, which did not grow during the 1950s, thrived during the 1960s, when massive resistance in the state failed to stop integration. For more on the failure of the Citizens' Council movement in the state, see McMillen, *Citizens' Council*, 80, 88.

77. For a look at the laws passed by the southern states during the years following the *Brown* decision, see Southern Education Reporting Service, *Statistical Summary of School Segregation-Desegregation in the Southern and Border States* (Nashville: Southern Education Reporting Service, November 1961); *Southern School News,* February 1956, March 1957; Southern Regional Council, *School Desegregation: The First Six Years* (Atlanta: Southern Regional Council, 1960).

78. Elbert Tuttle, interview by Cliff Kuhn, 21 September 1992, transcript, 22, GGDP. Robert Dubay, "Marvin Griffin and the Politics of the Stump," in Henderson and Roberts, *Georgia Governors,* 107; *Southern School News,* November 1955, September 1954, November 1954, November 1956, September 1956; Grace Towns Hamilton, interview by Cliff Kuhn, 26 June 1986, transcript, 16, GGDP; Ronald H. Bayor, *Race and the Shaping of Twentieth-Century Atlanta* (Chapel Hill: University of North Carolina Press, 1996), 222; Grant, *Way It Was,* 379; Sam Englehart is quoted in Sarratt, *Ordeal of Desegregation,* 34.

79. Judge Parker is quoted in Sarratt, *Ordeal of Desegregation,* 208.

80. Cook is quoted in Bartley, *Rise of Massive Resistance,* 236.

81. Grant, *Way It Was,* 378; *Southern School News,* June 1955. Other books banned included a history book for not giving the South proper credit in the Revolutionary war and a sociology book that claimed black Americans had been the victims of discrimination in elections, schools, and recreational activities.

82. Robert Dubay, "Marvin Griffin and the Politics of the Stump," in Henderson and Roberts, *Georgia Governors,* 110–11; *Southern School News,* January 1956; Carey Williams, interview.

83. Bartley, *Rise of Massive Resistance,* 192. Two long-time Georgia leaders discuss the race issue as being artificial: James Mackay, interview, transcript, 34; Hamilton Lokey, interview by Catherine Foster, 26 January 1989, transcript, 20, GGDP; Shipp, interview, transcript, 22.

84. George T. Smith, interview by T. Chaffin, 19 August 1992, transcript, 12, GGDP.

85. Harris is quoted in Sherrill, *Gothic Politics,* 46–47.

86. Mayer, "With Much Deliberation," 49.

87. Robert Dubay, "Marvin Griffin and the Politics of the Stump," in Henderson and Roberts, *Georgia Governors,* 104. For more on the myths and symbols of the massive resistance movement see Stephen Smith, *Southern Mind,* 42.

88. Bartley, *Rise of Massive Resistance,* 277. For more on the Little Rock crisis, see Elizabeth Jacoway, "Taken By Surprise: Little Rock Business Leaders and Desegregation," in Jacoway and David R. Colburn, *Southern Businessmen and Desegregation*

(Baton Rouge: Louisiana State University Press, 1982); Tony Freyer, *The Little Rock Crisis: A Constitutional Interpretation* (Westport, Conn.: Greenwood Press, 1984); Irving J. Spitzberg, *Racial Politics in Little Rock, 1954–1964* (New York: Garland Publishing, 1987); Virgil T. Blossom, *It Has Happened Here* (New York: Harper Collins, 1959).

89. In the two years following the crisis at Little Rock, the federal courts decided *Cooper v. Aaron, Aaron v. Cooper, United States v. Faubus,* and *James v. Almond,* each of which seriously damaged southern resistance strategy. Ely, *Crisis of Conservative Virginia,* 87; Bartley, *Rise of Massive Resistance,* 291, and for the idea of the massive resistance's peak, 273.

90. Ernest Vandiver is quoted in Charles Pyles, "S. Ernest Vandiver and the Politics of Change," in Henderson and Roberts, *Georgia Governors,* 155; and in Charlie Pou, "Epilogue: The Vandiver Years," *Atlanta Magazine,* December 1962, 45; McGill, *No Place to Hide,* 247.

Chapter 2

1. Ralph McGill, *The South and the Southerner* (Boston: Little, Brown, 1959), 252; Dr. Dow Kirkpatrick, president of the Georgia Council of Churches, quoted in *Southern School News,* December 1955, 12; *Southern School News,* April 1955, 11; Weltner, *Southerner,* 34; Eugene Patterson is quoted in Raines, *My Soul is Rested,* 367–68. For more on the repression of discussion during the massive resistance era, see Paul Quin's essay, "The Dominance of the Shadow in Southern Race Relations," *Louisiana History* 36 (winter 1995): 7–12.

2. Howard Zinn explores this choice in his *The Southern Mystique* (New York: Knopf, 1964). Zinn argues that the people of the South cared deeply about segregation, but when the moment of critical mass was reached, they retreated from their resistance stance because there were many things they cared about more than segregation. It is my contention that, during the 1950s, many people in Georgia searched to discover exactly where segregation fit into the public's priorities.

3. Klarman, "How *Brown* Changed Race Relations," 82.

4. Numan V. Bartley, "Another New South?" *Georgia Historical Quarterly* 65, no. 2 (summer 1981): 129; and his *Creation of Modern Georgia,* 170; Stephen Smith, *Southern Mind,* 30; James C. Cobb, "Cracklin's and Caviar: The Enigma of Sunbelt Georgia," *Georgia Historical Quarterly* 68, no. 1 (spring 1984): 22–23; Pete Daniel, *Standing at the Crossroads: Southern Life in the Twentieth Century* (New York: Hill and Wang, 1986), 11–12; Kirby, *Rural Worlds Lost,* 53–54.

5. Kytle and Mackay, "We Pass," 8, 16, and interview with Malcolm Bryan, 22 May 1947. For more on the relationship between segregation and economic development, see George Brown Tindall, *The Emergence of the New South, 1913–1945* (Baton Rouge: Louisiana State University Press, 1967), 70–110; C. Vann Woodward, "New South Fraud Is Papered by Old South Myth," *Washington Post,* 9 July 1961; and Quin, "Dominance of the Shadow," 11–12.

6. Kytle and Mackay, "We Pass," 12, 3, 15.

7. Talmadge's distrust in the federal government changed in pitch with his political position; while he was agricultural commissioner, Georgia faced the boll weevil infestation and agents of the Federal Extension Service came to the state to help farmers; while running for governor in 1934 and U.S. Senate in 1936, he fought the New Deal farm programs; and finally, in the last years of his life, he saw the massive changes in race relations brought on by training black soldiers from the North at southern military bases. Redeemer governments are described in C. Vann Woodward, *Origins of the New South* (1951; reprint, Baton Rouge: Louisiana State University Press, 1971), 14–16; Howard N. Rabinowitz, *The First New South, 1865–1920* (Arlington Heights, Ill.: Harlan Davidson, 1992), 88–98; Edward Ayers, *The Promise of the New South: Life After Reconstruction* (New York: Oxford University Press, 1992), 8–9.

8. Patton, "Southern Liberal," 605; Pyles, "Race and Ruralism," 94; Bass and Devries, *Transformation of Southern Politics,* 137–38; Tindall, *Emergence of the New South,* 511; interviews with Reverend Mac Anthony, 16 July 1947, and G. H. Moore, 5 June 1947, in Kytle and Mackay, "We Pass."

9. Bartley, *Creation of Modern Georgia,* 175, 177; Tindall, *Emergence of the New South,* 618.

10. Bartley, "Another New South?" 127; Sherrill, *Gothic Politics,* 50; Talmadge, interview, transcript, 80; Lester Maddox, Georgia Governor's Roundtable, 31 October 1985, transcript, 16, GGDP.

11. Roger Panjari, "Herman E. Talmadge and the Politics of Power," in Henderson and Roberts, *Georgia Governors,* 75; Bartley, *Rise of Massive Resistance,* 42; Cobb, *Selling of the South,* 161; Robert Dubay, "Marvin Griffin and the Politics of the Stump," in Henderson and Roberts, *Georgia Governors,* 107. See also Cobb, *Industrialization and Southern Society.*

12. The appeals to business came from a variety of sources—one of the earliest was the Southern Regional Council in 1956 (*Southern School News,* April 1956, 7)—and the Independent Party in its campaign against Roy Harris and his Cracker Party in Augusta in 1946 warned that his racist policies could harm the city's recruiting efforts (Cobb, "Politics in a New South City,"50). See also Bartley, *Rise of Massive Resistance,* 24; Frederick Allen, *Secret Formula,* 285–86; *Southern School News,* July 1956, 3.

13. As previously noted, the first major victory for the NAACP was *Missouri ex rel. Gaines v. Canada* (1938), which decided that a state had to provide equal facilities for black students or allow them into white schools. This decision, while a victory, did not challenge "separate but equal" tenets. That challenge came in the 1950 cases *Sweatt v. Painter,* where the Court ruled that a white law school and black law school were inherently unequal despite the equitability of school facilities, and the *McLaurin v. Board of Regents* case in Oklahoma, which maintained that a graduate school could not segregate a student within its program.

14. Paul Bolster, "Civil Rights Movements in Twentieth Century Georgia" (Ph.D. diss., University of Georgia, 1972), 132–33, 158–59; Grant, *Way It Was,* 375; O'Brien, "Georgia's Response," 139.

15. Susan M. McGrath, "From Tokenism to Community Control: Political Symbolism in the Desegregation of Atlanta's Public Schools, 1961–1973," *Georgia Historical Quarterly* 79 (Fall 1995), 846–47. See also Bartley, *Creation of Modern Georgia*, 196; Grant, *Way It Was*, 322–27, 367–77, registration figures, 371. For recent works on the African American leadership in Atlanta, see Bayor, *Shaping of Twentieth Century Atlanta*; and Gary M. Pomerantz, *Where Peachtree Meets Sweet Auburn: The Saga of Two Families and the Making of Atlanta* (New York: Scribner, 1996). For a comparative look at Atlanta and other southern cities, see Christopher Silver and John V. Moeser, *The Separate City: Black Communities in the Urban South, 1940–1968* (Lexington: University Press of Kentucky, 1995).

16. Hamilton, interview. Information on Hooper can be found in the *Georgia Official and Statistical Register, 1961* (Hapeville: State of Georgia, 1961). Bolster, "Civil Rights Movements," 162; McGrath, "Great Expectations," 108.

17. Hooper is quoted in J. W. Peltason, *Fifty-Eight Lonely Men* (Chicago: University of Illinois Press, 1971), 129.

18. As previously noted, Talmadge waited until after his victory in 1950 and then presented his tax to the General Assembly, which promptly passed the measure. Roger Panjari, "Herman E. Talmadge and the Politics of Power," in Henderson and Roberts, *Georgia Governors*, 80; Henderson, "1946 Gubernatorial Election," 111.

19. Bolster, "Civil Rights Movements," 149–52; *Southern School News,* December 1954, 6; Bartley, *From Thurmond to Wallace*, 23; Frances Pauley, interview by Cliff Kuhn, 11 April 1988, transcript, 50, GGDP.

20. *Southern School News,* January 1955, 6 June 1955, 3; Bartley, *Rise of Massive Resistance,* 224.

21. Bartley and Graham, *Southern Politics,* 26; *Southern School News,* December 1954, 7.

22. Hamilton Lokey, "The Low Key Life of Hamilton Lokey," unpublished manuscript, GGDP, 17, 24; George Goodwin, interview by Cliff Kuhn, 17 January 1992, GGDP; Lokey, interview, transcript, 21.

23. Hamilton Lokey, interview, transcript, 26; Everett Millican, interview by Lorraine Nelson Spritzer, 30 July 1977, transcript, 20–21, GGDP; O'Brien, "Georgia's Response," 191–95, 209; Hamilton Lokey, speech, 7 April 1959, reprinted in, "Low Key Life"; Weltner, *Southerner,* 30.

24. Roy Harris is quoted in *Southern School News,* June 1956, 9; Stevenson, "Personal History," 587; Lokey, interview, transcript, 11.

25. Jack L. Walker, "The Functions of Disunity: Negro Leadership in a Southern City," *Journal of Negro Education* 32 (March 1963): 227–28; and his "Protest and Negotiation: A Case Study of Negro Leadership in Atlanta, Georgia," *Midwest Journal of Political Science* 7 (May 1963), 116; Virginia H. Hein, "The Image of a 'City Too Busy to Hate': Atlanta in the 1960s," *Phylon* 33 (fall 1972), 209; Helen Fuller, *Southerners and Schools* (Washington: New Republic, 1959), 15–16. See also Silver and Moeser, *Separate City.*

26. Clarence Stone, *Regime Politics: Governing Atlanta, 1946–1988* (Lawrence: University of Kansas Press, 1989), 17; Manuel Maloof, interview by David Jordan, 13 and 15 June 1994, transcript, 19, GGDP; Frederick Allen, *Secret Formula,* 289; Celestine Sibley, interview by Cliff Kuhn, 4 and 5 March 1993, transcript, 82, GGDP.

27. Marvin Griffin and William B. Hartsfield were personal friends who understood that they needed to be political enemies to gain votes. Bowles and Tyson, *They Love a Man,* 60. Hartsfield is quoted in James L. Townsend, "Miracle in Atlanta," *Town and Country Magazine,* February 1963, 90; Harold Martin, *William Berry Hartsfield* (Athens: University of Georgia Press, 1978), 134, 138.

28. Bartley, *Rise of Massive Resistance,* 332–33; Charles Boykin Pyles, "S. Ernest Vandiver and the Politics of Change," in Henderson and Roberts, *Georgia Governors,* 149; McCain, "Reactions to the Segregation Decision of 1954," 375.

29. Bartley, *Rise of Massive Resistance,* 294; Len G. Cleveland, "Georgia Baptists and the 1954 Supreme Court Desegregation Decision," *Georgia Historical Quarterly* 59 (spring 1975), 108.

30. Cleveland, "Georgia Baptists," 110, 113.

31. Ibid., 112.

32. Cobb, "Politics in a New South City," 108; McGill, *South and the Southerner,* 273.

33. An excellent study of Atlanta ministers during the school crisis is Ray McCain, "Speaking on School Desegregation by Atlanta Ministers," *Southern Speech Journal* 29 (March 1964): 256–62. The Evangelical Council is quoted in McGill, *South and the Southerner,* 277; the States' Rights Council's statement is quoted in Grant, *Way It Was,* 379.

34. McCain, "Speaking on School Desegregation," 256–62; Gerald Reed to Muriel Lokey, 26 December 1958, and Harry Fifield to HOPE, 15 January 1959, Help Our Public Education (HOPE) papers, Library and Archives, Atlanta History Center, Atlanta, Georgia (hereafter cited as HOPE Papers).

35. Herman Talmadge had inherited his father's political mouthpiece, the *Statesman*; Roy Harris owned and edited the *Augusta Courier*; Marvin Griffin came from a newspaper background and edited the *Bainbridge Post-Searchlight*; and outspoken segregationist James Gray owned the daily *Albany Herald.*

36. Fuller, *Southerners and Schools,* 16; David L. Altheide and Robert P. Snow, *Media Logic* (Beverly Hills: Sage Publications, 1979), 87.

37. Ralph McGill, *Ralph McGill, Editor and Publisher: Ralph McGill Speaks,* vol. 2, comp. Calvin McLeod Logue (Durham, N.C.: Moore Publishing, 1969), xxvii, 48; McGill, *No Place to Hide,* 223.

38. Ralph McGill, *Editor and Publisher,* speech in Augusta, Georgia, 3 February 1959, 128–29.

39. Eugene Patterson interview is in Raines, *My Soul Is Rested*; *Southern School News,* July 1956, 3; Altheide and Snow, *Media Logic,* 87; William Shipp, interview, transcript, 17.

40. Ray Moore, interview by Cliff Kuhn, 8 May 1987, transcript, 50, GGDP.

41. Ray Moore, interview by Cliff Kuhn, 17 May 1987, transcript, 23, GGDP.

42. Nan Pendergrast, interview by Cliff Kuhn and Kathryn Nasstrom, 24 June 1992, transcript, 65, GGDP; Ray Moore, interview, 8 May 1987, transcript, 21; Ray Moore, interview, 17 May 1987, transcript, 22.

43. For a thorough examination of HOPE, see Mertz, "Mind Changing Time," 41–61.

44. Weltner, *Southerner,* 32; Muriel Lokey, interview, transcript, 57–58; Hamilton Lokey, interview, transcript, 17; Helen Bullard File, GGDP.

45. This decision prompted one early supporter of HOPE, Harry Boyte, to end his affiliation with the organization. Mertz, "Mind Changing Time," 50.

46. Nan Pendergrast, interview, transcript, 71–72, 74; Frances Pauley, interview, 3 May 1988, transcript, 14.

47. Bruce Galphin, *The Riddle of Lester Maddox* (Atlanta: Camelot Publishing, 1968), 48, 50, 22; Weltner, *Southerner,* 31; David Andrew Harmon, *Beneath the Image of the Civil Rights Movement and Race Relations: Atlanta, Georgia, 1946–1981* (New York: Garland Publishing, 1996), 109.

48. Frances Pauley, interview, 24 June 1992, transcript, 71–72, 74.

49. Muriel Lokey, interview, 26 January 1989, transcript, 64–65; Mertz, "Mind Changing Time," 50; Frances Pauley, interview 3 May 1988, transcript, 11; Townsend, "Miracle in Atlanta," 90; Nan Pendergrast, interview, transcript, 66; Stone, *Regime Politics,* 47.

50. Hamilton Lokey, interview, 26 January 1989, transcript, 23; MASE flyer, box three, HOPE papers; Lester Maddox to HOPE, March 1959, HOPE papers. Lester Maddox later became governor of Georgia on a segregationist platform. For more on Maddox's career, see Galphin, *Riddle of Lester Maddox*; and Lester Maddox, *Speaking Out: The Autobiography of Lester Garfield Maddox* (Garden City, N.Y.: Doubleday, 1975).

51. Minutes from HOPE meeting, 25 February 1960, HOPE papers; Barbara Davenport to Muriel Lokey, 7 January 1960, HOPE papers; Frances Pauley, interview, 3 May 1988, transcript, 17; Frances Pauley, interview, 11 April 1988, transcript, 51; *Americus Times-Recorder,* 8 February 1960; Mertz, "Mind Changing Time," 52.

52. Stickers found in HOPE Papers, box 1, file 3.

53. Copy of Lokey's letter found in HOPE papers, box 1, file 1; HOPE newsletter, February 1959, HOPE papers; Nan Pendergrast, interview, 24 June 1992, transcript, 78.

54. Muriel Lokey, interview, 26 January 1989, transcript, 74–76.

55. Ibid., transcript, 76; Frances Pauley, interview, 11 April 1988, transcript, 58–59.

56. Dubay, "Marvin Griffin," 107; Cobb, "Cracklin's and Caviar," 24; Helen Hill Miller, "Private Business and Public Education in the South," *Harvard Business Review* 8 (8 July 1960): 75–76; Georgia's economic expansion figures from Miller and an undated draft of a letter, Ernest Vandiver to Leroy Collins (Florida's governor), S. Ernest Vandiver Collection, Richard B. Russell Library, University of Georgia Libraries, Athens, Georgia (hereafter cited as Vandiver Papers).

57. Atlanta's population grew at a rate of 82 percent from 1940 to 1960. Neil Peirce, *The Deep South States of America: People, Politics, and Power in the Seven Deep South States* (New York: Norton, 1972), 310. Cobb, *Industrialization and Southern Society,* 101, 103; Frederick Allen, *Secret Formula,* 285.

58. Bartley, "Writing About the Post–World War II South," 4–5; Klarman, "How *Brown* Changed Race Relations," 86.

59. Miller, "Private Business and Public Education," 75, 76 (Ivan Allen is quoted on 76); Lane is quoted in Grant, *Way It Was,* 380; Rader is quoted in a pamphlet by Save Our Schools (New Orleans), "Our Stake in the New Orleans Schools," HOPE papers; Cobb, *Selling of the South,* 123.

60. Everett Tucker is quoted in Miller, "Private Business and Public Education," 78. Figures on Little Rock's business climate are on 75–76.

61. Miller, "Private Business and Public Education," 75. For a witty and insightful look at the business reaction to the public school crisis, see both Calvin Trillin, "Reflections: Remembrance of Moderates Past," *New Yorker,* 21 March 1977, 87–88; and Sherrill, *Gothic Politics,* 59.

62. M. Richard Cramer, "School Desegregation and New Industry: The Southern Community Leaders' Viewpoint," *Social Forces* 41 (May 1963), 386–87.

63. For more on individual cities' experiences with desegregation crises and business leaders' responses to those events, see Jacoway and Colburn, *Southern Business-men and Desegregation.* Other detailed studies of cites or states include: William Chafe, *Civilities and Civil Rights: Greensboro, North Carolina, and the Black Struggle for Freedom* (New York: Oxford University Press, 1980); Ely, *Crisis of Conservative Virginia*; Robert Pratt, *The Color of Their Skin: Education and Race in Richmond, Virginia, 1954–1989* (Charlottesville: University Press of Virginia, 1992). A good short overview of the South and North Carolina in particular is Davison M. Douglas, "The Rhetoric of Moderation: Desegregating the South During the Decade After *Brown,*" *Northwestern University Law Review* 89, no. 1 (1994): 92–139.

Chapter 3

1. S. Ernest Vandiver, interview by Charles Pyles, 20 March 1986, transcript, 12, 17, GGDP; Vandiver is quoted in *Southern School News,* May 1957, 6.

2. Charles Boykin Pyles, "S. Ernest Vandiver and the Politics of Change," in Henderson and Roberts, *Georgia Governors,* 146; James F. Cook, *Carl Sanders: Spokesman of the New South* (Macon, Ga.: Mercer University Press, 1993), 53; Vandiver, interview, 20 March 1986, transcript, 28; Marvin Griffin, interview by Gene Gabriel Moore, in Henderson and Roberts, *Georgia Governors,* 138.

3. McMillen, *Citizens' Council,* 86; Vandiver, interview, 20 March 1986, transcript, 28, 30; Pyles, "Race and Ruralism," 103; McGill, *No Place to Hide,* 249.

4. *Southern School News,* April 1957; Ernest Vandiver, Georgia Governors Roundtable, 31 October 1985, GGDP.

5. Vandiver used one basic speech during his campaign and modified it according to the group he was addressing.

6. Griffin Bell, interview by Cliff Kuhn, 12 June 1990, transcript, 23–26, GGDP; Earl Black, *Southern Governors and Civil Rights* (Cambridge, Mass.: Harvard University Press, 1976), 66; Vandiver, interview, 20 March 1986, transcript, 31; Ernest Vandiver, "Vandiver Takes the Middle Road," in Henderson and Roberts, *Georgia Governors,* 159.

7. Press Release of speech, 9 August 1958, box 13, Vandiver Papers.

8. Black, *Southern Governors,* 67; S. Ernest Vandiver, interview by Cliff Kuhn, 25 January 1994, transcript, 14–15, GGDP.

9. Griffin Bell to Ernest Vandiver, 18 December 1958, Vandiver Papers, box 49; Cook, *Carl Sanders,* 53–54; Southern Education Reporting Service, *Statistical Summary*; Vandiver is quoted in Pyles, "S. Ernest Vandiver and the Politics of Change," in Henderson and Roberts, *Georgia Governors,* 148.

10. Bass, *Unlikely Heroes,* 20; *Southern School News,* September 1956.

11. Peter Irons and Stephanie Guitton, eds. *May It Please the Court* (New York: New Press, 1993), 249, 260; Pou, "Epilogue," 45; undated manuscript describing federal court actions on massive resistance laws, Sibley Papers; Freeman Leverett to John Sibley, 29 February 1960, Sibley Papers; undated draft of laws that needed to be changed to overturn Georgia's massive resistance, Vandiver Papers, box 11; Mertz, "Mind Changing Time," 44.

12. Remarkably, these recommendations were almost identical to those of an earlier Virginia study committee—the Gray Commission—that submitted its report before Virginia committed itself to massive resistance.

13. Virginia's state supreme court also held the school closing laws unconstitutional. Ely, *Crisis in Conservative Virginia,* 75; undated manuscript of appropriate court decisions, Sibley Papers; a similar manuscript can be found in box 11, Vandiver Papers; Peltason, *Fifty-Eight Lonely Men,* 215; Bartley, *New South,* 246–47, 239; Harmon Caldwell to John A. Sibley, 4 April 1960, Harmon Caldwell Collection, box 65, Richard B. Russell Library, University of Georgia Libraries, Athens, Georgia (hereafter cited as Caldwell Papers). For more on Virginia see Ely, *Crisis in Conservative Virginia,* and Pratt, *Color of Their Skin.*

14. Chafe, *Civilities and Civil Rights,* 81, 82, 67; Douglas, "Rhetoric of Moderation," 107, 112, 120.

15. Iris Blitch's reaction can be found in *Southern School News,* December 1959; McGrath, "Great Expectations," 120; *Southern School News,* July 1959; Hartsfield quoted in *Southern School News,* August 1959; Vandiver quoted in *Southern School News,* July 1959.

16. McGrath, "Great Expectations," 140; undated manuscript describing the details of the Atlanta Plan, Sibley Papers; *Southern School News,* February 1960; Bayor, *Shaping of Twentieth-Century Atlanta,* 223.

17. Western Union telegram, Vandiver to Harris, Sanders, Bell, Perry, et al., 5 July 1959; Copy of a press release, 9 July 1959, describing events of meeting; William H. Burson to William Brooks, 14 July 1959, all in box 50, Vandiver Papers.

18. On 1 January 1960, Vandiver attended the Gator Bowl, where Georgia Tech was playing Arkansas. Before the game, Governors Faubus and Vandiver went down to the field, where Faubus was greeted with an incredible ovation. Vandiver described Faubus as the hero of the "whole South." S. Ernest Vandiver, interview, 25 January 1994, transcript, 6, GGDP.

19. Griffin Bell, interview by Cliff Kuhn, 12 June 1990, transcript, 26, GGDP.

20. Bartley, *Rise of Massive Resistance*, 334; Roy Harris to James S. Peters, 4 January 1960, box 26, Vandiver Papers. Peters's reply to Harris can be found in Sherrill, *Gothic Politics*, 53, and in *Southern School News*, February 1960. Roy Harris leaked the Peters letter to the press in an effort to gain support for his efforts to maintain resistance. However, the move backfired by bringing attention to the political pitfalls of massive resistance.

21. Pyles, "S. Ernest Vandiver and the Politics of Change," in Henderson and Roberts, *Georgia Governors*, 144, 152; statistics from an undated draft of a letter from Ernest Vandiver to Leroy Collins (Florida's governor), box 50, Vandiver Papers.

22. Stevenson, "Personal History," 584. Augusta poll found in Cobb, "Politics in a New South City," 114. The Sibley Commission hearings will also demonstrate that most white Georgians preferred to abandon public education rather than accept even token integration.

23. The idea of private schools being preferable comes from the president of the States' Rights Council of Georgia, R. Carter Pittman, in Bartley, *Rise of Massive Resistance*, 248; see also Weltner, *Southerner*, 30.

24. Herman Talmadge's reversal of position can be found in Osgood Williams, interview, 2 June 1988, transcript, 36; and in Sherrill, *Gothic Politics*, 53; Bartley, *Rise of Massive Resistance*, 333; Vandiver is quoted in Georgia Governors Roundtable, transcript, 7.

25. See Thomas R. Melton, "The 1960 Presidential Election in Georgia" (Ph.D. diss., University of Mississippi, 1985).

26. Bell, interview, 19 September 1990, transcript, 21.

27. Ibid., transcript, 18–19; Bell, interview, 12 June 1990, transcript, 26–27, 31; *Atlanta Constitution*, 31 January 1977; Ernest Vandiver, "Vandiver Takes the Middle Road," in Henderson and Roberts, *Georgia Governors*, 159.

28. One of the tenets of white supremacy and segregation was that it was not to be questioned or discussed. In Georgia, Roy Harris and the Talmadge faction of the party linked the principles of white supremacy and segregation with their own style of resistance. Doing this, they thought, would perpetuate not only the principles of segregation but their own political power.

29. George T. Smith, who served as Speaker of the House from 1963 to 1967, should not be confused with George L. Smith, who served as Speaker of the House from 1959 to 1963 and again from 1967 until his death in 1973. George T. Smith, interview, 19 August 1992, transcript, 8–10; Muriel Lokey, interview, 26 January 1989, transcript, 79.

30. Bell, interview, 19 September 1990, transcript, 32; S. Ernest Vandiver, "Van-

diver Takes the Middle Road," in Henderson and Roberts, *Georgia Governors*, 159; Bell, interview, 12 June 1990, transcript, 31.

31. George Busbee, interview by James F. Cook, 24 March 1987, transcript, 15, 16, GGDP; George T. Smith, interview, 19 August 1992, transcript, 9; Bell, interview, 19 September 1990, transcript, 34; *Atlanta Constitution*, 7 February 1960. Introducing the measure did not end George Busbee's career; he went on to serve as governor of Georgia from 1975 to 1983 and stressed his involvement with the creation of the Sibley Commission during his campaigns.

32. Bell, interviews, 30 June 1990, transcript, 21, 34, quote from 19; interview, 19 September 1990, transcript, 36.

33. Bell, interview, 19 September 1990, transcript, 30, 33; Vandiver, interview, 25 January 1994, transcript, 4; Bell, interview 12 June 1990, transcript, 36. See also Trillin, "Reflections"; *New Yorker*, 21 March 1977, for a detailed look at Bell's involvement with the Sibley Commission origins and the connections between Vandiver, Bell, and Sibley as well as the state government, King and Spalding, Trust Company Bank, and Coca-Cola.

34. Render Hill, telephone interview by author, 3 September 1995.

35. Although the panel's official title was the Georgia General Assembly Committee on Schools, the public referred to it as the Sibley Commission. For the purposes of this story the words committee and commission will be used interchangeably. See *Atlanta Journal and Constitution*, 14 February 1960. For more on modern paternalism in Georgia, see Bartley, *Creation of Modern Georgia*.

36. This change in strategy did not reflect on Sibley's skills as an attorney but on a change in Coca-Cola company policy in the 1940s. For almost three decades, the Woodruffs (first Ernest and then Robert) attempted to corner the soft drink market by aggressive marketing campaigns coupled with constant legal warfare on any company that sold a product similar to Coca-Cola. After World War Two, the company abandoned most of its litigation against competitors and concentrated more on marketing and advertising to retain its large share of the soft drink market. See Frederick Allen, *Secret Formula*, 234–35.

37. Jack Patterson, "The Unruffled Mr. Sibley," *Atlanta Magazine*, February 1962, 60–62; Frederick Allen, *Secret Formula*, 119, 269; Harold Martin, *Three Strong Pillars* (Atlanta: Trust Company of Georgia, 1974), 76.

38. Pomerantz, *Where Peachtree Meets Sweet Auburn*, 256; John Sibley to Carl Vinson, 30 January 1956; John Sibley to Robert Woodruff, 9 August 1954; John Sibley to William Tuck, 18 May 1956; undated memo from David Gambrell to John Sibley on the possibility of a Tenth Amendment case; copy of an undated memo from Eugene Cook to Marvin Griffin on the legality of the use of federal troops in Little Rock; States' Rights Council pamphlets and bulletins pamphlets mailed in bulk to John Sibley 13 October 1958; all items listed above, Sibley Papers.

39. Short biographical sketches of the commission membership can be found in the *Atlanta Journal and Constitution*, 14 February 1960, and the *Georgia Official and Statis-*

tical Register of 1960–61. Individual information can also be found in *Southern School News,* August and November 1954, on the early members of the Georgia Education Commission, who included not only Battle Hall but Robert Arnold, Harmon Caldwell, and the general counsel of the commission, Freeman Leverett. George B. Brooks, should not be confused with Vandiver advisor and speech writer William O. "B" Brooks, who also plays a prominent role in this story. See also John Greer, interview by Cliff Kuhn, 4 June 1987, transcript for his and Hollis's fight against the Klan, GGDP.

40. Georgia General Assembly Committee on Schools, "Majority and Minority Report," pamphlet, Atlanta, Georgia, April 1960.

41. Render Hill, telephone interview by author, 3 September 1995; *Atlanta Constitution,* 7 and 18 February 1960; minutes of Sibley Commission meeting, 17 February 1960, Sibley Papers.

42. Sibley received dozens of letters from all over Georgia, congratulating him for his opening statement, including from black ministers as well as members of segregationist groups. Among these letters were: Ivan Allen to John Sibley, 19 February 1960; Abner M. Israel to John Sibley, 20 February 1960; E. C. Hammond to John Sibley, 4 March 1960; Arthur Moore to John Sibley, 18 February 1960; and J. A. McCurdy to John Sibley, 22 February 1960; all letters, Sibley Papers.

43. *Augusta Courier,* 22 February 1960; *Bainbridge Post-Searchlight,* 25 February 1960; *Atlanta Constitution,* 7 February 1960; Pendergrast, interview, transcript, 69–70; Goodwin, interview.

44. Minutes of meeting, 17 February 1960, 10:00 A.M., Sibley Papers.

45. Render Hill, telephone interview by author, 3 September 1995.

46. Minutes of meeting, 26 February 1960, 10:00 A.M., and Howell Hollis to John Sibley, 22 February 1960, Sibley Papers.

47. Minutes of meeting, 26 February 1960, 10:00 A.M., Sibley Papers.

48. Minutes of meeting, 18 February 1960, 10:00 A.M., and Griffin Bell to John Sibley, 10 February 1960, Sibley Papers; Patterson, "Unruffled Mr. Sibley," 59; Ernest Vandiver, Georgia Governor's Roundtable, transcript, 6, GGDP.

49. Minutes of meeting, 23 February 1960, 10:00 A.M., Sibley Papers.

50. Population statistics from John C. Belcher and Carolyn N. Allman, *The Non-White Population of Georgia* (Athens: Institute of Community and Area Development, 1967); Charles Cowan to John Sibley, copy of draft read before the commission, Sibley Papers.

51. John Sibley to James Childress, 12 August 1954; to Robert W. Woodruff, 9 August 1954; and to Bob Lanier, 9 August 1954; handwritten note by John Sibley about black testimony; list of prospective questions for black witnesses; Sibley Papers.

52. John Sibley to Erwin Sibley, 5 May 1960, U. Erwin Sibley Collection, Russell Library, Georgia College, Milledgeville; Opening Statement, to be read at the opening of each hearing, Sibley Papers. The freedom of choice measure was the idea of Leon Dure, a Virginia gentleman farmer. He and Sibley corresponded frequently throughout the latter part of 1959 and all of 1960. Ely, *Crisis in Conservative Virginia,* 129.

53. Sibley quoted in Sam Hopkins, "A Georgia Patriarch," *Atlanta Journal,* 6 August 1977.

54. *Atlanta Constitution,* 11 March 1960; John Greer, interview, 27 May 1987; copy of Original Schedule of Hearings, Sibley Papers. The reason for the move from Savannah to Sylvania was probably due to the strong NAACP presence in Savannah. Sibley and Greer originally scheduled the meeting in Savannah because, up to that point, no meeting had been held in a city. Parker recommended that Sylvania be used as the hearing site because it was more centrally located. Although Sylvania was easier to reach from the northern counties of the district, it was a long distance from the district's southern counties. Statesboro or Claxton would have been more central locations. It may very well be that Parker requested the move because he wanted to impress his hometown or he knew that the St. Patrick's Day celebration in Savannah, a city with a huge Irish-American population, could distract from the commission's purpose. As it turns out, the black population of Savannah, led by the local NAACP, began a boycott of downtown stores on 16 March. Minutes of meeting, 26 February 1960, Sibley Papers. For more on the black boycott, see Paul Bolster, "Civil Rights Movements," 225–35, and W. W. Law, interview by Cliff Kuhn and Tim Crimmins, 15 November 1990, GGDP.

55. Minutes of meeting, 25 February 1960, 3:00 P.M., and "Formal Statement, for all districts," 2 March 1960, Sibley Papers.

Chapter 4

Kueltne's poem can be found in Sibley Papers.

1. Harris is quoted in Sherrill, *Gothic Politics,* 48.

2. General Assembly Committee on Schools, "Summary of Hearings, By Districts," undated manuscript, Sibley Papers; John Greer, interview, 27 May 1987; Patterson, "Unruffled Mr. Sibley," 57; Claude Purcell, "Georgia Public School Enrollment, January 1960," draft of manuscript prepared at John Sibley's request, Sibley Papers; Belcher and Allman, *Non-White Population of Georgia.*

3. *Americus Times Recorder,* 2, 3 March 1960.

4. Transcript, Georgia General Assembly Committee on Schools, Hearing, 3 March 1960 (Americus hearing transcript), 1, and "Formal Statement for All Districts," 1–5, Sibley Papers.

5. "Formal Statement for All Districts," 6–10, Sibley Papers.

6. Americus hearing transcript, 24–27; Render Hill, telephone interview by the author, 3 September 1995. Hill expressed surprise that anyone would choose the first option after Sibley's careful explanation of the choices. The testimony before the Sibley Commission was recorded by a court reporter and later transcribed and printed as the official transcript. Where appropriate I have made minor changes in punctuation.

7. Americus hearing transcript, 27–34.

8. Ibid., 35. Most married women used their husband's name when testifying.

9. Ibid., 34–38.

10. Ibid., 63, 85.

11. Ibid., 58–59.

12. Ibid., 70.

13. For the record, John Greer then took the names of those delegation members who did not testify, and these individuals did not appear on the witness stand nor in the official transcript to express their choice. Ibid., 94–105.

14. Americus hearing transcript, 79–81

15. Greene's speech and subsequent correspondence, Sibley Papers; Americus hearing transcript, 81–83.

16. Americus hearing transcript, 107–22; *Bainbridge Post-Searchlight,* 10, 17 March 1960; *Albany Herald,* 4 March 1960, devoted much of its coverage of the Americus hearing to describing the black testimony and witnesses in detail.

17. Sam Hopkins, "A Georgia Patriarch," *Atlanta Journal,* 6 August 1977.

18. Those testifying gave Sibley their membership figures. They did not represent any accurate or scientific polling. Many of the groups' membership overlapped, and a certain amount of exaggeration must be taken into account.

19. Pauley, interview, 11 April 1988, transcript, 53–57.

20. Ibid.; Muriel Lokey, interview, 26 January 1989, transcript, 84.

21. Ray Moore, interview, 18 June 1987, transcript, 61–62; Joe Fain, interview by the author, 29 January 1993, Decatur, Georgia; Render Hill, telephone interview by the author, 3 September 1995.

22. Jo Allyn Clark to John Sibley, 27 June 1960; Dr. M. B. Smith to John Sibley, 1 June 1960; Malcom S. Cone to John Sibley, 9 May 1960; all in Sibley Papers.

23. Manuel Maloof, interview, 13 June 1994, transcript, 61–62; Render Hill, telephone interview by the author, 3 September 1995; Howard Stahlman to John Sibley, 31 March 1960; Erwin Sibley to John Sibley, 25 March 1960; John Good to John Sibley, 12 April 1960; Sibley Papers.

24. Stevenson, "Personal History," 594.

25. The idea of changing tactics can be found in Freeman Leverett to John Sibley, 8 March 1960, Sibley Papers. A reporter for Marvin Griffin's newspaper correctly surmised that the reason Sibley served as the sole spokesperson for the commission was to avoid disclosing the personal feelings of the rest of the commission's membership or the political motivation behind the origins of the committee and its hearings. *Bainbridge Post-Searchlight,* 17 March 1960.

26. Margaret Shannon, "Sibley Panel Goes to Douglas Next," *Atlanta Journal,* 13 March 1960.

27. *Athens Banner-Herald,* 7, 8 March 1960; Transcript, Georgia General Assembly Committee on Schools, Hearing, 7 March 1960 (Washington hearing transcript), 14, Sibley Papers.

28. Ibid., 25.

29. Ibid., 30.

30. Ibid., 195.

31. Ibid., 64.

32. Ibid., 32–73, 184, 193.

33. Ibid., 129, 187.

34. Ibid., 60.

35. Ibid., 137. Langham referred to chapters from Gen. 9, Deut. 7, and Neh. 13, and Matt. 25:14.

36. Washington hearing transcript, 107–8.

37. Ibid., 108.

38. Ibid., 78–82.

39. For more on Harris and Grant, see Cobb, "Politics in a New South City," 102–3; Grant's testimony can be found in Washington hearing transcript, 97.

40. Washington hearing transcript, 100–104. Wilburn's testimony appeared on the national NBC news that evening. After he expressed his desire that Sibley experience being a black man for a half hour, he changed his mind and said so softly that the transcriber did not hear (but the TV camera did), "No, I wouldn't wish that on anyone." Joe Fain, interview by the author, 29 January 1993, Decatur, Georgia.

41. Washington hearing transcript, 115.

42. Ibid., 160.

43. Ibid., 155–56.

44. Ibid., 198.

45. Ibid., 117.

46. Ibid., 173.

47. The official commission record shows that ninety-eight people favored option one and forty-eight option two. This discrepancy between the number of individuals testifying and the official record, created by the filing of the entire county delegation's votes with John Greer, accelerated the pace of the hearings and softened the impact of those testifying for the first option.

48. Belcher and Allman, *Non-White Population of Georgia.*

49. Charles Pou, "Seventh District Asks Local Option," *Atlanta Journal,* 11 March 1960.

50. Transcript, Georgia General Assembly Committee on Schools, Hearing, 10 March 1960 (Cartersville hearing transcript), 5–7, 10–20, Sibley Papers. *Atlanta Journal,* 10, 11 March 1960; *Atlanta Constitution,* 11 March 1960.

51. *Atlanta Constitution,* 7 March 1960. Quote from *Atlanta Journal,* 9 March 1960; Cartersville hearing transcript, 9.

52. Cartersville hearing transcript, 121–24.

53. Ibid., 23, 45.

54. Ibid., 111.

55. Ibid., 92.

56. Cartersville Hearing Transcript, 90, 93. For more on organized labor and seg-regation, see Alan Draper, *Conflict of Interests: Organized Labor and the Civil Rights Movement in the South, 1954–1968* (Ithaca, N.Y.: ILA Press, 1994).

57. Cartersville Hearing Transcript, 139.

58. Ibid., 141.

59. Ibid., 33–34.

60. Mrs. Howell Hollis (widow of commission member), telephone interview by the author, 2 August 1995. Transcript, Georgia General Assembly Committee on Schools, Hearing, 11 March 1960 (LaGrange hearing transcript), 21; *Carroll County Georgian*, 10, 24 March 1960; *Atlanta Constitution*, 23 March 1960; *Atlanta Journal*, 11, 12 March 1960.

61. LaGrange hearing transcript, 22–23, 77.

62. LaGrange hearing transcript, 22.

63. Sibley's thinking and questions to black witnesses were very similar to the sit-uation in North Carolina during the Pearsall Committee's meetings. William Chafe explains that the white men who made up that committee could not "conceive of any blacks questioning the white view of reality." Chafe, *Civilities and Civil Rights*, 73–74.

64. LaGrange hearing transcript, 37.

65. Ibid., 84.

66. Ibid., 33.

67. Ibid., 95.

68. Ibid., 135.

69. Ibid., 65.

70. Ibid., 120.

71. Clayton, Troup, Carroll, Heard, and Coweta counties (with an average black population of 24.2 percent) supported local option. Fayette, Spalding, Meriwether, Lamar, Upson, and Butts counties (with an average black population of 37 percent) favored the first option, thus reflecting the trend of the previous three hearings; coun-ties with a lower black population percentage usually voted for the local option plan.

72. Transcript, Georgia General Assembly Committee on Schools, Hearing, 14 March 1960 (Douglas hearing transcript), 10.

73. The divergent reports of testimony were the result of the timesaving practice of recording delegations' preferences away from the witness stand.

74. Douglas hearing transcript, 97–99.

75. Ibid., 29.

76. Douglas Kiker, "Pro, Anti Public School Vote 'May Do Good in Valdosta,'" *Atlanta Journal*, 21 March 1960. Douglas hearing transcript, 45, 52, 113, 150.

77. Douglas hearing transcript, 48.

78. Douglas hearing transcript, 48; Downing Musgrove, interview by Jane Hern-don, 2 October 1988, transcript, 57–58, GGDP. Meyer, editor of the *Gainesville Times*, is widely credited as describing the fall of 1960 as "mind changing time," but the pro-cess for many Georgians came after the excitement of the commission hearings ebbed

and they confronted the possible loss of public education. See Mertz, "Mind Changing Time," 36.

79. Thirteen counties (with an average black population of 28.5 percent) expressed a desire for the first option. Only seven counties (with an average black population of 24 percent) preferred the second option. The two urban counties split on the question: Lowndes County almost unanimously supported massive resistance, and Glynn County was 100 percent behind local option. These figures come from the newspaper accounts of the hearing, the *Atlanta Journal*, 14 March 1960; *Atlanta Constitution*, 15 March 1960; and *Americus Times-Recorder*, 15 March 1960; and from the Douglas hearing transcript, 148.

80. Douglas hearing transcript, 152, 153.

81. *Atlanta Constitution*, 12 January 1960.

82. *Americus Times-Recorder*, 9 February 1960.

83. Bodenhamer quoted in *Atlanta Journal*, 16 March 1960; and *Albany Herald*, 20 March 1960; *Atlanta Journal*, 20 March 1960. The hearings proved invaluable to state politicians in offering them a revealing glimpse into how their constituents felt about the school issue. The men would then be free to follow their wishes with few political repercussions. *Atlanta Journal*, 18 March 1960.

84. *Augusta Courier*, 14, 21 March 1960; *Bainbridge Post-Searchlight*, 17 March 1960.

85. *Atlanta Constitution*, 11 March 1960. For increase in Klan and Citizens' Councils' testimony, see transcripts for the LaGrange, Douglas, Sandersville, Sylvania, Moultrie, and Atlanta hearings. *Atlanta Journal*, 18 March 1960; *Americus Times-Recorder*, 22 March 1960; Mosely, *Invisible Empire*, 181.

86. For more on the Greensboro sit-ins, see Chafe, *Civilities and Civil Rights*.

87. Bolster, "Civil Rights Movements," 192; Walker, "Protest and Negotiation," 114; and Walker, "Functions of Disunity," 228. Vandiver is quoted in *Atlanta Constitution*, 10 March 1960. For more on the Atlanta sit-in movement, see David Garrow, *Atlanta, Georgia, 1960–1961* (Brooklyn: Carlson Publishing, 1989); Raines, My Soul is Rested, 84–87; Harmon, *Beneath the Image*, 131–38.

88. Bolster, "Civil Rights Movements," 226, 194.

89. Minutes of meeting of Sibley Commission, 28 February 1960, box 68, Caldwell Papers. Render Hill, telephone interview by the author, 3 September 1995; Lutrelle Tift Rankin, interview by the author, 1 August 1995.

90. Jasper, Monroe, Jones, Hancock, Glascock, Jefferson, Crawford, Twiggs, Wilkinson, Washington, Johnson, and Bleckley counties, with an average black population of 50 percent, were largely rural and chose option one. Two of the counties for option two, Bibb (Macon) and Baldwin (Milledgeville), had substantial urban populations and an average black population of 36 percent. Laurens and Putnam counties were more evenly divided in their testimony; they had black populations of 37 percent and 54 percent respectively.

91. Transcript, Georgia General Assembly Committee on Schools, Hearing, 16 March 1960 (Sandersville hearing transcript), 23, 74.

92. Margaret Shannon, "Sibley Lauds Local Option," *Atlanta Journal,* 16 March 1960; Sandersville hearing transcript, 62, 102.

93. Harmon Caldwell to John Sibley, box 65, Caldwell Papers; Sandersville hearing transcript, 26. For more information on the North Carolina plan and its efforts to limit desegregation, see Douglas, "Rhetoric of Moderation"; and Chafe, *Civilities and Civil Rights.*

94. Sandersville hearing transcript, 145, 73. The Ku Klux Klan of Bibb County was also present, and its representative and Groover were two of the limited number of resistance advocates from that county.

95. Sandersville hearing transcript, 87, 152.

96. The representative of the "Chittlin Eaters Club," Cecil Ferguson, made Sibley an honorary member. Sibley's membership certificate hung on the wall of his Trust Company Bank office for years after the hearings and can be found in the Sibley Papers. Render Hill, telephone interview by the author, 3 September 1995.

97. Long, Bryan, and McIntosh were not represented at the hearing, and Liberty County sent only white resisters. *Atlanta Journal,* 17 March 1960; *Americus Times-Recorder,* 18 March 1960.

98. Transcript, Georgia General Assembly Committee on Schools, Hearing, 17 March 1960, Sibley Papers (Sylvania hearing transcript), 13, 25, 27.

99. Sylvania hearing transcript, 97; *Americus Times-Recorder,* 17 March 1960; *Savannah Morning News,* 18 March 1960.

100. Sylvania hearing transcript, 29; *Americus Times-Recorder,* 17 March 1960.

101. Gillis was also the son of the state's highway board chairman, Jim Gillis. In 1960, that position was even more politically powerful than it is today. *Americus Times-Recorder,* 18 March 1960; Sylvania hearing transcript, 53, 82.

102. For other examples of black opinion on segregated schools following the *Brown* decision, see Robert Penn Warren, *Segregation: The Inner Conflict in the South* (New York: Random House, 1956) especially 36 and 58, the quote is on 74.

103. Render Hill, telephone interview by the author, 3 September 1995; Warren, *Segregation,* 36, 58; O'Brien, "Georgia's Response," 66; George B. Tindall, "The Cost of Segregation," in Haws, *Age of Segregation,* 124. Many black witnesses throughout the course of the hearings expressed these or similar ideas.

104. See also O'Brien, "Georgia's Response," 119; Warren, *Segregation,* 74; Calvin Trillin, *An Education in Georgia: The Integration of Charlayne Hunter and Hamilton Holmes* (New York: Viking Press, 1964), 13.

105. *Atlanta Journal,* 7 March 1960, *Atlanta Constitution,* 7 March 1960. The state's NAACP leadership also expressed this concern and wired John Sibley with the same request.

106. *Americus Times-Recorder,* 9 March 1960.

107. Sylvania hearing transcript, 118–19.

108. Sylvania hearing transcript, 122. For more on the NAACP in Savannah, see Tuck, "City Too Dignified to Hate."

109. Sylvania hearing transcript, 93, 112.

110. *Albany Herald,* 20 March 1960. The unqualified support for the first option in this extreme southwest corner of Georgia had its roots in the black population percentages in the district's counties. Although only one had more than 60 percent (Calhoun), five had between 45 percent and 60 percent, and all but one had more than 30 percent. Six counties, Decatur, Mitchell, Brooks, Worth, Seminole, and Miller unanimously supported option one.

111. *Albany Herald,* 20 March 1960; Bainbridge *Post-Searchlight,* 3, 10, 17, 24 March 1960. Seventy-five people took part in the motorcade, and ten testified (*Bainbridge Post-Searchlight,* 24 March 1960). See also Transcript, Georgia General Assembly Committee on Schools, Hearing, 21 March 1960, Sibley Papers (Moultrie hearing transcript), 7–10; Charles Pou, "Integration Opposed By Negroes in Second," *Atlanta Journal,* 22 March 1960; Marion Gaines, "Segregation At All Costs Backed 5–1 at Moultrie Before Cheering Crowd," *Atlanta Constitution,* 22 March 1960.

112. Moultrie hearing transcript, 46–47.

113. Charles Pou, "Integration Opposed by Negroes in Second." *Atlanta Journal,* 22 March 1960; Moultrie hearing transcript.

114. *Albany Herald,* 15, 20, 18 March 1960.

115. Moultrie hearing transcript, 201.

116. Ibid., 73.

117. Ibid., 198.

118. Ibid., 35.

119. Bruce Galphin, "Mackay Says Only Assembly Can Shut All Schools," *Atlanta Constitution,* 22 March 1960.

120. Mike Edwards, "Sibley Panel in Atlanta Wednesday," *Atlanta Journal,* 22 March 1960; *Atlanta Constitution,* 22 March 1960; *Bainbridge Post-Searchlight,* 17 March 1960.

121. Bruce Galphin, "100 Here Ask To Testify to Sibley Panel," *Atlanta Constitution,* 23 March 1960; *Atlanta Journal,* 22 March 1960.

122. *Atlanta Journal,* 20, 21, 22, and 23 March 1960; *Atlanta Constitution,* 21, 22, 23 March and 2 April 1960.

123. Douglas Kiker, "They All Turn Out for School 'Rally,'" *Atlanta Journal,* 23 March 1960.

124. Ibid. See also Transcript, Georgia General Assembly Committee on Schools, Hearing, 23 March 1960, Sibley Papers. This transcript is not in the Committee on Schools Collection and can be found in the bound version of the hearing transcripts in what is known at the Robert W. Woodruff Library, Special Collections Department, as the "original" Sibley Collection (Atlanta hearing transcript, 23 March— there were two Atlanta hearings).

125. Atlanta hearing transcript, 23 March, 24–28, 31, 34. *Atlanta Journal,* 17, 18, 19, 20 March 1960.

126. Atlanta hearing transcript, 23 March, 41.

127. Ibid., 52.

128. Ibid., 66.

129. Ibid., 60.

130. An excellent look at the breakdown of the Atlanta black community's leadership in the face of increased militancy brought on by the student sit-in movement is offered in Walker, "Protest and Negotiation," and Walker, "Functions of Disunity." For Savannah, see Tuck, "City Too Dignified to Hate."

131. Atlanta hearing transcript, 23 March, 67.

132. Atlanta hearing transcript, 23 March, 149. Other unions represented at the Atlanta hearing took an opposing stance. The International Association of Machinists, Local 2616, and Brick Layers Union, Local 9, both voted for open schools.

133. Atlanta hearing transcript, 23 March, 92.

134. Ibid., 160.

135. Ibid., 120.

136. Ibid., 98.

137. Ibid., 167. For more on John Wesley Dobbs, see Pomerantz, *Where Peachtree Meets Sweet Auburn.*

138. Atlanta hearing transcript, 23 March, 182.

139. Transcript, Georgia General Assembly Committee on Schools, Hearing, 24 March 1960 (Gainesville hearing transcript).

140. Gainesville hearing transcript, 82–84.

141. Ibid., 104, 108. *Americus Times-Recorder,* 25 March 1960; *Atlanta Constitution,* 25 March 1960; Belcher and Allman, *Non-White Population of Georgia.*

142. Draft of separate Columbus and Atlanta statement, Sibley Papers.

143. *Columbus Enquirer,* 31 March 1960; Transcript, Georgia General Assembly Committee on Schools, Hearing, 31 March 1960 (Columbus hearing transcript), 26.

144. Columbus hearing transcript, 29, 45.

145. Ibid., 43, 90.

146. Ibid., 90.

147. Ibid., 85.

148. Ibid., 100.

149. Ibid., 59.

150. Ibid., 99. *Atlanta Constitution,* 1 April 1960.

151. Columbus hearing transcript, 34–35.

152. Transcript, Georgia General Assembly Committee on Schools, Hearing, 31 March 1960.

153. Render Hill, telephone interview by the author, 3 September 1995.

Chapter 5

Stevenson, "Personal History," 593.

1. Sibley Commission, "Summary of Findings," Sibley Papers; *Atlanta Constitution,* 1 April 1960.

2. This division in Georgia can be traced throughout its political history. The state divided along these same lines in the Secession Convention in the days preceding the Civil War. The state again split at the fall line during the Populist revolt in the last decade of the nineteenth century. And during the rise of massive resistance in the state, the Piedmont always lagged in its support of the program. Numan Bartley's seminal examination of the political effects of the civil rights movement in Georgia, *From Thurmond to Wallace,* clearly demonstrates this division. The Wiregrass and Black Belt areas of Georgia offered the strongest support for expanding Herman Talmadge's county unit amendment. In the 1954 private school amendment fight that created the miasma leading to the Sibley Commission, the two southern sections of Georgia overwhelmingly voted for the plan. Bartley's examination also reveals the same rural-urban split on the amendment that the Sibley Commission discovered when polling the state about its possible implementation. Indeed, the urban support for the private school plan dropped off by 10 percent in the two southern regions. It was only a 5 percent drop in the Piedmont, but that area had offered only lukewarm support for the idea.

3. John Sibley to Erwin Sibley, 28 March 1960, Sibley Papers.

4. John Duncan to John Sibley, 31 March 1960, and Sibley's same-day reply, Sibley Papers; Harmon Caldwell to John Sibley, 4 April 1960, Sibley Papers; Render Hill, telephone interview by the author, 3 September 1995.

5. Freeman Leverett to John Sibley, 8 April 1960, Sibley Papers. Render Hill, interview.

6. "Commission Summary," 13 April 1960, Sibley Papers; Margaret Shannon, "Sibley Panel Drafting Report," *Atlanta Journal,* 12 April 1960.

7. Render Hill, telephone interview by the author, 3 September 1995.

8. Bernice McCullen, "Tales Out of School" newsletter, Sibley Papers; General Assembly Committee on Schools, Majority Report, Sibley Papers (hereafter cited as Majority Report).

9. The Majority Report went through three major drafts: Harmon Caldwell wrote the first and stressed a constitutional amendment to adopt local option; Howell Hollis drafted a new version after reading Caldwell's report; Sibley then composed the final draft that he submitted to the General Assembly (Sibley Papers; various versions of Caldwell's attempts can be found in box 65, Caldwell Papers). The quotations that follow in the next few paragraphs all come from this report.

10. John Sibley to Pope Brock, 20 May 1960, Sibley Papers. For another interpretation of the commission's report, see McGrath, "Great Expectations," 145–50. McGrath argues that Sibley's hostility toward the *Brown* decision, linking desegregation to communism, and his paternalistic outlook shaded the report. Although this impression is certainly true, Sibley's main goal was an end to massive resistance as a tactic to preserve segregation. He and other like-minded individuals sought an end to the school crisis and the threat to public education, but they also wanted to preserve segregation.

11. Render Hill, telephone interview by the author, 3 September 1995; Georgia General Assembly Committee on Schools, Minority Report, Sibley Papers.

12. "Separate Statement from Render Hill," Sibley Papers; Render Hill, interview.

13. In spite of the commission's three different reports, most Georgians understood the "Sibley report" to mean only the majority report. John Sibley to Ernest Vandiver, Richard B. Russell, and Herman Talmadge, 28 April 1960; and John Sibley to Dugas Shands, 13 June 1960, Sibley Papers.

14. Charles Pou and Raleigh Bryans, "Vandiver Won't Call Assembly," and Charles Pou, "Analysis," *Atlanta Journal,* 28 April 1960.

15. This "Editorial Roundup" can be found in the *Atlanta Journal,* 29 April 1960; *Augusta Courier,* 9 May 1960.

16. Frank Hooper to John Sibley, 18 May 1960; John Sibley to Frank Hooper, 13 May 1960; Robert O. Arnold to John Sibley, 12 May 1960; John Sibley to Howell Hollis, 10 May 1960; John Sibley to Erwin Sibley, 5 May 1960; all in Sibley Papers.

17. Danny Sloan to John Sibley, (no date), Sibley Papers; John Sibley to John Greer, 2 May 1960, Sibley Papers; printed copy of Murrow interview, box 26, Vandiver Papers.

18. Rankin and Bodenhamer's comments, Sibley Papers; O'Brien, "Georgia's Response," 260; James F. Cook, *Carl Sanders,* 67–68; rough draft of Greer's September statement, Sibley Papers; Greer's Macon speech, John Greer Papers, Special Collections, Pullen Library, Georgia State University, Atlanta, Georgia.

19. John Sibley, "The Urgency of Education and the Georgia School Situation," speech, 10 November 1960, Sibley Papers.

20. Undated minutes of a HOPE meeting, HOPE papers; Paul E. Mertz, "Mind Changing Time," 57–59.

21. Fran Breeden to John Sibley, 11 November 1960, Sibley Papers.

22. Muriel Lokey, interview, 26 January 1989, transcript, 89.

23. Robert W. Woodruff to John Sibley, 1 June 1960, Robert W. Woodruff Papers, letters, box 1, Special Collections Department, Emory University, Atlanta, Georgia. Both men's personal and business papers, deposited at Emory University, include heavy correspondence between them every year except 1960. That year's holdings are particularly sparse and include only thank-you notes and other trifling letters. The invitation to the "orientation" is the lone exception.

24. For more on the sit-in movement in Atlanta, see Jack Walker, "Protest and Negotiation," and his "Functions of Disunity." See also David Garrow, *Atlanta, Georgia.*

25. Ivan Allen to John Sibley, 12 January 1961, Sibley Papers; John Sibley to Howell Hollis, 19 December 1960, Sibley Papers; Sherrill, *Gothic Politics,* 59.

26. For an in-depth examination of these events, see Melton, "1960 Presidential Election," especially 26–27, 36, 60, 98.

27. Melton, "1960 Presidential Election," 83–84.

28. Melton, "1960 Presidential Election," 140; S. Ernest Vandiver interview, 20 March 1986, transcript, 45; S. Ernest Vandiver interview, 25 January 1994, transcript, 5–7.

29. This assessment is taken from a handwritten note found in Vandiver's personal papers, in which he listed the commission members on two sides, with those he was unsure about labeled with a horizontal, two-sided arrow (box 27, Vandiver Papers); Bell, interview, 12 June 1990, transcript, 37; Griffin Bell, Hearings before the Committee on Judiciary, United States Senate, 95th Congress, January 1977, transcript, 127.

30. Almost all of the correspondence on the segregation question in Vandiver's papers is addressed to or from "B" Brooks, which leads to the assumption that he was a key advisor in this crisis. He was also the recipient of a 14 July 1959 letter from Virginia lawyer William H. Burson, which presented a plan to abandon resistance in Georgia that parallels the Sibley recommendations. See also Pou, "Epilogue," 55; James F. Cook, Carl Sanders, 67–68; Griffin Bell to "B" Brooks, 30 November 1960, box 113, Vandiver Papers; Freeman Leverett to "B" Brooks, 1 December 1960, box 27, Vandiver Papers; Freeman Leverett to Eugene Cook (acknowledging Hall's participation), 19 February 1961, box 11, Vandiver Papers; Atlanta Journal, 1 January 1961; Carl Sanders, interview by James F. Cook, 5 August 1986, transcript, 22–23, GGDP.

31. See Clifford M. Kuhn, " 'There's a Footnote to History!' Memory and the History of Martin Luther King's October 1960 Arrest and Its Aftermath," Journal of American History 84 (September 1997), 583–95.

32. Atlanta Journal, 1, 2, 3, 5 January 1961; Atlanta Constitution, 1, 2, 3, 5 January 1961; Joe Fain, interview by the author, 29 January 1993, Decatur, Georgia; Pou, "Epilogue," 50.

33. For a detailed look at the integration crisis, see Trillin, Education in Georgia, and Atlanta Journal, 7 January 1961.

34. Atlanta Journal, 7 January 1961; Elbert Tuttle, interview, 21 September 1992, transcript, 24; Bass, Unlikely Heroes, 217–18; Ernest Vandiver, "Vandiver Takes the Middle Road," in Henderson and Roberts, Georgia Governors, 161.

35. Atlanta Journal, 10 January 1961.

36. John Pennington and Gordon Roberts, "Integration Follows Fast Court Ruling," Atlanta Journal, 11 January 1961; Albany Herald, 8, 12 January 1961; Athens Banner-Herald, 10 January 1961.

37. Atlanta Journal, 12 January 1961; Atlanta Constitution, 12 January 1961; Joe Fain, interview by the author, 29 January 1993, Decatur, Georgia; James F. Cook, Carl Sanders, 67–68; Trillin, Education in Georgia, 52; Stevenson, "Personal History," 589; Pou, "Epilogue," 52.

38. Harris is quoted in Sherrill, Gothic Politics, 47, and in Atlanta Journal, 12 January 1961, with Vandiver's response.

39. Grant, Way It Was, 384; Trillin, Education in Georgia, 59; Silver and Moeser, Separate City, 107.

40. Atlanta Constitution, 14 January 1961.

41. Vandiver, interview, 20 March 1986, transcript, 51–53.

42. Atlanta Journal, 15 January 1961; Ivan Allen to John Sibley, 12 January 1961, Sibley Papers.

43. Vandiver, Georgia Governors Roundtable, transcript, 11, GGDP.

44. Vandiver, interview, 20 March 1986, transcript, 52; George T. Smith, interview, 19 August 1992, transcript, 11; Bell, interview, 12 June 1990, transcript, 32.

45. Render Hill, telephone interview by the author, 3 September 1995; Brooks's actions and statement can be found in Shipp, interview, 22 April 1987, transcript, 38, and Osgood Williams, interview, 2 June 1988, transcript, 53.

46. Vandiver, interview, 20 March 1986, transcript, 54; *Atlanta Journal*, 17 January 1961; Bell, interview, 19 September 1990, transcript, 28.

47. Vandiver, "The Fate of Public Education in Georgia," reprinted in the *Atlanta Journal*, 19 January 1961.

48. Celestine Sibley, interview, 5 March 1987, transcript, 74, GGDP.

49. Legislative reaction can be found in the *Atlanta Journal*, 19 January 1961; Freeman Leverett to John Sibley, 21 June 1961, Sibley Papers.

50. *Atlanta Journal*, 19 January 1961.

51. Ibid.; 1961 House Education Committee minutes, Georgia Department of Archives and History, Atlanta, Georgia; *Augusta Courier*, 23 and 30 January 1961.

52. *Bainbridge Post-Searchlight*, 19 and 26 January 1961; *Albany Herald*, 19 January 1961.

53. Hamilton Lokey to Saunders Jones, 31 June 1961, HOPE papers; Jesse Hill quoted in McGrath, "Great Expectations," 161.

54. McCain, "Speaking on School Desegregation," 258–59; Charles Weltner, "Pride and Progress," *American Education* 2 (September 1966): 25; David R. Goldfield, *Cotton Fields and Skyscrapers: Southern City and Region* (1982; reprint, Baltimore: Johns Hopkins University Press, 1989), 173; Susan M. McGrath, "From Tokenism to Community Control: Political Symbolism in the Desegregation of Atlanta's Public Schools, 1961–1973," *Georgia Historical Quarterly* 79 (winter 1995), 852–53; and her "Great Expectations," 165–72; Bayor, *Shaping of Twentieth-Century Atlanta*, 225.

55. Ray Moore, interview, 8 May 1987, transcript, 34–35; Townsend, "Miracle in Atlanta"; *New York Times*, 27 August 1961.

56. Townsend, "Miracle in Atlanta"; Ray Moore, interview, 8 May 1987, transcript, 34–35. For more on the continuing efforts to integrate Atlanta's schools, see McGrath, "Great Expectations," and Bayor, *Shaping of Twentieth-Century Atlanta*, 227–51.

57. Erwin Sibley to John Sibley, 30 January 1961, Erwin Sibley Collection.

58. Nan Pendergrast, interview, 24 June 1992, transcript, 69–70.

59. Bell, interview, 12 June 1990, transcript, 37.

Epilogue

1. HOPE mail-out, October 1961, HOPE Papers.

2. Joe Fain, interview by the author, 29 January 1993, Decatur, Georgia.

3. *Atlanta Journal*, 6 August 1977; *Atlanta Journal*, 7 May 1961; *Atlanta Constitution*, 16 February 1975; speech by Herman Talmadge, 30 April 1977, Sibley Papers.

4. The opinions of Sam Nunn, Herman Talmadge, and Griffin Bell can be found in U.S. Congress, Senate, Griffin Bell, Hearings before the Committee on Judiciary,

United States Senate, 95th Cong., January 1977 (Bell confirmation hearings); Vandiver, interview, 20 March 1986, transcript, 57; Osgood Williams, interview, 2 June 1988, transcript, 56; Bell, interview, 19 September 1990, transcript, 33; A. T. Walden to John Sibley, 14 June 1961, Sibley Papers; Erwin Sibley to John Sibley, 3 May 1960, Erwin Sibley Collection; John Sibley quoted in Patterson, "Unruffled Mr. Sibley," 38.

5. *U.S. News and World Report,* 6 November 1961; Kiwanis Club of Birmingham Speech, 7 May 1963, Sibley Papers; Southern States Conference of Certified Public Accountants speech, 15 June 1964, Sibley Papers.

6. Carolyn Hansen to John Sibley, 17 February 1975, Sibley Papers.

7. Griffin Bell, Confirmation Hearings, 126–27, 277, 253, 282.

8. Bartley and Graham, *Southern Politics,* 19, 53, 71.

9. Sanders quoted in Ben Hibbs, "Progress Goes Marching Through Georgia," *Saturday Evening Post,* 13 February 1963, 69. See also James F. Cook, *Carl Sanders,* and Cobb, *Selling of the South.*

10. Trillin, *Education in Georgia,* 43; Render Hill, telephone interview by the author, 3 September 1995.

SELECTED BIBLIOGRAPHY

Manuscript Collections

Caldwell, Harmon. Collection. Richard B. Russell Library. University of Georgia Libraries, Athens, Georgia.

Greer, John. Private papers. Pullen Library. Georgia State University, Atlanta, Georgia.

Help Our Public Education (HOPE) papers. Library and Archives. Atlanta History Center, Atlanta, Georgia.

Sibley, John A. Papers. Georgia General Assembly Committee on Schools Collection. Special Collections Department, Robert W. Woodruff Library. Emory University, Atlanta, Georgia.

Sibley, U. Erwin. Collection. Russell Library. Georgia College, Milledgeville, Georgia.

Vandiver, S. Ernest. Collection. Richard B. Russell Library. University of Georgia Libraries, Athens, Georgia.

Woodruff, Robert W. Private papers. Special Collections Department, Robert W. Woodruff Library. Emory University, Atlanta, Georgia.

Newspapers

Albany Herald
Americus Times-Recorder
Athens Banner-Herald
Atlanta Constitution
Atlanta Daily World
Atlanta Journal
Augusta Courier
Bainbridge Post-Searchlight

Bartow Herald
Carroll County Georgian
Columbus Enquirer
Macon Telegraph
Montgomery Advertiser
New Jersey Afro-American
New York Times
Savannah Morning News
Southern School News
Washington (Georgia) News-Reporter

Interviews

Arnall, Ellis. Interview by Jane W. Herndon. 24 July 1971. Georgia Government Documentation Project. Special Collections, Georgia State University, Atlanta, Georgia.

Bell, Griffin. Interview by Cliff Kuhn. 12 June and 19 September 1990. Georgia Government Documentation Project. Special Collections, Georgia State University, Atlanta, Georgia.

Bullard, Helen. Interview by Lorraine Nelson Spritzer. 27 July 1977. Georgia Government Documentation Project. Special Collections, Georgia State University, Atlanta, Georgia.

Busbee, George D. Interview by James F. Cook. 21 and 24 March 1987. Georgia Government Documentation Project. Special Collections, Georgia State University, Atlanta, Georgia.

Calloway, William. Interview by Cliff Kuhn. 21 October 1992. Georgia Government Documentation Project. Special Collections, Georgia State University, Atlanta, Georgia.

Goodwin, George. Interview by Cliff Kuhn. 17 January 1992. Georgia Government Documentation Project. Special Collections, Georgia State University, Atlanta, Georgia.

Greer, John. Interviews by Cliff Kuhn. 27 May and 4 June 1987. Georgia Government Documentation Project. Special Collections, Georgia State University, Atlanta, Georgia.

Hamilton, Grace Towns. Interview by Cliff Kuhn. 26 June 1986. Georgia Government Documentation Project. Special Collections, Georgia State University, Atlanta, Georgia.

Harris, Roy. Interview by Jane Walker Herndon. 20 August 1971. Georgia Government Documentation Project. Special Collections, Georgia State University, Atlanta, Georgia.

Johnson, Leroy. Interview by Cliff Kuhn. 1991. Georgia Government Documentation Project. Special Collections, Georgia State University, Atlanta, Georgia.

Law, W. W. Interview by Cliff Kuhn and Tim Crimmins. 15 November 1990. Georgia

Government Documentation Project. Special Collections, Georgia State University, Atlanta, Georgia.

Lokey, Hamilton, and Muriel Lokey. Interview by Catherine Foster. 26 January 1989. Georgia Government Documentation Project. Special Collections, Georgia State University, Atlanta, Georgia.

Mackay, James. Interviews by Cliff Kuhn. 18 and 31 March 1986. Georgia Government Documentation Project. Special Collections, Georgia State University, Atlanta, Georgia.

Maloof, Manuel. Interviews by David Jordan. 13 and 15 June 1994. Georgia Government Documentation Project. Special Collections, Georgia State University, Atlanta, Georgia.

Millican, Everett. Interview by Lorraine Nelson Spritzer. 30 July 1977. Georgia Government Documentation Project. Special Collections, Georgia State University, Atlanta, Georgia.

Moore, Ray. Interviews by Cliff Kuhn. 8 May and 18 June 1987. Georgia Government Documentation Project. Special Collections, Georgia State University, Atlanta, Georgia.

Musgrove, Downing. Interview by Jane Herndon. 2 October 1988. Georgia Government Documentation Project. Special Collections, Georgia State University, Atlanta, Georgia.

Pauley, Frances. Interviews by Cliff Kuhn. 11 April and 3 May 1988. Georgia Government Documentation Project. Special Collections, Georgia State University, Atlanta, Georgia.

Pendergrast, Nan. Interview by Kathryn Nasstrom and Cliff Kuhn. 24 June 1992. Georgia Government Documentation Project. Special Collections, Georgia State University, Atlanta, Georgia.

Sanders, Carl. Interview by James F. Cook. 5 August 1986. Georgia Government Documentation Project. Special Collections, Georgia State University, Atlanta, Georgia.

Shipp, William (Bill). Interview by Cliff Kuhn. 22 April 1987. Georgia Government Documentation Project. Special Collections, Georgia State University, Atlanta, Georgia.

Sibley, Celestine. Interview by Cliff Kuhn. 4 and 5 March 1993. Georgia Government Documentation Project. Special Collections, Georgia State University, Atlanta, Georgia.

Smith, George T. Interview by T. Chaffin. 19 August 1992. Georgia Government Documentation Project. Special Collections, Georgia State University, Atlanta, Georgia.

Talmadge, Herman. Interview by Harold Henderson. 17 July 1987. Georgia Government Documentation Project. Special Collections, Georgia State University, Atlanta, Georgia.

Tuttle, Elbert. Interviews by Cliff Kuhn. 4 April and 21 September 1992. Georgia

Government Documentation Project. Special Collections, Georgia State University, Atlanta, Georgia.

Vandiver, S. Ernest. Interviews by Charles Pyles. 20 March and 28 July 1986. Georgia Government Documentation Project. Special Collections, Georgia State University, Atlanta, Georgia.

———. Interview by Cliff Kuhn. 25 January 1994. Georgia Government Documentation Project. Special Collections, Georgia State University, Atlanta, Georgia.

Williams, Carey. Interview by Cliff Kuhn. 23 February 1989. Georgia Government Documentation Project. Special Collections, Georgia State University, Atlanta, Georgia.

Williams, Osgood. Interview by Cliff Kuhn. 2 June and 2 October 1988. Georgia Government Documentation Project. Special Collections, Georgia State University, Atlanta, Georgia.

Other Works

Adamson, June N. "Few Black Voices Heard: The Black Community and the Desegregation Crisis in Clinton, Tennessee, 1956." *Tennessee Historical Quarterly* 53 (spring 1994): 30–41.

Allen, Frederick. *Secret Formula.* New York: Harper Collins Publishers, 1994.

Allen, Ivan, Jr. *Mayor: Notes on the Sixties.* New York: Simon and Schuster, 1971.

Altheide, David L. *Creating Reality.* Beverly Hills: Sage Publications, 1976.

Altheide, David L., and Robert P. Snow. *Media Logic.* Beverly Hills: Sage Publications, 1979.

Anderson, William. *The Wild Man From Sugar Creek: the Political Career of Eugene Talmadge.* Baton Rouge: Louisiana State University Press, 1975.

Ashmore, Harry S. *An Epitaph for Dixie.* New York: Norton, 1957.

Ayers, Edward L. *The Promise of the New South: Life After Reconstruction.* New York: Oxford University Press, 1992.

Bartley, Numan V. *The Rise of Massive Resistance: Race and Politics in the South During the 1950s.* Baton Rouge: Louisiana State University Press, 1969.

———. *From Thurmond to Wallace: Political Tendencies in Georgia, 1946–1968.* Baltimore: Johns Hopkins Press, 1970.

———. "Moderation in Maddox Country?" *Georgia Historical Quarterly* 58, no. 4 (winter 1974): 340–48.

———. "Another New South?" *Georgia Historical Quarterly* 65, no. 2 (summer 1981): 119–37.

———. *The Creation of Modern Georgia.* Athens: University of Georgia Press, 1983.

———. "Writing About the Post-World War II South." *Georgia Historical Quarterly* 68, no. 1 (spring 1984): 1–18.

———. *The New South: 1945–1980.* Baton Rouge: Louisiana State University Press, 1995.

————. "Social Change and Sectional Identity." *Journal of Southern History* 66, no. 1 (February 1995): 3–16.

Bartley, Numan V., and Hugh Graham. *Southern Politics and the Second Reconstruction.* Baltimore: Johns Hopkins University Press, 1975.

Bass, Jack. *Unlikely Heroes.* New York: Simon and Schuster, 1981.

Bass, Jack, and Walter DeVries. *The Transformation of Southern Politics: Social Change and Political Consequences Since 1945.* New York: Basic Books, 1976.

Bayor, Ronald H. "The Twentieth-Century Urban South and the Atlanta Experience." *Georgia Historical Quarterly* 75, no. 3 (fall 1991): 557–65.

————. *Race and the Shaping of Twentieth-Century Atlanta.* Chapel Hill: University of North Carolina Press, 1996.

Belcher, John C., and Carolyn N. Allman. *The Non-White Population of Georgia.* Athens: Institute of Community and Area Development, 1967.

Belknap, Michal R. *Federal Law and Southern Order: Racial Violence and Constitutional Conflict in the Post-Brown South.* Athens: University of Georgia Press, 1987.

Bernd, Joseph L. "White Supremacy and the Disenfranchisement of Blacks in Georgia, 1946." *Georgia Historical Quarterly* 66, no. 4 (winter 1982): 492–513.

Black, Earl. "Southern Governors and Political Change: Campaign Stances on Racial Segregation and Economic Development, 1950–1969." *Journal of Politics* 33 (August 1971): 703–34.

————. *Southern Governors and Civil Rights.* Cambridge, Mass.: Harvard University Press, 1976.

Bloom, Jack M. *Class, Race, and the Civil Rights Movement.* Bloomington and Indianapolis: Indiana University Press, 1987.

Blossom, Virgil T. *It Has Happened Here.* New York: Harper, 1959.

Bolster, Paul. "Civil Rights Movements in Twentieth Century Georgia." Ph.D. diss., University of Georgia, 1972.

Boone, Buford. "Southern Newsmen and Local Pressure." In *Race and the News Media,* edited by Paul Fisher and Ralph Lowenstein. New York: Frederick A. Praeger Publishers, 1967.

Bowles, Billy, and Remer Tyson. *They Love a Man in the Country: Saints and Sinners in the South.* Atlanta: Peachtree Publishers, 1989.

Boyle, Sarah-Patton. *The Desegregated Heart: A Virginian's Stand in Time of Transition.* New York: Morrow, 1962.

Brauer, Carl M. *John F. Kennedy and the Second Reconstruction.* New York: Columbia University Press, 1977.

Campbell, Will D. *The Stem of Jesse: The Costs of Community at a 1960s Southern School.* Macon, Ga.: Mercer University Press, 1995.

Carmine, Edward G., and James A. Stimson. *Issue Evolution: Race and the Transformation of American Politics.* Princeton: Princeton University Press, 1989.

Carter, Dan T. *The Politics of Rage: George Wallace, the Origins of the New Conservatism, and the Transformation of American Politics.* New York: Simon and Schuster, 1995.

———. *From George Wallace to Newt Gingrich: Race in the Conservative Counter-revolution, 1963–1994.* Baton Rouge: Louisiana State University Press, 1996.

Carter, Hodding. *The South Strikes Back.* 1959. Reprint, Westport, Conn.: Negro Universities Press, 1970.

———. "The Wave Beneath the Froth." In *Race and the News Media,* edited by Paul Fisher and Ralph Lowenstein. New York: Frederick A. Praeger Publishers, 1967.

Carter, Jimmy. *Turning Point.* New York: Times Press, 1992.

Cash, W. J. *The Mind of the South.* 1941. Reprint, New York: Vintage Books, 1991.

Chafe, William H. *Civilities and Civil Rights: Greensboro, North Carolina, and the Black Struggle for Freedom.* New York: Oxford University Press, 1980.

Chalmers, David M. *Hooded Americanism: The First Century of the Ku Klux Klan, 1865–1965.* Garden City, N.Y.: Doubleday, 1965.

Cleveland, Len G. "Georgia Baptists and the 1954 Supreme Court Desegregation Decision." *Georgia Historical Quarterly* 59, no. 1 (spring 1975): 107–17.

Cobb, James Charles. "Politics in a New South City: Augusta, Georgia, 1946–1971." Ph.D. diss., University of Georgia, 1975.

———. *The Selling of the South: The Southern Crusade for Industrial Development, 1936–1980.* Baton Rouge: Louisiana State University Press, 1982.

———. *Industrialization and Southern Society.* Lexington: University Press of Kentucky, 1984.

———. "Cracklin's and Caviar: The Enigma of Sunbelt Georgia." *Georgia Historical Quarterly* 68, no. 1 (spring 1984): 19–39.

Cook, Eugene. "The Georgia Constitution and Mixed Public Schools." Pamphlet, Georgia Attorney General's Office, October 1954.

Cook, James F. *Carl Sanders: Spokesman of the New South.* Macon, Ga.: Mercer University Press, 1993.

Cramer, M. Richard. "School Desegregation and New Industry: The Southern Community Leaders' Viewpoint." *Social Forces* 41 (May 1963): 384–89.

Dallek, Robert. *Lone Star Rising: Lyndon Johnson and His Times.* New York: Oxford University Press, 1991.

Daniel, Pete. *Breaking the Land: The Transformation of Cotton, Tobacco, and Rice Cultures Since 1880.* Urbana: University of Illinois Press, 1985.

———. *Standing at the Crossroads: Southern Life in the Twentieth Century.* New York: Hill and Wang, 1986.

Douglas, Davison M. "The Rhetoric of Moderation: Desegregating the South During the Decade After *Brown.*" *Northwestern University Law Review* 89, no. 1 (1994): 92–139.

Draper, Alan. *Conflict of Interests: Organized Labor and the Civil Rights Movement in the South, 1954–1968.* Ithaca, N.Y.: ILA Press, 1994.

Dykeman, Wilma, and James Stokely. "The Klan Tries a Comeback." *Commentary* (January 1960): 45–51.

Edsall, Thomas B., and Mary D. Edsall. *Chain Reaction: The Impact of Race, Rights, and Taxes on American Politics.* New York: Norton, 1991.

Egerton, John. *The Americanization of Dixie: The Southernization of America.* New York: Harper's Magazine Press, 1974.

———. *Speak Now Against the Day: The Generation Before the Civil Rights Movement in the South.* New York: Knopf, 1994.

Ely, James W. *The Crisis of Conservative Virginia: The Byrd Organization and the Politics of Massive Resistance.* Knoxville: University of Tennessee Press, 1976.

Fanning, Lawrence S. "The Media: Observer or Participant?" In *Race and the News Media,* edited by Paul Fisher and Ralph Lowenstein. New York: Frederick A. Praeger Publishers, 1967.

Fifteen Southerners. *Why the South Will Survive.* Athens: University of Georgia Press, 1981.

Freyer, Tony. *The Little Rock Crisis: A Constitutional Interpretation.* Westport, Conn.: Greenwood Press, 1984.

Fuller, Helen. *Southerners and Schools.* Washington: New Republic, 1959.

Galphin, Bruce. *The Riddle of Lester Maddox.* Atlanta: Camelot Publishing, 1968.

Garrow, David J. *Atlanta, Georgia, 1960–1961.* Brooklyn: Carlson Publishing, 1989.

Gates, Robin L. *The Making of Massive Resistance: Virginia's Politics of Public School Desegregation, 1954–1956.* Chapel Hill: University of North Carolina Press, 1964.

Georgia General Assembly Committee on Schools. "Majority and Minority Report." Pamphlet, Atlanta, Georgia, April 1960.

Georgia Governors Roundtable. 31 October 1985. Georgia Government Documentation Project. Special Collections, Georgia State University, Atlanta, Georgia.

Gerster, Patrick, and Nicholas Cords, eds. *Myth and Southern History.* Vol. 2, *The New South.* 2d ed. Urbana: University of Illinois Press, 1989.

Goldfield, David R. *Cotton Fields and Skyscrapers: Southern City and Region.* 1982. Reprint. Baltimore: Johns Hopkins University Press, 1989.

———. *Black, White, and Southern: Race Relations and Southern Culture, 1940 to the Present.* Baton Rouge: Louisiana State University Press, 1990.

Grant, Donald L. *The Way It Was in the South: The Black Experience in Georgia.* New York: Birch Lane Press, 1993.

Grantham, Dewey W. *The Life and Death of the Solid South: A Political History.* Lexington: University Press of Kentucky, 1988.

———. *The South in Modern America: A Region at Odds.* New York: Harper Collins Publishers, 1994.

———, ed. *The South and the Sectional Image: The Sectional Theme Since Reconstruction.* New York: Harper and Row, 1967.

Harmon, David Andrew. *Beneath the Image of the Civil Rights Movement and Race Relations: Atlanta, Georgia, 1946–1981.* New York: Garland Publishing, 1996.

Hartman, Paul, and Charles Husband. "The Mass Media and Racial Conflict." In *The Manufacture of News,* edited by Stanley Cohen and Jock Young. London: Constable, 1981.

Haws, Robert, ed. *The Age of Segregation: Race Relations in the South, 1890–1945.* Jackson: University Press of Mississippi, 1978.

Hein, Virginia H. "The Image of 'A City Too Busy to Hate': Atlanta in the 1960s." *Phylon* 33 (fall 1972): 205–21.

Henderson, Harold P. "The 1946 Gubernatorial Election in Georgia." Master's thesis, Georgia Southern College, 1967.

———. *The Politics of Change in Georgia: A Political Biography of Ellis Arnall.* Athens: University of Georgia Press, 1991.

Henderson, Harold P., and Gary L. Roberts, ed. *Georgia Governors in an Age of Change: From Ellis Arnall to George Busbee.* Athens: University of Georgia Press, 1988.

Inscoe, John C., ed. *Georgia in Black and White: Explorations in the Race Relations of a Southern State, 1865–1950.* Athens: University of Georgia Press, 1994.

Irons, Peter, and Stephanie Guitton, eds. *May It Please the Court.* New York: New Press, 1993.

Iyengar, Shanto, Mark D. Peters, and Donald R. Kinder. "Experimental Demonstrations of the 'Not-So-Minimal' Consequences of Television News Programs." In *Media Power in Politics,* edited by Doris A. Graber. Washington, D.C.: Congressional Quarterly, 1984.

Jacoway, Elizabeth, and David R. Colburn. *Southern Businessmen and Desegregation.* Baton Rouge: Louisiana State University Press, 1982.

Jacoway, Elizabeth, Dan T. Carter, Lester C. Lamon, and Robert C. McMath, Jr. *The Adaptable South.* Baton Rouge: Louisiana State University Press, 1991.

Key, V. O. *Southern Politics in State and Nation.* New York: Vintage Books, 1949.

Kirby, Jack Temple. *Rural Worlds Lost: The American South, 1920–1960.* Baton Rouge: Louisiana State University Press, 1987.

Klarman, Michael J. "How *Brown* Changed Race Relations: The Backlash Thesis." *Journal of American History* 81 (June 1994): 81–118.

Kluger, Richard. *Simple Justice: The History of Brown v. Board of Education and Black America's Struggle for Equality.* New York: Vintage Books, 1977.

Kuhn, Cliff. " 'There's a Footnote to History!' Memory and the History of Martin Luther King's October 1960 Arrest and Its Aftermath." *Journal of American History* 84 (September 1997): 583–95.

Kytle, Calvin, and James Mackay. "We Pass . . . On Democracy: Who Runs Georgia." Unpublished manuscript. Special Collections Department. Robert W. Woodruff Library. Emory University, Atlanta, Georgia.

Lokey, Hamilton. "The Low Key Life of Hamilton Lokey." Unpublished manuscript. Georgia Government Documentation Project. Special Collections. Georgia State University, Atlanta, Georgia.

Lougue, Calvin McLeod, ed. *Eugene Talmadge: Rhetoric and Response.* New York: Greenwood Press, 1989.

Maddox, Lester Garfield. *Speaking Out: The Autobiography of Lester Garfield Maddox.* Garden City, N.Y.: Doubleday, 1975.

Martin, Harold. *Three Strong Pillars.* Atlanta: Trust Company of Georgia, 1974.

———. *William Berry Hartsfield.* Athens: University of Georgia Press, 1978.

Martin, John Barlow. *The Deep South Says Never.* Westport, Conn.: Negro Universities Press, 1957.

Matthews, John Michael. "Studies in Race Relations in Georgia, 1890–1930." Ph.D. diss., Duke University, 1970.

Mayer, Michael S. "With Much Deliberation and Some Speed: Eisenhower and the *Brown* Decision." *Journal of Southern History* 52 (February 1986): 43–76.

McCain, Ray. "Speaking on School Desegregation by Atlanta Ministers." *Southern Speech Journal* 29 (March 1964): 256–62.

———. "Reactions to the United States Supreme Court Segregation Decision of 1954." *Georgia Historical Quarterly* 52 (December 1968): 371–87.

McCombs, Maxwell E., and Donald L. Shaw. "The Agenda-Setting Function of the Press." In *Media Power in Politics,* edited by Doris A. Graber. Washington, D.C.: Congressional Quarterly, 1984.

McGill, Ralph. "How It Happened Down in Georgia." *New Republic* 116 (26 January 1947): 12–15.

———. *The South and the Southerner.* Boston: Little, Brown, 1959.

———. *Ralph McGill, Editor and Publisher: Ralph McGill Speaks.* Vol. 2. Compiled by Calvin McLeod Lougue. Durham, N.C.: Moore Publishing, 1969.

———. *No Place to Hide.* 2 vols. Macon, Ga.: Mercer University Press, 1984.

McGrath, Susan Margaret. "Great Expectations: The History of School Desegregation in Atlanta and Boston, 1954–1990." Ph.D. diss., Emory University, 1992.

———. "From Tokenism to Community Control: Political Symbolism in the Desegregation of Atlanta's Public Schools, 1961–1973." *Georgia Historical Quarterly* 79 (winter 1995): 842–72.

McMillen, Neil R. *The Citizens' Council: Organized Resistance to the Second Reconstruction.* Chicago: University of Illinois Press, 1971.

Melton, Thomas R. "The 1960 Presidential Election in Georgia." Ph.D. diss., University of Mississippi, 1985.

Mertz, Paul E. "'Mind Changing Time All Over Georgia': HOPE Inc. and School Desegregation, 1958–1961." *Georgia Historical Quarterly* 77 (spring 1993): 41–61.

Miller, Helen Hill. "Private Business and Public Education in the South." *Harvard Business Review* 8 (8 July 1960): 75–88.

Monroe, William B. "Television: The Chosen Instrument of the Revolution." In *Race and the News Media,* edited by Paul Fisher and Ralph Lowenstein. New York: Frederick A. Praeger Publishers, 1967.

Moore, Noellene J. *I Saw a Tear.* Macon, Ga.: Macon Press Services, 1978.

Mosely, Clement Charlton. "Invisible Empire: A History of the Ku Klux Klan in Twentieth Century Georgia, 1915–1965." Ph.D. diss., University of Georgia, 1968.

Muse, Benjamin. *Virginia's Massive Resistance.* Bloomington: Indiana University Press, 1961.

Norris, Hoke, ed. *We Dissent.* 1962. Reprint, Westport, Conn.: Greenwood Press, 1973.

O'Brien, Thomas Victor. "Georgia's Response to *Brown v. Board of Education*: The

Rise and Fall of Massive Resistance, 1949–1961." Ph.D. diss., Emory University, 1992.

Paletz, David L., and Robert M. Entman. "Accepting the System." In *Media Power in Politics,* edited by Doris A. Graber. Washington, D.C.: Congressional Quarterly, 1984.

Paschall, Eliza. *It Must Have Rained.* Atlanta: Center for Research in Social Change, Emory University, 1975.

Patterson, Jack. "The Unruffled Mr. Sibley." *Atlanta Magazine,* February 1962, 38–39, 58–63.

Patton, Randall L. "A Southern Liberal and the Politics of Anti-Colonialism: The Governorship of Ellis Arnall." *Georgia Historical Quarterly* 74, no. 3 (fall 1990): 597–621.

Peirce, Neal R. *The Deep South States of America: People, Politics, and Power in the Seven Deep South States.* New York: Norton, 1972.

Peltason, J. W. *Fifty-Eight Lonely Men.* Chicago: University of Illinois Press, 1971.

Pendergrast, Mark. *For God, Country, and Coca-Cola: The Unauthorized History of the Great American Soft Drink and the Company That Makes It.* New York: Charles Scribner's Sons, 1993.

Pomerantz, Gary M. *Where Peachtree Meets Sweet Auburn: The Saga of Two Families and the Making of Atlanta.* New York: Scribner, 1996.

Potenziani, David Daniel. "Look to the Past: Richard B. Russell and the Defense of Southern White Supremacy." Ph.D. diss., University of Georgia, 1981.

Pou, Charlie. "Epilogue: The Vandiver Years." *Atlanta Magazine,* December 1962, 43–63.

Pratt, Robert A. *The Color of Their Skin: Education and Race in Richmond, Virginia, 1954–1989.* Charlottesville: University Press of Virginia, 1992.

Pyles, Charles Boykin. "Race and Ruralism in Georgia Elections, 1948–1966." Ph.D. diss., University of Georgia, 1967.

Quin, Paul. "The Dominance of the Shadow in Southern Race Relations." *Louisiana History* 36 (winter 1995): 5–30.

Rabinowitz, Howard N. *The First New South, 1865–1920.* Arlington Heights, Ill.: Harlan Davidson, 1992.

Raines, Howell. *My Soul is Rested: The Story of the Civil Rights Movement in the Deep South.* 1977. Reprint, New York: Penguin Books, 1983.

Rich, Evelyn. "Ku Klux Klan Ideology, 1954–1988." Ph.D. diss., Boston University, 1988.

Sarratt, Reed. *The Ordeal of Desegregation.* New York: Harper and Row, 1966.

Schulman, Bruce J. *From Cotton Belt to Sunbelt: Federal Policy, Economic Development and the Transformation of the South, 1938–1980.* New York: Oxford, 1991.

Sherrill, Robert. *Gothic Politics in the Deep South.* New York: Grossman Publishers, 1968.

Silver, Christopher, and John V. Moeser. *The Separate City: Black Communities in the Urban South, 1940–1968.* Lexington: University Press of Kentucky, 1995.

Smith, R. C. *They Closed Their Schools: Prince Edward County, Virginia, 1951–1964.* Chapel Hill: University of North Carolina Press, 1965.

Smith, Stephen A. *Myth, Media and the Southern Mind.* Fayetteville: University of Arkansas Press, 1985.

Southern Education Reporting Service. *Statistical Summary of School Segregation-Desegregation in the Southern and Border States.* Nashville: Southern Education Reporting Service, November 1961.

Southern Regional Council. *School Desegregation: The First Six Years.* Atlanta: Southern Regional Council, 1960.

———. *School Desegregation: Old Problems Under a New Law.* Atlanta: Southern Regional Council, 1965.

Southern Regional Council and Robert F. Kennedy Memorial. *The Student Pushout.* Atlanta: Southern Regional Council, 1973.

Spitzberg, Irving J. *Racial Politics in Little Rock, 1954–1964.* New York: Garland Publishing, 1987.

Stevenson, Elizabeth. "A Personal History of Change in Atlanta." *Virginia Quarterly Review* 41 (April 1965): 580–95.

Stone, Clarence. *Regime Politics: Governing Atlanta, 1946–1988.* Lawrence: University of Kansas Press, 1989.

Talmadge, Herman. *You and Segregation.* Birmingham: Vulcan Press, 1955.

"Talmadge and Segregation: He Makes His Stand." *Newsweek,* 31 May 1954, 31–32.

Tindall, George Brown. *The Emergence of the New South, 1913–1945.* Baton Rouge: Louisiana State University Press, 1967.

Townsend, James L. "Miracle in Atlanta." *Town and Country Magazine,* February 1963, 90–96.

Trillin, Calvin. *An Education in Georgia: The Integration of Charlayne Hunter and Hamilton Holmes.* New York: Viking Press, 1964.

———. "Reflections: Remembrance of Moderates Past." *New Yorker,* 21 March 1977.

Tuck, Stephen. "A City Too Dignified to Hate: Civic Pride, Civil Rights, and Savannah in Comparative Perspective." *Georgia Historical Quarterly* 79 (fall 1995): 539–59.

U.S. Congress. House. Committee on Un-American Activities. *The Present Day Ku Klux Klan Movement.* 90th Cong., 1967.

U.S. Congress. Senate. Griffin Bell. Hearings before the Committee on Judiciary. 95th Cong., January 1977.

Walker, Jack L. "The Functions of Disunity: Negro Leadership in a Southern City." *Journal of Negro Education* 32 (March 1963): 227–36.

———. "Protest and Negotiation: A Case Study of Negro Leadership in Atlanta, Georgia." *Midwest Journal of Political Science* 7 (May 1963): 99–124.

Warren, Robert Penn. *Segregation: The Inner Conflict in the South.* New York: Random House, 1956.

Weltner, Charles Longstreet. *Southerner.* Philadelphia: Lippincott, 1966.

———. "Pride and Progress." *American Education* 2 (September 1966): 23–25.

Wilhoit, Francis M. *The Politics of Massive Resistance.* New York: George Braxiller, 1973.

Woodward, C. Vann. *Origins of the New South.* 1951. Reprint. Baton Rouge: Louisiana State University Press, 1971.

———. "New South Fraud Is Papered by Old South Myth." *Washington Post,* 9 July 1961.

———. *The Strange Career of Jim Crow.* New York: Oxford University Press, 1974.

———. *The Burden of Southern History.* 3d ed. Baton Rouge: Louisiana State University Press, 1993.

Ziemke, Caroline F. "Senator Richard B. Russell and the 'Lost Cause' in Vietnam, 1954–1968." *Georgia Historical Quarterly* 72, no. 1 (spring 1988): 30–54.

Zinn, Howard. "The Southern Mystique." *American Scholar* 33 (January 1963): 49–56.

———. *The Southern Mystique.* New York: Knopf, 1964.

INDEX